# Summer Days

✺

## WRITERS ON CRICKET

*Edited by*
MICHAEL MEYER

OXFORD UNIVERSITY PRESS

1983

Oxford University Press, Walton Street, Oxford OX2 6DP

London Glasgow New York Toronto
Delhi Bombay Calcutta Madras Karachi
Kuala Lumpur Singapore Hong Kong Tokyo
Nairobi Dar es Salaam Cape Town
Melbourne Auckland

and associates in
Beirut Berlin Ibadan Mexico City Nicosia

Oxford is a trade mark of Oxford University Press

© Methuen London Ltd. 1981
Introduction © Michael Meyer 1981
First published in 1981 by Eyre Methuen Ltd.
First issued as an Oxford University Press paperback 1983

British Library Cataloguing in Publication Data

Summer days—(Oxford paperbacks)
1. Cricket—Literary collections
2. English literature
I. Meyer, Michael
820.908' 0355 PR1111.C/
ISBN 0-19-28137-8

Printed in Great Britain by
Richard Clay (The Chaucer Press) Ltd
Bungay, Suffolk

# SUMMER DAYS
# WRITERS ON CRICKET

# Contents

# Introduction

William Blake wrote a short poem about cricket, Lord Byron played for Harrow and described it in *Childish Recollections,* James Joyce was an enthusiast, Samuel Beckett is the only Nobel Prize-winner for Literature to have appeared in *Wisden* (in 1926 he opened both the batting and the bowling for Dublin University against Northamptonshire, scoring only 4 and 1 but bowling fifteen economical overs, o for 47). Cricket figures prominently in English literature from Dickens, Trollope and Meredith to the present day. But comparatively few authors, other than those who are lucky enough to write about it professionally, have set down their considered reflections on the game, and I thought it would be fun to ask a few present-day *aficionados* to do this.

Originally the plan was to limit this book to such specially commissioned pieces; Mr Alan Ross seemed to have covered the field of already published material in his excellent anthology, *The Cricketer's Companion*. But some of those whom I approached replied that they had said all they had to say about cricket in publications which had evaded even Mr Ross's sharp eye, and it seemed a pity to exclude these, the more so as their existence is probably unknown even to students of cricket literature. So I have stretched my net to include V. S. Naipaul's diary of the 1963 England v West Indies Lord's Test, poems by Gavin Ewart, Ted Hughes, Harry Kemp and David Wright, Laurie Lee's thoughts on Hill Cricket and Arthur Marshall's shameful admissions of early misdemeanours on the field; also two poems by dead writers, Drummond Allison and Francis Meynell, which I have long admired.

I decided against including professional cricket writers, though several are distinguished authors in their own right. Some of those whom I asked replied that they would have contributed but could not do so within the required time. Some intriguing facts emerged; Samuel Beckett, in reply to my enquiry whether he had bowled off-breaks or seam (remembering that he had opened the bowling in that match against Northants), replied: 'Off-breaks endlessly. Least unsuccessful round the wicket to left-handers,' but added mystifyingly: 'Seam? I suppose so.' Contrary to what has sometimes been asserted, Mr Beckett assures me that he never played for Ireland.

As well as those whom I knew to be interested in the game, I wrote to several authors whom I admired without knowing whether they were what Julian Symons, later in these pages, calls 'cricketeers' or not. Some, such as Kingsley Amis, A. J. Ayer, Beryl Bainbridge and the late Jacky Gillott, proved happily willing; others expressed their apathy or distaste in vivid terms. 'My father's passion for sport,' declared Sir Angus Wilson, 'effectively killed any interest I might have had in the game.' Graham Greene, invited to express what I supposed to be his distaste for the game, replied: 'Alas, I don't even know enough about cricket to attack it. Anyway I wouldn't attack it as I much prefer it to the muddied oafs.'

I would have liked to have included a foreigner's view, but none of those whom I approached felt bold enough to take the field. Arthur Koestler confessed: 'Cricket has remained a kind of mumbo-jumbo to me, compared with civilized games like soccer,' and Paul Theroux: 'I feel greatly hampered by my ignorance of cricket because I am aware that it is a metaphor everywhere in English life. I know I'm missing something. I don't know what it is.' Only two, one a Member of Parliament and 'media personality', the other a Very Big Seller Indeed (living in tax exile), refused because the money wasn't enough, the former in the kind of peremptory manner in which, I suppose, he dismisses hecklers. When I gently suggested that, remembering our earlier acquaintance before he became so famous, he might have replied a little more courteously, he returned my letter with a scribble at the foot: 'You asked me to write an article. I refused.

What kind of grovelling do you expect?' I reflected (and replied) that it must be a high price to pay for fame and wealth if one loses the ability to distinguish between courtesy and grovelling.

I note with regret a certain southern bias in this book, though I hope that the excellence of the poems about Verity, Boycott and Rhodes, and of the prose pieces by Beryl Bainbridge, Melvyn Bragg, Roy Fuller and Sir Bernard Lovell will balance this. I am happy that Australia, the West Indies and South Africa find a place. Sir Bernard Lovell asks me to assure readers that the match he describes 'did happen – although of course I have changed the names of the cricketers mentioned', and Andrew Sinclair stresses that 'there really is a Spoty (*sic*) Dog and Dirty Dick's side by side in the Corfu docks.'

I am grateful to the following for permission to reprint copyright material: Ralph Allison and the Whiteknights Press for *Verity* (from *The Poems of Drummond Allison*, edited by Michael Sharp); Gavin Ewart and the *Guardian* for *Geoffrey*; Ted Hughes and Faber & Faber Ltd for *Sunstruck* (from *Remains of Elmet*); V. S. Naipaul and *Harpers & Queen* for *Test*; Laurie Lee and *Wisden Cricket Monthly* for *Hill Cricket*; Harry Kemp for *Wilfred Rhodes* (from his *Poems in Variety*, privately printed); The Bodley Head Ltd for *Mirage at Mickleham* (from Sir Francis Meynell's autobiography, *My Lives*); Arthur Marshall and Hamish Hamilton Ltd for *The Crooked Bat* (from *Girls Will be Girls*); David Wright and A. D. Peters & Co. for *A Poet at the Tavern* (from *To the Gods the Shades*). Also to David Wright for drawing my attention to Mr Kemp's poem, and to my editor Richard Johnson for repeating the encouragement and tactful criticism which he has handed out to me on numerous cricket fields.

MICHAEL MEYER

# *Verity*

## DRUMMOND ALLISON

The ruth and truth you taught have come full circle
On that fell island all whose history lies.
Far now from Bramall Lane and far from Scarborough,
You recollect how foolish are the wise.

On this great ground more marvellous than Lord's
– Time takes more spin than nineteen thirty-four –
You face at last that vast that Bradman-shaming
Batsman whose cuts obey no natural law.

Run up again, as gravely smile as ever,
Veer without fear your left unlucky arm
In his so dark direction, but no length
However lovely can disturb the harm
That is his style, defer the winning drive
Or shake the crowd from their uproarious calm.

Hedley Verity was mortally wounded in action in Sicily (the 'fell island')
and died in enemy hands on 31 July 1943, which coincidentally was
Drummond Allison's 22nd birthday. Allison himself was killed in action on
the Italian mainland just over four months later.

Nineteen thirty-four was the year when Verity took fourteen wickets in
a single day against Australia at Lord's, a feat unique in Test cricket.

# Ten to Make and the Match to Win

KINGSLEY AMIS

I was never much of a cricketer, though as a boy I dreamed of being a famous one, and instantly echoed my cousin John's avowal, when we were both about twelve, that he meant to become a professional at the game. Circumstances were against me. The sports ground of my school, the City of London, lay out beyond Deptford and Lewisham at Grove Park, only half a dozen miles from my home in Norbury, but unreachable without a car except by a savage dog-leg journey that also involved plenty of walking. I used to moan about this when reproached by master or fellow-pupil for lack of keenness. Also, I found batting, which in my ignorance I thought outshone bowling by miles, a nervous business. I was afraid of being hit by the ball and, more scurvily, of making a fool of myself. What with one thing and another, over the years I played less and tended more to read, spin fancies and waste time on book-cricket.

And watch, of course. The Oval was easier to get at than Grove Park. But I went to fewer matches there than at the ground belonging to the club my father played for, Streatham. Good club cricket, between the wars at any rate, could be very good indeed, skilful, adventurous and sporting. It fostered individualists, not just big hitters or demon bowlers, but characters like the fellow some visiting side brought, played entirely for his fielding, they said. He had hit the stumps in profile to run out one of the home side, and caused another to leap for dear life before it dawned on them what they were up against. Thereafter, if the ball went any-where on his side of the field, both batsmen stood in their creases as if carved out of stone. Another time there was a round-arm bowler, the only one I ever saw and, in the 1930s, surely among the last of his line. He caused some discreet amusement till two of our chaps had fatally played over the top of him in the same over.

All this and much more I watched and enjoyed. But I never achieved spectatorial mastery of the game, the capacity to see exactly and in full what happens to every ball bowled. Perhaps this is only open to those who have played a great deal of competitive cricket, or to the unusually persistent. I fancy that the estimable Harold Pinter, not the only successful dramatist one might mention in this context, falls into the second category. One fine day in 1970 he and I were guests of Huw Wheldon in a box at Lord's, England v Australia. I arrived at about 11.29. Huw's hospitality was such that by 11.50 I had my second gin and tonic in my hand and had taken in no more of the cricket than that England were batting. This inattention struck me as unseemly and, hearing a moment later the sound of leather on willow, I glanced over my shoulder just in time to see the ball reaching the third-man boundary.

'Good shot,' I said without much warmth.

Harold, who had been watching the play past my waistcoat, so to speak, put his glass down and looked me in the eye. 'Good shot?' he asked me. 'That was the late outswinger.' His tone moderated to the patiently expository. 'He got a thickish edge to it; if first slip had been a yard finer he'd have been caught, and third man was asleep. Really, what do you think you're talking about, *good shot*?'

'I'm awfully sorry,' I croaked, 'I didn't realise you were Dennis Lillee's cousin.' No, actually I thought of the last bit later.

It was many years before that, at the Oval, fittingly enough, that I saw a day's cricket worth all the attention I or anybody else could have given it. The date was 9 August 1932. That was the year the Nazis won the largest number of seats in the last Reichstag, Shirley Temple appeared in her first film and John Galsworthy was awarded the Nobel Prize for Literature. I was ten years old and accompanying my father. He was a far better and more active cricketer than I would ever be, a natural stroke-player who at this stage of his life could and would hit the ball very hard. He clearly knew much more about the game as it is played, but even at that early age I reckon I knew more than he did of what could be learned from books: record-breaking scores, fastest hundreds, remarkable analyses, the – then – solitary occasion on which the Champion County had beaten the Rest. (I can still remember it was Yorkshire and the margin was 65 runs, but am no longer sure about the year. 1906?)*

We had seats in the open with the pavilion on our left. The sun was shining; London was in the middle of what was then called a heat-wave. Before I saw the score-card I was already well aware of what had happened up to that point. It was full of interest. On the Saturday the visiting side, Middlesex, had won the toss, batted, started well, collapsed, ended up with only 141 on the board. Surrey had started badly, recovered and reached 184 for four, thanks largely to a 'masterly' (*Wisden*) 92 from Jack Hobbs, then in his fiftieth year; he was seemingly unfit for the rest of the match. At 3.30 on the Monday Surrey had declared, having increased their score to 540 for nine. The top scorer was F. R. Brown, with an innings of 212 that is still occasionally mentioned. So far from being utterly demoralised by the lashing Brown and others had given them and by their position (399 behind on the first innings), Middlesex had scored 134 for one at the close. They thus needed 265 to avoid an innings defeat that Tuesday.

Out came Sims and Hearne at 11 o'clock to resume their innings. Everything went sufficiently well for them at first, till Brown came on to bowl and almost at once took Hearne's valuable wicket. Patsy Hendren joined Sims and the runs came, but not in any very steady manner: Sims kept looking like getting out and Hendren took what I thought were terrible risks, not that I had any objection – playing all sorts of shots with a cross bat, though *Wisden* says 'his batting was of the highest class' and he seems to have given only one actual chance. Sims achieved his century and went soon afterwards. Then Brown took four more

---

* Not bad – 1905, actually. – Ed.

wickets in succession, the last of them that of Haig, the Middlesex captain, thrillingly caught at slip by Allom off his first ball.

From then on the tension was continuous. There were two hours left for play and Middlesex were 338 for eight, 61 behind. But Hendren went on cutting and hooking and pulling as before, including a six on to the pavilion roof specially for me. In the end he was brilliantly run out by Hobbs's sub for 145; 443 for nine, 44 ahead, forty minutes to go. But Durston, the last man in, survived for half of that time and helped Price, the wicket-keeper, to add another dozen. Middlesex were all out for 455, leaving Surrey to make 57 in a time recorded by both *The Times* and *Wisden* as twenty minutes, though I have always maintained, and always will, that only nineteen minutes elapsed between the start of the first over and the last run being scored. Ten-year-old boys are good witnesses to that sort of thing; they are childish enough to make sure several times more than strictly necessary.

Anyway, the innings began like part of an ordinary cricket-match. The opening pair, Shepherd and Brown, walked briskly but without hurry to the crease, Shepherd took guard and Durston ran up to bowl. He started with a wide, probably out of nervousness, but that was normal enough. Then, after a safe two, Shepherd aimed a mighty hit which misfired and was nearly caught. Any doubt anywhere about Surrey going for the runs was dispelled. The batsmen having crossed, the tall fair figure of Brown faced Durston. He hit a solitary four, rather a chancy one as I remember, and was caught at slip off the next ball, the last of the over. It was not going to happen in the way I had hoped, almost expected, the rest of the runs coming from Brown in consecutive sixes. Haig started to bowl at the other end. Shepherd took a single off his first ball and the new batsman, Percy Fender, instantly dealt another mistimed blow but with less luck and was caught at mid-on. S. A. Block replaced him.

The outlook was mediocre: two wickets down – no matter; 9 runs on the board – unsatisfactory; five minutes gone – appalling. A fair part of those minutes had been spent in the outgoing of the outgoing batsmen and the incoming ones' incoming. Somebody had evidently noticed that, and soon the next man – Ratcliffe – came and stood padded and gloved just inside the gate at the foot of the pavilion steps. This was no longer an ordinary cricket-match, as was fully demonstrated by his running nearly all the way to the wicket when Block (I think) skied one, and back to his post when the fieldsman put it on the floor. The crowd was excited but watchful, wildly applauding every run and then at once shushing itself so as not to distract or delay.

Runs turned up, nearly all from hearty drives for four and gentle pats for quick singles to mid-off or mid-on or even back to the bowler. That sort of single must be more upsetting to a fielding side than almost any sort of four, but Middlesex kept their head and ran both batsmen out in Haig's third over, Shepherd for 22 and Block for 19. They had played like angels, but Surrey were still woefully behind the clock: 46 scored and almost no time left.

Ratcliffe was joined by Jardine. I am sure I have never since experienced the kind of stillness that had fallen all round the ground before Durston began to run up for the first ball of what was going inexorably to be, as everyone there understood, the last over of the match. Most of the crowd must have been supporters of Surrey if anything, but I am just as sure that they – we – were not sitting there poised for victory, let alone impatient of it, as might well have been while Durston and Price were defying the Surrey attack. No, clearly we were expecting a great event, a piece of history, something that absent thousands would envy us for having witnessed.

Would it come? Durston bowled and there was immediate anti-climax: Ratcliffe struck him for a single. Try as he might, Jardine at the gasometer end was unable to score off the next two deliveries. 10 to make; I felt I dared not move. Off the fourth ball of the over Jardine should have been caught at mid-off and the match have ended. But he was dropped and they ran two. The fifth ball went for four, stylishly cut through the slips according to *The Times*. And the last ball came skipping across the grass in the evening sunshine to the pavilion rails – that I clearly remember.

I have a mass or mess of memories of that day but none of what happened then. Did we swarm on to the pitch? Or was that impossible in 1932 even after what had just taken place? The question is not urgent. Having been there is enough. But I find it hard to resist a mild resentment that that wonderful day's cricket came my way when I had so little to compare it with. And – a quite different point – I can think of nothing that could have suggested to me how impossible the more attractive parts of the match would have been half a century later in the 1980s.

When drafting this essay I tried all sorts of ways to develop that last theme without sounding peevish or being boring or both. It could not be done, so I will pass on to the contribution made to the fourth innings by the fielding side. Perhaps because of my early partiality for the bat, it was quite a long time before I apportioned the credit properly. All honour is due to Surrey, but the real heroes were Middlesex. They bowled off short runs, and unchanged, and at the wicket, and when over was called they *ran* to their new positions; they were not going to have it said that they had saved the match by not giving Surrey the chance to win it. Their part in their own defeat earned them the admiring gratitude of all those present at it and everybody else who has ever cared for cricket.

# Middlesex Cricket

A. J. AYER

I began to play cricket and, what does not necessarily follow, to take an interest in the game, at the age of seven, when I first went to my preparatory school at Eastbourne. It was the fashion at this school to support one or other of the first-class counties and since my home in London was within a penny bus ride of Lord's I naturally chose Middlesex. I had fantasies in my childhood of playing for the county, or even for England, as an all-rounder, but they had no foundation in fact. I could bowl off-breaks and make a few runs off long hops and half-volleys, but my performances were not good enough for me to retain a place even in my preparatory school eleven, let alone win any kind of cricketing colour at Eton, and by the age of 17 I forsook the game for lawn tennis at which I did show rather more skill. This did not, however, take away my interest in cricket. In those days sport of every kind was more fully covered in the newspapers than it is now and I read the reports of all the county cricket matches. I acquired a small cricketing library and regularly bought and studied *Wisden's Almanack*. As a result I was well-informed about all the county elevens, but my allegiance to Middlesex never wavered.

Unfortunately, in spite of my living so near to their home ground, I seldom had the opportunity to see them play. In May and June when they played most of their home matches, I was away at school, and in the early part of my summer holidays the Lord's fixture list was filled with a series of two-day matches between schools, not only Eton versus Harrow, which was then a great social occasion to which one went in top hat and tails, but Clifton versus Tonbridge, Rugby versus Marlborough and

Cheltenham versus Haileybury, culminating in Lord's Schools against the Rest, and the Public Schools against the Army. As a small boy I used to watch all these matches, always taking sides, though for the most part quite arbitrarily. I remember seeing Duleepsinhji play for Cheltenham in a match in which he enjoyed more success as a slow bowler than as a batsman. He was, indeed, an exception, in that very few of the schoolboys concerned developed into first-class cricketers. The relatively low standard of play in these matches did not mar my enjoyment of them, but I sometimes wished that the Lord's fixture list was arranged differently. For my father took his annual holiday in August and the return of Middlesex to Lord's to complete their programme in the county championship nearly always found me with my parents abroad.

The result was that I followed their fortunes mainly in the press. My earliest reward came in the season of 1920 when they won the county championship for the first time since 1903. They had been runners-up to Surrey in 1914, but in 1919, when county cricket was resumed after the war, they fell as low as thirteenth. This was the season in which the experiment was made of limiting county cricket matches to two days, but lengthening the hours of play. The experiment proved a failure and in 1920 the first-class counties reverted to what remained the standard practice of three-day matches with a daily maximum of six hours play. Since not every county played every other, or the same number of matches, positions in the table were decided by the percentage of points obtained, five points being allotted for a win and two for a lead in the first innings in a drawn match. Cricket was still sufficiently popular and played with sufficient abandon for there to be no need to attempt to attract spectators by awarding bonus points for the rapidity of either scoring or wicket-taking or by setting any upper limit to the numbers of overs that could be bowled in an innings. Nor were there any single-innings competitions to distract attention from the county championship.

Though it soon became clear that they were going to do better in 1920 than they had in 1919, it was not until August that

Middlesex showed any serious prospect of becoming champions. They achieved it by winning all of their last nine matches, finishing less than three percentage points ahead of Lancashire. Their final match, on which the result depended, was against Surrey at Lord's. The match attracted such interest that the gates had to be closed on the first two days and there were some 15,000 spectators on the third. It was memorable also for the last appearance in the county championship of the Middlesex captain P. F. (subsequently Sir Pelham) Warner who had first played for the county in 1895 and had twice led English tours to Australia. An opening batsman in his prime, he now went in fifth and saved the day for Middlesex in their first innings, coming in with the score at 35 for three and making the top score of 79 out of a total of 268. He was helped by Hendren, Middlesex's best batsman, who made 41, and by G. T. S. Stevens, an all-rounder still up at Oxford, who made 53.

Warner made his runs slowly, so that the Middlesex innings was not completed until the second morning. Surrey then scored so fast that they were able to declare at 341 for nine, with forty minutes left for play on the day. Hobbs did nothing of note but his partner Sandham batted throughout the innings for 167. So Middlesex began their second innings 73 runs in arrears. Their opening batsmen were C. H. L. Skeet, another recruit from the Oxford eleven, and Lee, and both of them made centuries. The other wickets fell cheaply, but Warner, who had dropped himself to ninth place and made 14 not out, was able to declare at a total of 316 for seven. This left Surrey with 244 runs to win and a little under three hours to make them. Nowadays most counties in this position would play for a draw but Surrey went for the runs. Hobbs again failed, but Sandham made 68 and with help from Shepherd took the score past 100 in 75 minutes. The total was 120 when the third wicket fell, but then the Middlesex spin bowlers, Stevens and Hearne, took charge and Surrey were all out for 188 with forty minutes of play unused. Middlesex had won by 55 runs.

The Middlesex eleven contained only five professionals, its three leading batsmen, Elias (commonly known as 'Patsy') Hendren, J. W. (or 'Young Jack') Hearne, and Harry Lee, its fast bowler Durston and the wicket-keeper H. R. Murrell. Besides Plum Warner, the two amateurs who played regularly were F. T. Mann, a hard-hitting middle-order batsman, and Nigel Haig, an all-rounder who bowled at a fast-medium pace and opened the bowling with Durston. Various amateurs filled the remaining places, before Stevens and Skeet became available. In the Surrey match the last place was filled by H. K. Longman, who did not bowl and batted at number nine. He justified his inclusion by making over 60 runs out of a Middlesex total of 318, when as champion county they played a very strong Rest of England side. The Rest's reply of 603 for five declared included an innings of 215 by Hobbs, made at a rate of more than a run a minute, but thanks mainly to Hendren, Middlesex achieved a draw with a second-innings total of 192 for four. Hendren had, indeed, been in great form throughout the season, heading the first-class averages with 2,520 runs at an average of 61·46, while Hearne was not far behind him with 2,148 runs made at an average of 55·07. Hearne also took 142 wickets at an average cost of 17·83.

It had been characteristic of Middlesex ever since the county club was formed in 1864 to rely preponderately on amateurs. In fact only three professionals of note played regularly for them before 1914, the all-rounders F. A. Tarrant and A. E. Trott, both imported from Australia, and their most successful opening bowler J. T. Hearne, a cousin of J. W. Hearne's. Many of the amateurs such as A. E. Stoddart, C. T. and G. B. Studd, the Hon. Alfred Lyttelton and B. J. T. Bosanquet, the inventor of the googly (still known as the bosie in Australia), were exceptionally gifted cricketers, but the constant changes in the side, occasioned by the inconstancy of their appearances in it, were a weakening factor. It largely accounts for the fact that Middlesex, apart from being the most successful county in 1865 and again in 1870, were champions only once – in 1903 – in the period between 1895 when the championship was formally organised and the outbreak of the First World War.

At least until the Second World War the difference between amateurs and professionals was taken very seriously. It was marked not only by the annual match of Gentlemen versus Players, which continued until some time after the Second World War, but in various other ways. At Lord's only the amateurs emerged from and returned to the pavilion. The professionals were quartered in a small lodge by its side. On the score-cards, which were so far as possible kept up to date throughout the match, the amateurs had their initials printed before their surnames, the players after. Sometimes, as in *Wisden*, where the professionals were allowed to have their initials printed before their names, the amateurs were distinguished by the prefix 'Mr' or any superior title to which they could lay claim. The abolition of this distinction, which it took some years to effect even after the Second World War, reflects a change in economic as well as in social values.

Though relatively few in number, the professionals played the most important part when Middlesex again won the championship in 1921, under the captaincy of F. T. Mann. Hendren, Hearne and Lee were the leading batsmen and Durston the most successful bowler, with greater support from Nigel Haig. Lee also advanced as a bowler, though neither Hearne, whose health was precarious, nor Stevens, who became available only at the end of the Oxford term, repeated their success of the previous year.

For no very obvious reason Middlesex then entered into a period of decline. They were runners-up to Yorkshire in 1924, but were not again in serious contention for the championship until 1936 when they came second to Derbyshire and remained in second place, with Yorkshire as champions, for the three following years. Throughout almost the whole of this period, Hendren was by far their most successful batsman. He first played for the county in 1908 but did little of note before the First World War. After the war, if the records of those who played fewer than ten innings for the county are disqualified, he headed the Middlesex batting average for sixteen consecutive seasons. His highest score of 301 not out was made against Worcestershire in 1933 when he was 44 years old. By the time that he retired five years later he had scored over 40,000 runs in county matches and made 119 centuries. The last of them, which I had the good fortune to see him make, was on the occasion of his final appearance at Lord's, in the Middlesex first innings of a match against Surrey. It more than compensated for his failure to score in the second innings. He was a small man, rotund in figure, but an excellent fielder, largely because of his speed. He was a professional footballer in his youth, and played for Brentford as an outside-right. Brentford were then, as they usually have been, in the third division of the Football League and Hendren was no longer playing for them when they made their brief ascent to the first division before the war. He had a fair record in Test cricket, failing against the fast bowling of Gregory and Macdonald in the triumphant Australian tour of 1921, but holding a place in A. P. F. Chapman's side which regained the Ashes in 1926. He was a fast-scoring batsman with a penchant for the hook. A humorous Irishman, he was exceedingly popular both with his fellow-players and with the English and even the Australian crowds.

The other Middlesex player to appear in the decisive Test match of 1926 was G. T. S. Stevens, who played ten times for England between 1922 and 1930. He was chosen mainly for his bowling, which combined leg-breaks with googlies, but he was also a very gifted batsman who sometimes went in first for Middlesex. I think that it was in 1926 in a match played at Lord's against Somerset that I saw him open an innings with four successive boundaries. Unfortunately he could not spare the time to play very often and with the virtual retirement of Jack Hearne early in the 1930s and the decline of Lee, the county badly needed a professional batsman to give Hendren regular support. The man who came closest to supplying it was Joe Hulme, better known as the regular outside-right of the all-conquering Arsenal sides of the 1930s, but though he played some good innings for Middlesex, and fielded consistently well, his cricket never reached the international standard of his football.

The most talented recruit to Middlesex in the 1920s was G. O. Allen, who was one of the many amateurs who came to them from Cambridge. He may well have been the best fast bowler ever to play for the county and in his later years he developed into a successful hard-hitting batsman. In 1929 he took all ten Sussex wickets in an innings. He toured Australia in 1932–3 under D. R. Jardine and played in the Tests, which gave rise to the notorious controversy about body-line bowling, but himself refused to employ body-line tactics. He himself led a tour to Australia in 1936–7, when the Ashes were narrowly lost, and came out of retirement to lead a tour to the West Indies in 1948. In all he played in 25 Test matches. His appearances for Middlesex were, however, only intermittent. This was the more to be regretted as the county was short of fast bowling. In the latter part of his career Durston preferred to bowl slow-medium off-breaks and too much work fell upon Nigel Haig, who inherited the captaincy from F. T. Mann and retained it until 1934, having shared it in his last two years with H. J. Enthoven, another amateur from Cambridge, who showed promise as an all-rounder which he never quite fulfilled.

By contrast, during this period, Middlesex had almost a plethora of leg-spin and googly bowlers. In addition to Hearne and Stevens, there were Peebles, Robins, Bettington, Owen-Smith and Sims. Of these only Jim Sims was a professional. He started playing for Middlesex in 1930 as a batsman, often going in first, but soon became primarily a bowler, developing so quickly that within half a dozen years he was playing Test cricket, touring Australia under G. O. Allen. A very tall man, noted for his wit, he spun the ball powerfully and had good control of length. He was at his best at the end of the 1930s and would almost certainly have played more often for England had his career not been interrupted by the war. As it was, he had taken nearly 1,600 first-class wickets when he finally retired in 1952.

Of the amateurs, Ian Peebles, R. H. Bettington and H. G. Owen-Smith joined the side from Oxford and R. W. V. Robins from Cambridge. Initially, Peebles was the most promising. He was taken on an MCC tour to South Africa in 1927 at the age of nineteen and played in thirteen Test matches between 1927 and 1931. He was also successful for Middlesex until a muscular injury turned him into a less dangerous googly bowler, without the power to bowl leg-breaks. He continued to play occasionally for Middlesex, taking over the captaincy in 1939, but was never again the force that he had been in his youth. After the war he earned a good reputation as a writer about cricket.

The other three were all talented all-rounders. Bettington, an Australian who was studying to be a medical doctor, had played especially well for Oxford, and Owen-Smith, also a medical student, played Test cricket for his native South Africa, though he was even better known as a Rugby football player, at which he played for England, but neither of them appeared at all regularly for Middlesex, any more than did Walter Robins until he took over the captaincy in 1935. A small bird-like man, very fast in the field, Robins first made his reputation as a schoolboy batsman at Highgate, playing for the Public Schools at Lord's in 1924. It was only at Cambridge that he developed into a leg-break bowler, with such success that he was capped for England in 1929 and played in eighteen more Test matches between then and 1937. His chief service to Middlesex, however, was as a captain, where his enterprising and aggressive tactics quickly brought results. Middlesex rose to third place in the championship in the first season of his captaincy and, as I have said, were runners-up in each of the three seasons that followed. They were again runners-up in 1946, when Robins resumed the captaincy, and in 1947, his last full season as captain, they won the championship with the strongest batting side that ever played for them, possibly the best side altogether.

Robins was most greatly assisted by the emergence of the famous 'Middlesex twins', Denis Compton and W. J. Edrich. Bill Edrich came from Norfolk and had played several seasons of minor counties cricket before he joined Middlesex in 1937 at the age of twenty-one. He was immediately successful as an opening or first-wicket batsman and made over 2,000 runs in each of the three seasons in which he played before the war. In 1938 he reached his 1,000 runs before the end of May and was chosen to play against Australia. It took him some time to find his form in

Test matches, though he played an innings of over 200 against South Africa in the winter of 1938–9. By the time his first-class career came to a close in 1958, he had played in 39 Tests with an aggregate of 2,440 runs made at an average of 40. A short slender man, he hit the ball surprisingly hard and was a good player of fast bowling, being never afraid to hook. He was also a fine slip-fielder and a tempestuous fast bowler, making up in energy for what he lacked in strength.

Though often bracketed with Edrich, Denis Compton was an even better batsman, indeed probably the best batsman ever to play for Middlesex, not excluding Hendren. I saw him make his first appearance for their first eleven, when he was eighteen years old, in the Whitsuntide match at Lord's against Sussex in 1936. He batted last but made his 14 runs so stylishly that he was soon moved up the order and before the end of the season had achieved his 1,000 runs. By the following season he had improved so much that he was picked to play for England against New Zealand and in 1938 he made a century in his first appearance against Australia. In the course of his career, which also ended in 1958, he played in no fewer than 74 Test matches with an aggregate total of 5,807 runs made at an average of over 50. His total of runs in first-class cricket reached nearly 39,000, made at an average of just under 52. He also took over 600 wickets as a slow left-arm bowler, though like nearly all the other Middlesex batsmen of note he batted right-handed. An excellent fielder in his youth, he might have achieved even greater feats in all departments of the game if he had not been handicapped by a knee injury which troubled him in the last ten years of his career. His batting showed the power of a well-built man and the speed of his footwork enabled him to play many unorthodox as well as all the orthodox strokes. His eyesight was so keen that he had no need to watch the bowler's hand but could tell from its movement in the air which way the ball would turn. If he had a weakness it was as a judge of a run and he often incurred too great a risk of running either himself or his partner out.

Denis Compton was also a professional footballer in the years just preceding and following the war, playing outside-left for Arsenal, and being good enough to play for England in a wartime international match. His elder brother Leslie, who played centre-half for Arsenal and England, was the better footballer but not so outstanding a cricketer, though he kept wicket competently for Middlesex in the 1947 side and for several seasons afterwards.

Another asset to Robins in the late 1930s was the arrival from Wiltshire of a dependable fast bowler, 'Big Jim' Smith. Though he was a good enough bowler to play five times for England, his main attraction for the crowd was as a slogger. Going in usually at number ten, he treated every ball alike, advancing his left leg more or less straight down the pitch, and swiping as hard as he could. In 1938, again in a Whitsuntide match against Sussex, in which Middlesex made no fewer than 577 runs on the first day, I saw him make over 60 in a quarter of an hour, including six sixes, three of which went out of the ground. The same tactics brought him a century against Kent at Canterbury in the following season. The young Laurie Gray supported him well as an opening bowler but did not try to emulate his batting.

Smith did not play for Middlesex after the war and until J. J. Warr, a fast bowler from Cambridge, joined the side in August 1949, Gray had Edrich for his opening partner. Edrich was more properly a change bowler and the shortage of fast bowling was the only serious weakness in the Middlesex elevens of 1946 and 1947. It was partially compensated by the development of Jack Young, an orthodox slow left-hander, who had played once or twice for the county before the war. He shared the brunt of the bowling with Sims and took over 100 wickets in each of the first four post-war seasons. He was not so successful in Test cricket, though he played eight times for England between 1947 and 1949. Another reinforcement was the schoolboy Ian Bedford, a leg-break and googly bowler, who came into the side at the age of seventeen in 1947 and took 25 wickets, finishing second in the averages to Young. He never repeated this early success and when he returned to captain the side for two or three seasons in the early 1960s he hardly ever put himself on to bowl.

It cannot, therefore, be said that the Middlesex bowling in the years immediately following the war was altogether negligible. Nevertheless what made them into so powerful a side was the strength of their batting. Their innings were opened by Robertson and Brown with Edrich coming in at number three and Denis Compton following him. While Brown was a dependable county batsman and a very good fielder in the deep, Robertson was in a higher class and was unlucky not to be chosen in more than eleven Tests. He was an attractive batsman to watch and his individual score of 331 not out, made in a day against Worcestershire in 1949, is still a record for the county. Both he and Brown scored heavily in 1947, but they were outshone by Edrich and Compton whose totals for the season, including large scores made for England against the South Africans in both cases, were respectively 3,539 at an average of 80·43 and 3,816 at an average of 90·85. Edrich hit 12 centuries and Compton 18, of which 13 were made for Middlesex. This also remains a county record. Middlesex ended the season by defeating a strong Rest of England side by nine wickets, a feat hitherto accomplished only by Yorkshire. Compton contributed 240 to the Middlesex first-innings total of 543 for nine declared and Edrich 180.

In 1948 Robins handed over the captaincy to F. T. Mann's son, F. G. Mann, who led the county to third place in his first year as captain and to a championship, shared with Yorkshire, in his second. As his father had done before him, twenty-six years earlier, he captained a successful MCC side in South Africa, in the winter of 1948-9. That Middlesex did not win the championship in both the years of George Mann's captaincy was largely due to the fact that Compton and Edrich missed nine championship matches in the first of them through being chosen to play against the Australians, and Young seven for the same reason.

Mann relinquished the captaincy in 1950 and Robins resumed it yet again, but did not find the time to play in more than ten matches, a number of different players deputising for him in the remainder. From then until 1964 the captaincy passed from Edrich and Compton jointly, to Edrich alone, then Warr who succeeded in 1958, then Ian Bedford and then Colin Drybrough, a left-handed bowler who joined the side from Oxford. If this was a disappointing period for Middlesex cricket it was mainly because of the gradual decline of their four leading batsmen and their disappearance from the side by 1959 as well as that of all the leading bowlers of the late 1940s. Nevertheless some good cricketers emerged in their place. J. G. Dewes, who made a great many runs for Cambridge and appeared in five Test matches, played some good innings for the county in the early 1950s. Bob Gale and Eric Russell developed later into a good pair of opening batsmen and Alan Moss in the 1950s and Jack Price in the 1960s were fast bowlers of Test-match standard. So was John Murray, as a wicket-keeper. Don Bennett, who became the county coach, was an all-rounder who promised rather more than he eventually performed, but Mike Smith, who was first recruited as a slow left-arm bowler, turned into a very good right-handed opening batsman. A better batsman still was Peter Parfitt, a left-hander going in first wicket down and a brilliant fielder, especially in the slips. In the course of the 1960s he was chosen no less than thirty-four times to play for England.

The best player of all, however, to be produced by Middlesex during these two decades was Fred Titmus, who made his first appearance for the county in 1949 at the age of 16, was still playing for them in 1980 and for England in the early 1970s. Altogether he played in over fifty Test matches. Originally chosen by Middlesex for his batting, he made his reputation as an off-break bowler relying less on spin than on control of length and flight. The 158 wickets that he took for Middlesex in the season of 1955 remains a county record.

Titmus took over the captaincy in 1965 but seemed to have little relish for the office and relinquished it to Parfitt towards the close of the summer of 1968. After Parfitt had served for two more seasons the Middlesex committee offered the captaincy to J. M. Brearley, who was at that time a lecturer in philosophy at Newcastle University. Mike Brearley had kept wicket for Cambridge in the early 1960s but had excelled as a batsman, to the point where he was chosen for a tour to South Africa in 1964–5. He did not then do well enough to play in any of the Test matches and no one could have foreseen that within a dozen years he would be a successful captain of England. There have always been doubts whether his batsmanship was quite up to Test-match standards, but none about the quality of his captaincy. During the past decade he has led Middlesex to three county championships, one of them shared with Kent, and in one-day cricket, where their form has been more erratic, to two victories in the final of the Gillette Cup. Their 1980 side, which won both the championship and the Gillette Cup, with the West Indian Wayne Daniel, the South African Van der Bijl, and a former England player Mike Selvey, from Cambridge and Surrey, as fast bowlers, with Clive Radley, Graham Barlow, Mike Gatting and Roland Butcher, all of whom have played for England, supporting Brearley as batsmen, with yet another England player and recruit from Cambridge, Phil Edmonds, a slow left-arm bowler and attacking right-handed batsman, and John Emburey, replacing Titmus, in the England side also, as an off-break bowler, and with Paul Downton as wicket-keeper – was probably the strongest that Middlesex had mustered since 1947.

An eleven picked from all those who have ever appeared for Middlesex would have to include several players like Tarrant, Trott and J. T. Hearne who played before the First World War. It should probably be captained by P. F. Warner, whom I never saw in his prime. If I had to pick an eleven from those whom I have seen in their prime, I think its order of batting would run: Edrich, Robertson, J. W. Hearne, Denis Compton, Hendren, Allen, Robins (captain), Titmus, Murray (wicket-keeper), Jim Smith and Daniel. An objection to my choice is that Edrich was happier at number three than as an opening batsman, but to drop Edrich in the order, bring in Stevens or Brearley as an opener and leave out Smith would yield too high a proportion of slow to fast bowling. This result would be avoided if Robins were omitted instead of Smith and the captaincy given to Brearley, but though the captaincy would not suffer I think that Robins was too good an all-rounder not to be included. As it is, I believe the side which I have chosen would be more than a match for the one that any other county could produce over the same period, with the possible exceptions of Yorkshire and Surrey.

# The Longstop

BERYL BAINBRIDGE

Words and cricket seem to go together. Whenever I watch the game, by mistake, on television, I think it's not true that you can't get blood from a stone.

I only ever played the game once myself, in the park with some evacuees from Bootle. I was allowed to join in because I held a biscuit tin filled with shortbread that my mother had baked. They said I could have a turn if I gave them a biscuit afterwards. I didn't make any runs because I never hit the ball, and when I kept my promise and began to open the tin the evacuees knocked me over and took every piece of shortbread. They threw the tin over the wall into the gentlemen's lavatory. I had to tell my mother a six-foot-high naughty man with a Hitler moustache had chased me; she would have slapped me for playing with evacuees.

Mr Baines, who was my maternal grandfather, was a lover of cricket. Mr Bainbridge, my father, didn't care for the game. He cared even less for my grandfather. In his humble estimation Mr Baines was a mean old bugger, a fifth columnist, and, following his self-confessed denouncing of a neighbour in Norris Green for failing to draw his curtains against the black-out, a Gauleiter into the bargain. He was also a lounge lizard, a term never satisfactorily explained, though it was true that my grandfather fell asleep between meals.

Apart from words, my father was keen on sailing ships. He subscribed to a monthly magazine on the subject. If he was to be believed, he had, when no more than a child, sailed as a cabin boy to America. In middle age, his occupation a commercial traveller, he prowled the deserted shore beyond the railway line, peering of an evening through the barbed wire entanglements at the oil tankers and the black destroyers that crawled along the bleak edge of the Irish Sea; it was a gloomy mystery to him where that fearless lad before the mast had gone.

Every week Mr Baines came for Sunday dinner. There had been a moment at the outbreak of the war when he had contemplated coming to live with us, but after three days he returned home. He said he preferred to take his chances with the Luftwaffe. His conversation during the meal was always about cricket, and mostly to do with a man called Briggs. Briggs, he said, had just missed greatness by a lack of seriousness. If only Briggs had taken batting more seriously he would have been, make no bones about it, the best all-round cricketer in England after W. G. Grace. Briggs, he informed, took bowling and fielding in deadly earnest, but as a batsman he was a disaster; he seemed far more anxious to amuse the crowd than to improve his average.

Nobody listened to my grandfather, certainly not my father who was often heard to remark quite loudly that, had he been in control, he wouldn't give the old skinflint the time of day, let alone Sunday dinner, world without end.

However, one particular Sunday in the summer of 1944, Mr Baines, without warning, excelled himself when describing a cricketer called Ranjitsinhji.

'Just to set eyes on him,' said Mr Baines, 'was a picture in motion. The way his shirt ballooned –'

'A black chappie,' my father exclaimed, taken aback at my grandfather speaking civilly of a foreigner.

'An Indian Prince,' said Mr Baines. He was equally taken aback at being addressed in the middle of his monologue. He was used to conversing uninterrupted throughout the devouring of the blackmarket roast pork.

'They're two a penny,' my father said.

'More potatoes?' asked my mother, worriedly.

'Even when it wasn't windy,' continued Mr Baines, 'his shirt ballooned. Whether half a gale was blowing on the Hove ground or there wasn't enough breeze to shift the flag at Lord's, the fellow's shirt flapped like the mainsail of a six-tonner on the Solent.'

'Blithering rubbish,' said my father. He stabbed at a sprout on his plate as though it was alive.

My mother told Mr Baines that they played cricket in the park every Sunday afternoon. Not a proper team, just old men and young lads. Not what he was used to, of course. 'But,' she said, eyeing my father contemptuously, 'it will do us good to get out into the pure air.'

She didn't mean my father to come. We were never a family who went anywhere together. My father's opinion, had he voiced it, would have been that the family who stood together fell out together. Often we would attempt an outing, but between the closing of the back door and the opening of the front gate, misunderstandings occurred and plans were abruptly abandoned. She was astonished when, having washed up and taken off her pinny, she found my father in the hall putting on his trilby hat. She didn't like it, you could tell. Her mouth went all funny and the lipstick ran down at one corner. Shoulder to shoulder, more or less, we set off for the park.

I wanted to nip over the garden fence and through the blackberry bushes into Brows Lane, but my mother said my grandfather wasn't about to nip anywhere, not at his age. We trotted him down the road past the roundabout and the Council offices. The brass band was practising in the hut behind the fire station. When he heard the music Mr Baines began to walk with his arms held stiffly at his sides, only the band kept stopping and starting and the tune came in bits and after a little while he gave up playing at soldiers and shuffled instead. My father looked at the ground all the time; there was a grey splodge on the brim of his hat where a pigeon had done its business.

The park was quite grand, even though it had lost its ornamental gates at the entrance. My mother said they'd been removed to make into tanks. My father swore they were mouldering away in a brick field down by the Docks, along with his mother's copper kettle and a hundred thousand front railings. The park had a pavilion, a sort of hunting lodge with mullioned windows and a thatched roof. People were worried about incendiary bombs. The park keeper kept his grass roller inside and buckets of water. In front of the pavilion was a sunken bowling green and beyond that a miniature clock-golf course. We used to ride our bikes up and down the bumps. Behind the pavilion, within a roped enclosure, was a German Messerschmidt. It had been there for two years. It hadn't crash-landed anywhere near our village; it was on loan. The park-keeper was always telling the Council to tell someone to come back for it. At first we had all run round it and shuddered, but after a few weeks we hardly noticed it any more. It just perched there, propped on blocks, one wing tipped up to the sky, the cockpit half burned away, its melted hood glittering beetle-black in the sunlight.

When he saw the aeroplane, my father cried out, 'Good Lord, look at that!' He flung his arms out theatrically and demanded, 'Why wasn't I told?'

No one took any notice of him; he was always showing off. He stared up at the plane with an expression both fearful and excited, as though the monster was still flying through the air and he might yet be machine-gunned where he stood.

My mother and Mr Baines sat on wooden chairs pressed against the privet hedge. My mother was worried in case we were too near the wicket. She was for ever ducking and flinching, mistaking the white clouds that bowled across the sky for an oncoming ball. It wasn't an exciting game as far as I could tell but my grandfather sat on the edge of his chair and didn't fall asleep once. There was a man fielding who was almost as old as Mr Baines, and when the bowler was rubbing the ball up and down the front of his trousers preparing to run, the old man rested in a deck-chair on the pitch. The butcher's boy from the village shop was crouching down behind the wicket wearing a tin hat and smoking a cigarette.

'That fellow,' said Mr Baines, pointing at the elderly batsman in Home Guard uniform, 'is taking a risk. If he misses the ball he'll be out leg before or he'll get his skull stove in.'

'Heavens,' cried my mother, cringing backwards on her chair.

'Briggs used to play that sort of stroke,' said Mr Baines. 'Of course, he knew what he was doing.'

My father came and sat down beside him. He said: 'I never knew it was there. I never knew.' He still looked excited. He'd taken his hat off and there was a mark all round his forehead.

'As soon as he saw what ball it was,' Mr Baines said, 'he'd stand straight in front of the wicket and wait until it looked as if it would go straight through his body –'

'I never knew,' repeated my father. 'I never even guessed.' He was very unobservant. He'd been morosely loping to and from the railway station night and morning for twenty years and never bothered to look through the trees.

'Be quiet,' said my mother. 'We're concentrating.'

'At the last moment,' Mr Baines said, 'Briggs would hook it. Glorious stroke. Poetry in motion.'

'If I could have served,' remarked my father, 'I would have chosen the Merchant Navy.'

'Mind you,' Mr Baines said. 'It had to be a fast ball.'

'Failing that, I think I'd have fancied the Air Force,' said my father.

There wasn't anything one could reply to that piece of poppy-cock. If my father had been healthy enough to join up, he wouldn't have been any use. When Wilfred Pickles said on the wireless – 'And how old are you, luv? Ninety-seven!' – my father had to blow his nose from emotion. If he happened to hear 'When the lights go on again all over the world' on Forces' Favourites, he had to go out into the scullery to take a grip on himself. According to my mother, Auntie Doris had turned him into a cissy. He was a terrible cry-baby. He cried one time when the cat went missing. My mother said that most of the time his carrying on like that was misplaced. Once he went all over South-port pressing shilling pieces into the hands of what he called our gallant boys in blue. They were soldiers from the new hospital down by the Promenade. My father told them he was proud of them, that they were the walking wounded; he had a field day with his handkerchief. Afterwards it turned out there was nothing wrong with them, nothing wounded that is, it wasn't that sort of hospital. They were soldiers all right, my mother said, but they'd all caught a nasty disease from just being in the army, not from fighting or anything gallant like that and it was certainly nothing to be proud of.

'I'm not criticising,' said Mr Baines, looking at the fielder resting in his deck-chair, 'but these fellows lack self-discipline. The true sportsman is a trained athlete. He dedicates himself to the game. Only way to succeed. Same with anything in all walks of life, cotton, fishing, banking, shipping –'

'Doesn't he ever get tired of his own voice?' said my father savagely.

I sat on the grass with my back propped against my mother's knees. I could feel her trembling from indignation. My grandfather began to clap, slapping the palms of his hands together above my head as the elderly batsman left the crease and began to trail towards the pavilion. Mr Baines was the only one applauding; there were few spectators and most of those had swivelled round the other way to look at the bowling green. The new batsman was younger and he had a gammy leg. When he heard Mr Baines clapping he glared at him, thinking he was being made fun of.

'One time,' said Mr Baines, 'Briggs got stale. The Lancashire committee suggested that he should take a week's holiday. He went to a remote village in Wiltshire –'

'Don't think I don't know what the old beggar's getting at,' said my father. 'Talking about cotton like that. Did he think I wanted to come a cropper in cotton –?'

'Word got round as it will,' Mr Baines said. 'Second day there a fellow came up to Briggs and asked him how much he'd take for playing in a local match. Ten pound, said Briggs, thinking that would be prohibitive – '

The park was shimmering in sunshine. You couldn't see the boundary by the poplar trees; all the leaves were reflecting like bits of glass. The man with the gammy leg was out almost at once.

I didn't know why, the bails were still standing. I couldn't follow the rules. A fat man came out in a little peaked cap. I could hear the dull clop of the ball against the bat and the click of the bowls on the green as they knocked against each other. Behind me the voices went on and on, another game in progress, more dangerous than either cricket or bowls, and the rules were always changing.

'Briggs's side lost the toss,' said Mr Baines, 'and he had to begin the bowling. His first ball was hit out of the ground for six –'

'If I'd had any appreciation all these years,' my father said, 'things might have been different. When I think how I tramp from door to door in all weathers while you and your blasted Dad put your feet up –'

'Finally he had two wickets for a hundred and fifty runs. The crowd was looking quite nasty,' Mr Baines said. 'But what finished them off was that when he went into bat he was bowled second ball.'

'All I needed was a few bob at the right moment,' said my father. 'Just a few measley quid and the old skinflint wouldn't put his hand in his pocket –'

'Don't speak about him like that,' cried my mother. 'I won't have him called names.'

'Only a stalwart policeman and the train to London saved him from a jolly good hiding,' said Mr Baines. 'He never tried village cricket again.'

'If you'd been any proper sort of woman,' groaned my father, 'you'd have been a help-mate.'

'Be quiet,' my mother cried. 'Shut your mouth.'

'You've only been a bloody hindrance,' my father shouted. He jumped up and knocked over his chair. He walked away in the direction of the aeroplane, leaving his hat on the grass.

'What's up?' I asked. Though I knew. 'Is he off home, then?'

'Ssh,' said my mother. 'He's gone for a widdle.' Her voice was all choked.

'Don't upset yourself,' said Mr Baines. 'It's not worth it.'

'He sickens me,' my mother said. 'Sickens me. Whimpering

over the least thing when inside he's like a piece of rock. He's hard. He's got no pity for man nor beast.'

'Don't waste your tears,' said Mr Baines. 'You can't get blood from a stone.'

At that moment the ball flew past the wicket and striking the ground rolled to my grandfather's feet. He leapt up and striding to the side of the pitch chucked the ball at the batsman. He didn't exactly bowl it; he sort of dipped one shoulder and flung the ball like a boy skimming a stone on water. The batsman, taken by surprise at such an accurate throw, swung his bat. The scarlet ball shot over Mr Baines's shoulder and went like a bullet from a gun after my father.

When we ran up to him he was stood there in the shadow of the Messerschmidt with his hand clutched to the side of his head. The ball hadn't hit him full on, merely grazed the side of his temple. But he was bleeding like a pig.

'That's a turn-up for the book,' said Mr Baines.

# On the Boundary

## MELVYN BRAGG

I have just watched yet another 'collapse of English batting'. I tried everything to prevent it. I employed the prime superstition of profound pessimism, i.e. 'I bet Lillee gets Boycott this time' and 'Gower can't sweep! Next time he tries that sweep he'll come unstuck' and 'The Aussies are bound to walk it – walk it.' The idea – a sub-Roman notion, in origin, I'm told – is that by calling on the gods as if I already knew that they would do their worst, I just might taunt them into changing that frown for a smile to show that they are fully able to alter the world at their convenience. Not the most convincing props for the middle order of the present (or past, in my doleful experience) English batting order – but it is my trump card which I rather ruin by playing every ball of every over, especially when Lillee 'powers up' (copyright – all BBC commentators) to bowl. Yet superstition is all a committed spectator has to offer.

Clearly the gods rule cricket, and to that extent I am in tune with the deepest influences on the game. A spot of rain, a flash of sun, a swathe of wind, a flick of hail, a yield of earth, a tuft of turf, an errant mole, a humid noon, a pollen surge – all or any of these natural and uncontrollable forces of the weather can be crucial. Cricket is the rawest game left on the planet. For Nature old in tooth (why only one tooth? P. G. Wodehouse ought to have stayed to give us an answer) and claw (somehow a single claw is much more acceptable than a single tooth: in fact, Nature, to me, often seems nothing but a claw – mark you, that could be to do with life in the minor counties region of Cumbria) – anyway – for the sight of man pitting and falling against Nature –

go to a cricket match. None of the coddled securities of ice hockey
or American football here: none of the pampered conditions of
all-in wrestling or judo: none of the fancifulness of rugby league
or water polo – just man against the elements any one of which
could get him out just when his eye is in. *Fortuna* – she's the name
of the game and so when I watch the television and wince at the
English batting and send off missives to Delphos every time the
bowler walks back for his 440-yard run-up, I am in the right area.
We are indeed in the hands of the gods – especially when Lillee's
on song and our middle order will not play down the line as
John Arlott tells it to!

Nature – gods - we are in deep waters as we always knew we
were in this most ancient of games. 'Ancient', you cry – knowing,
perhaps, of the present state of scholarship on the game which
merits Antique more than Ancient – but Ancient has it, I think,
especially after a discovery I made in Cumbria this summer.

You might be surprised to learn that Cumbria is the home of
cricket. I have been spending the summer working on a history
of the place and found myself up against the so-called Stone
Circles. There are several here: smaller, neater, better located,
more romantic Stonehenges always brilliantly placed inside a
sweep of fell top or cresting a plain. What were they for? Once
it was thought that they were the local Druid's hall where one
sun was celebrated and another sacrificed. That fell by the way-
side of progressive academic theories. Then it was thought that
these circles represented meeting places – 3,500 years ago –
something between a market and a parliament, where stone-age
and iron-age man came to trade axes and local gossip. Again,
though, that theory lacked a real clincher. Why were the circles
*there*? Why positioned so and not so? An Egyptologist has
proposed that all those stone circles which run across Europe and
up its western fringe are, in fact, clocks, put there by the Egyptian
priesthood to correct those great clocks on the Nile whose un-
folded mysteries gave the priesthood its absolute authority for so
long. As all cricket-lovers will be aware, the Egyptian clock,
wonderful though it was, could not cope with a leap year and

so gradually became confused and thus prevented the magic of foretelling eclipses and other marvels. Reports, then, were supposed to have been sent from Brittany and Cumbria to correct the timing.

This attractive theory finally fell down because of the withering weight of academic indifference. And, possibly, the weather, in Cumbria, would allow about one sighting a month and not on the same day either.

No, these stone circles are undoubtedly the earliest cricket pitches. It was a primitive form then, as you might expect. The wicket was that big stone at the end, facing the east so that a brisk and early start could be made to the morning's play. The other stones were for the fielders to lean against during periods of dull play (hence the term 'stone-walling') and to dodge behind when a particularly vicious shot was struck: for the ball (or 'bowull' as it was known) was made from porcellenite, a substance as hard and sharp as flint, and if a full toss were to be slammed to the boundary you would be a right ass to try to catch it (hence the colloquial Cumbrian term for the full toss – the 'donkey drop'). It is worth observing that all these stone circles (and 'circle', of course, was what put me on to it: there could be no other final reason for this choice of geometric shape) are planted on dry, short, turf-land, better by far than many current-day cricket pitches in Australia and Wales. No, the case is proved: cricket began in Cumbria in about 1550 BC and it is simply and solely because of this discovery and the fame it has brought to this area that envy has so unfairly relegated us to the minor counties ever since.

Being a minor county had one advantage. When you were at school you were allowed to adopt another county so that you could get properly (i.e. with a complete range of prejudices, statistics, jeers and boasts) involved in the League championship. Most of my friends picked Yorkshire. One or two who had spent memorable days in Blackpool lighted on Lancashire. I opted for Middlesex. Denis Compton – of course!

Since then there have been lean years: and even leaner years. It has to be admitted that I became involved – in a purely cricketing sense – with Fred Trueman and I am somehow caught up in the picturesque drama of Geoffrey Boycott which made me list towards Yorkshire. But the strength of that secondary loyalty has not really wavered and when I was in India recently I found myself blessing that great nation's fine journal *The Times* for printing the English county cricket scores: and the eye went straight to Middlesex. You will have noticed that we have come up trumps again.

Secondary loyalties, though, are not quite powerful enough. The real energy went into – (a) becoming a world authority on facts and figures (an ambition I junked at thirteen, and that painstaking period of memory-bashing has left little but speckles of *Wisden* to disturb me now and then when Boycott is at the crease); (b) watching, and (c) playing.

As a cricket watcher I had one of the best strokes of luck it is historically possible to have had. I went to the 1948 Australia v England Test at Headingley. Pause for the thought to percolate slowly and with relish.

It was my father's idea of a holiday and he was absolutely right. He proposed it, though, in the most serpentine way. An old friend of his, he said, from the RAF (a sacred trilogy of letters to my mother) had asked us all to stay with him in Leeds over a long weekend. My mother was moved. There had been no holidays in the war, of course, and none since. A long weekend in Leeds! We went by British Rail and caught the bus up to Headingley. My father was so wily that he did not even let on to me that the Test was his objective. He knew I could not have kept the secret. And he knew, also, that I was usefully ignorant. I was aware that the match was going to be played and indeed on the Sunday before our departure we sat beside the radio with full concentration waiting for the team to be announced. But my geography was patchy. 'Headingley' was somewhere north-east of Paradise as far as I knew: Leeds was that poorish football team in the middle of Yorkshire. My mother bought a new skirt and blouse.

We arrived on Wednesday afternoon and behaved with all the expected awkward niceness to each other. There was a daughter who was younger than me but quite merry and a boy next door who had the right idea and a bat. I'd brought a couple of old tennis balls, naturally. In about an hour we had our own Test series arranged in the park at the bottom of the street. My mother and her hostess cautiously but firmly motored towards friendship. My father looked like a very happy man. The next morning our holiday began in earnest.

My father, his friend with whom he had been in the RAF and myself, got up at about 6.30 a.m., had breakfast and waited around the small kitchen while the two wives prepared our bait-tins for lunch. Enough sandwiches were put in these tins to promise a feast for any stray Australian eleven who might gather the left-overs. It was agreed that we would buy our own lemonade, sweets, apples and ice cream at the ground.

We walked. The city was silent but from this steady, happy shuffle of feet as the hundreds and thousands of Yorkshiremen around us bent their way on a glorious morning towards that magnificent Test where nineteen-year-old Neil Harvey made a century in his first innings, Australia got 400 in their second innings, we failed to bowl them out on a spinners' wicket and – the pen trembles as I write – I handed the ball back to Denis Compton Himself after it had crossed the boundary and he said 'Thanks, son'. It was almost worth the Australian victory.

It's Australia I want us to beat. More than anyone and all the time. As you'll realise I have had a very frustrating life in this respect. The lust to beat them bites in very deeply. The other year, after a sad defeat at the bats of our antipodean friends, I had a drink or six with a few cricket-lovers in the Earls Court area before proceeding in an easterly direction to Mayfair to meet my wife and accompany her to the Curzon Cinema. Ingmar Bergman's *Scenes from a Married Life* was showing. Now I esteem Mr Bergman so highly that I would defend him as the best film-maker alive today. But his made-for-television condensed-for-cinema piece did not catch my interest. In the comfort of the

Curzon and rather cast down by another inglorious English defeat, I dozed: well, slept. My wife tells me that she prodded me several times before the last prod got through and I woke up instantly, shouting 'Bloody Australians!'

The audience, by then enwrapt in Liv Ullmann's long monologue, were surprised, I think, judging from the freeze which came in from all about me. But as I explained to my wife again and again – it's all very well to try to gather up insights on the deeper currents in contemporary relationships, and painful, profound and moving it certainly is: but what were we going to do about the bloody Australians winning all the important matches?

When we can't beat Australia I'm afraid to say that I like the West Indies to beat them. Another great fluke in my life was being at the Oval in the one-day world cricket final when little Kallicharran hooked Lillee all around the ground. That was deeply enjoyable.

They are very good, the Australians: at cricket: the sense of fair play bred in every cricket-lover's bone-marrow makes me record that.

Watching, otherwise, has most often been contained in those lazy sunny English afternoons which seemed to disappear from my life with the arrival of the last Government but two. Until then there seemed to be time to step into the world of 'Well caught!' and 'Well held, sir!' evoked by John Moore in his fiction. Ragged village green with worn rug of playing pitch sloppily roped off; clatter of tea-cups in the wooden pavilion as the wives and girl-friends arrived to make the tea; deck-chairs with rotting canvas; wet grass which stained the raincoat; children who wanted to go to the lavatory in the crucial over; the vicar making an appearance for the fishpaste sandwiches; calm, even no rain if you were fortunate, and the sharp sounds of cricket lighting up a drowsy Sabbath. Beer in the pub after the game; lifts back home; a perfect day's watching.

I was about eleven when I decided not to captain England and if I may say so I now regard that as a wise decision. At eleven I arrived at the grammar school which then plumped out its numbers by taking in boys from other small towns and villages in the neighbourhood. Some of them were good. Not that I was bad. I was dreadful. Always out in the first over, mostly at the first straight ball; always hurt my hands fielding; always bowled either to second slip or silly mid-on; always hoping that some miracle would turn me into Denis Compton. I used Brylcreme every day.

But it was not to be. Colours came for other games, but for cricket, which colonised most of my young fantasies for most of the sunny weeks of the year, I had no aptitude at all.

I would spend literally days on end, from post-breakfast to a late fish-and-chip supper, with a bat and ball and a piece of chalk to draw stumps on a wall, sweet-talking anyone I could find to play with me. I would promise to 'field for both sides', to get a game in any scratch match I nosed out down on the common, called the Show Fields, or in the breaks at school. I cut out those educational strip cartoons in the comics where the famous taught you how to square-cut and how to off-spin; I even came to P. G. Wodehouse via cricket; the great *Mike*. But nothing happened.

Perhaps it was eyesight. At about eleven it was discovered that I was almost as blind as a mole and the introduction of those National Health specs changed my life. Before that, I tell myself, I couldn't see precisely enough. And after that, at school, moved by the usual schoolboy macho, I would whip them off, stride to the crease, blink and be clean bowled. It was hellish.

But later, when I took to the invisible aids of contact lenses, the expected improvement failed to materialise. My last games were at Roseley in Derbyshire where Philip Whitehead, MP was born, where he lives and to which he takes a gaggle of metropolitan friends of his every year to play the cunning-beyond-human-kenning local team. They have a fifty-two-year-old medium-slow bowler with a low lope and an arc-armed delivery. He got me every time. Nowadays I am not invited to Roseley for the cricket. Such setbacks could ruin your life.

That I am still resilient is due to the wonderfully organic diversity of the game itself. I can't play any more – no team, let me put an end to my excuses – no team which plays anywhere above the level of multi-geriatrical and sexually integrated British beach cricket – will have me. And I don't seem to get to see as many games as I used to, although I still manage to call in at St John's Wood now and then on the way between Hampstead where I live and the South Bank where I work. There is the television for which much thanks. And there are the ageing addicts like myself who can be warmed to a glow all evening by the nod of recognition following a remark such as 'Pity old Lillee had such a rotten day today'.

It seems to be in the family. My father, in his retirement, is a fully paid-up 11.30–6.30 five-day television Test man. My mother backs away from the ground (or lounge) to make refreshments in the pavilion (or kitchen). The phone is not answered and everyone encountered for the rest of the evening is expected by my father to be 100% up on all aspects of the day's play or they are simply cut out of the conversation. He's an example for us all.

Yet, I once saw my father play. He was scorer for Wigton at the time and he did not know it but I had come along to watch the end of the game but preferred to stay in the trees on the opposite side of the ground from the pavilion. This anti-social stance was not unconnected with embarrassment as I was with someone described to myself as 'my girl-friend' and we had had our first real argument: whether to go to the cinema café for a coffee or catch the end of the game. It was mid-week, summer, an evening, about half-past eight.

To my horror my father strode in to bat. Later I learnt they were a man short and he had been persuaded. He had never played cricket at his school, yet his devotion to the game is a mixture of the aesthetic and the obsessive. He was wearing grey trousers which made me blush. He had never admitted to having played, I realised. In all our talk of cricket – summers in and out since the war – he had never once fantasised or even referred to his own play. But he looked quite acceptable: a little plump, perhaps, but OK.

He let the first ball alone. Didn't move. It flew into the wicket-keeper's hands as if a strong stretch of elastic were holding it. I sighed with the beginnings of relief: but when he made no move at the next and yet again the third ball, I became dimly aware – as did everyone else – that having taken his guard, he was either stuck, petrified, or, as I prefer to think, entranced. For there he was – last man in – Wigton, like England, in trouble again: it all depended on him. I'm sure that his heroes marched through his mind as he faced up to the fourth ball. Bradman, Washbrook, Edrich – all of them were rooting for him as the bowler came up, and delivered, and my father leapt out of the crease to describe a stupendous hook. The bat wrapped itself around his neck, the three stumps were splayed out before my eyes and I walked away quietly before I should be seen.

He told me about it, in a roundabout way, a year or two later. Two or three years after that, I admitted I had seen it. A year or so later it became a joke between us. Cricket encourages that kind of intimacy.

# Geoffrey

GAVIN EWART

See Boycott, nonchalant, with flat bat pat
approvingly the friendly pitch, which, rich
in runs, helps him, as loud fans roar, score more!
And now he sees the elbow-peeled field yield,
the tired outfielder (once in slips) dips, trips . . .
each fluent stroke so calmly flows, those toes
aid him to cut, to glide and glance, dance, prance
and slam the ball for four. What fun! *Run, run!*
they shout. The bowlers, sad in soul, bowl, bowl . . .
unhelped by any well-worn patch (natch!), catch
or batsman's over-confident mistake, fake break,
bad timing. He just stands and picks, flicks . . . SIX!
No one could call this bat-and-pad lad bad!

# Not Quite Cricket?

Watching cricket is habit-forming, it can become habitual.
It's a kind of long-lasting white-robed ritual;
and (until recently) it's been a male prerogative,
played by big hairy bowlers and blacksmiths who were slog-
     gative.
And in village cricket, which was where it all began,
it was a straightforward matter (as in Milton) between God and
     Man –

in spite of the bumpy pitch and the blinding light
the idea was that, if you tried hard, the Deity would see you right.
The ladies just watched – in crinolines that were both broad and
  high,
which would have made the l.b.w. law hard to apply.
Notice, by the way, that cricket doesn't have *Rules*, like any
  ordinary game; it has LAWS
and many a staunch cricketer is ready to die for the Cause.
In low-grade cricket they sometimes get hit on the head
and left on the field (as at Eton and Waterloo) for dead.
Personally I think you don't have to be much of a detective
to work out that all those devices categorised as protective,
gloves, pads, boxes, helmets, are *a good thing*. Though the fans,
  stiff-upper-lipping and bobbysoxing,
consider it should be A Man's Game and lethal – like boxing.

You can imagine cricket going on eternally in Heaven.
Perhaps the Devil would be allowed up to bowl, with the Seven
Deadly Sins all clustered round the bat, fielding.
They once had Demon Bowlers and 'fast' meant yielding
(in the case of young ladies) to a sexual attraction;
but I think the Devil would bowl leg-breaks with an off-break
  action,
the classical googly, as invented by Bosie.
Such games, going on for ever, could get quite cosy.

Or perhaps the angels would be fielding, in their white flannels,
and it would be compulsory viewing on all the heavenly channels.
Certainly many Englishmen are so enamoured of cricket
that in Paradise, rather than a pretty girl, they'd like to see a
  wicket.

## *Appeal to a Cricketing Publisher*

Honest, if you publish my novel I'll lend you
my personal copy of *Cricket Rebel* by John Snow –
    or at least let you have a read of it!

I want people to say 'There goes Ewart – the *novelist!*'
as they write 'Barbara Skelton, the novelist' in gossip columns.
    Believe me, my reputation has need of it!

Some sort of boost, to get me out of the limbo
inhabited by poets the public has never heard of –
    Fame equals Fortune, we've made a creed of it.

And, since it's really only prose that turns them on,
if you want to make a lot of money or be thought highly of
    it's fiction or biography – the likeliest seed of it.

To be called 'a considerable poet' by some highbrow reviewer
doesn't cut very much ice among the paperbacks –
    except years afterwards (that's the Proust and the Gide of it).

So I want instant publication of my naive fantasy.
I implore you: increase the scoring rate, the running between
  wickets –
    I'm calling for a quick single. Take heed of it!

I want to be numbered with Dickens and Dostoievski –
not labelled 'did not bat' on the literary score-sheet,
    it's more *honour* that impels me, not the greed of it.

Let's get ahead of the game (any sporting metaphor will do),
keep up with the clock, increase the over-rate, go for the bowling,
    get that book out, make a first-innings lead of it!

## Cricket, Lovely Cricket

It's an experimental congruence!
It's a probationary similarity!
It's a proving lucifer!
It's an investigating rapport!
It's a probing likeness!
It's a dry-run flamethrower!
It's a try-out igniter!
It's a fact-finding similitude!
It's a researchful correspondence!
It's a trial contest!
It's a *Test Match!*

# From Sparrow Park to Stanley Park

ROY FULLER

Was Fuller ever more
  than a good tail-ender?
  Gavin Ewart: *The Cricket of my Friends*

My father died in 1920 when I was eight. I do not recall ever
watching cricket with him, though he took me to Boundary
Park and Watersheddings, where the Oldham soccer and rugby
league teams played. There would have been Lancashire League
cricket in Oldham; and Old Trafford would not have been too
awkward of access if he had used his Overland motor car, later
the Crossley – at any rate before we moved at the end of the
1914–18 War to Waterhead, on the side of Oldham farthest from
Manchester. Being brought up in Scotland, perhaps he was less
attached to cricket than football. And yet, having written that,
don't I associate those villages and small towns not far from
Waterhead – Delph, Upper Mill, Milnrow, Crompton – not only
with dark stone walls and mills but also little cricket league-
tables in the Oldham paper and white figures against the lush
green of levels on the valley sides? And that was a country we
quickly left after my father's death.

I first played cricket myself when I went to boarding-school in
Blackpool in 1923, though I participated in a species of the game
at earlier times on Blackpool sands or in the informally-named
Sparrow Park, a local patch of grass, with benches, rockeries and
a mast like a yacht. The sand pitches could be hard, recently left
by the tide; or soft, non-tide-washed, clogging the feet as in
nightmares. I was never any good at cricket, but in the end
played for the school XI, a non-bowler going in at a bowler's
number, rather like some of the county captains, obligatorily
amateurs in those days.

A few of these facts, and the strange nature of the school that played such a duffer, are dilated on in *Souvenirs*, memoirs of my childhood and youth. I did not think I should write further about those days, least of all about cricket, but I see now there are some matters of interest, which I hope I shall be able to communicate. So I start off, despite having come across the following the other night in *The Life of Henri Brulard* (Stendhal's autobiography), very apropos and off-putting: 'Who the deuce will have the courage to wade through it [i.e. his early memoirs], to read this excessive pile of *Is* and *Mes*? I even find it stinking myself. That's the weakness of this sort of writing in which, moreover, I cannot season the insipidity with any sauce of charlatanism.' I remember several of the cricket bats we played with at school. One was known as 'the Hobbs', a heavy implement bearing the Master's signature in facsimile, which I tried to avoid in early days but disliked less as I grew taller and stronger. Another, smaller in size, was almost equally heavy because someone had once over-zealously left it in linseed oil overnight. Insipidity!

In one way I liked cricket; in another, not. In the playground at school during the summer term cricket of a kind was played by senior boys, to which I eventually graduated, initially insinuating myself at the edge of the 'field', in fact the walls of the bogs. A solid rubber ball and the asphalt surface provided passable conditions. The oil-soaked bat was available for use, for I recall its toe leaving a mark on the asphalt when one pressed on it taking guard. Sometimes a master joined in the game, Mr David, who was good enough to play on occasions for Blackpool's Second XI. I enjoyed these sessions: late in my schooldays I began to see what cricket was about. Two elementary instances may be given. A boy called Burton used to attack the leg-stump with good-length balls. He was below medium pace but not a spinner, extreme accuracy the secret of his success, though perhaps doing a little both ways. Eventually I realised one had to play forward to the pitch of the ball, bat close to the forward leg, if one wasn't to be bowled at an early stage (topography required that the stumps be chalked on a wall, and all fielders positioned on the on side). A boy called Hayes did bowl at medium pace, and his getting his head almost too well out of the way of his arm at the moment of delivery (faintly reminiscent of Alec Bedser, then aged about nine) demonstrated what for years I had only dimly perceived – that the arm should be vertical when the hand released the ball. Real cricketers will smile in their sleeves at such confessions.

I imitated the foregoing and other players, particularly Mr David's bowling action (which included in the run-up an exaggerated but catchy piston motion of the fist holding the ball), but never had a word of coaching. Without natural ability, therefore, improvement was meagre. I visualised clearly the actions my body ought to perform but it was not well enough co-ordinated to perform them. I watched with amazement a younger and quite ordinary boy called Bancroft dance down the wicket to drive. What unjust deity had conferred such professional ability? In all this I see a parallel to my first attempts to write: imitation, snail-like improvement, execrable performance.

The side of cricket I didn't like was to be found at the school's playing fields. Soon after I joined the school it lost its playing field to the speculative building of the day, just gathering pace, and moved out to what had been agricultural land at Squires Gate. The pitches followed the slope of the land, not inconsiderable. I remember well their location being chosen – stones removed, coarse grass cut, the big roller pulled by ropes; the boarders' labour being lavishly applied, like that of Israel in Egypt. A cricket table was a thing unknown, even for the 'first game', so bowling of any accuracy was formidable, medium pace or over inclining to the lethal. Most, including myself, played in gym-shoes; no guard at all against a rap by the ball on ankle or toe. In the lower games one pad or none was *de rigueur*, simply through shortages. Late in my school career I won a pair of batting gloves in the school sports, perhaps had a season, or the rump of a season, wearing them: presumably they slightly relieved my apprehension at standing up to a bowler of any pace. Even on the first pitch we sometimes had pick-up games, first choice decided by tossing a coin. If I won I was torn between

picking Burton, the soundest first choice, and the demon Fore-
shew, wanted so one would not have to face his speed, which his
captain took care to augment by letting him bowl down the
aforesaid slope. It comes to me as I put pen to paper that at the
last I was cricket secretary (chosen no doubt for literary ability,
limited though that was in wider spheres), sending the ritual
postcards to other school secretaries – 'We can offer you 9th or
23rd June for the match here . . .' This would account for me
sometimes choosing a pick-up side (Captain's XI v Secretary's
XI), perhaps the principal reason why I got a place in the First XI.

The main school fixture to arrange was with Southport College, whose team included Caldwell, a bowler Mr David had
pronounced the fastest schoolboy bowler he had ever seen; no
mean bat, either. Did I face him twice? I remember only the
home game, when I actually caught him in the deep, falling back
into a gorse-bush (if boundaries were ever marked at Squires
Gate they would anyway incorporate extraneous vegetation),
having previously dropped him from another towering whack.
When I came in to bat he had turned to bowling enormous but
extremely slow off-breaks from the bottom of the slope, the sort
of undeserved luck I've been conscious of all my life. Plainly,
Caldwell had become one of those prodigies whose talents are
so ripe they decay a little even in youth. I had scored half a dozen
when the ball slipped from his hand as he attempted a great tweak,
and rolled gently towards me. I stood watching it fail to reach
the batting crease, gravelled to know what to do, perhaps even
joining in the derisory laughter. 'Why didn't you go down the
pitch and hit it hard with a golf shot?' Mr David asked afterwards. 'You couldn't have been caught – the ball was on the
ground.' The lost opportunity nagged and nagged me, particularly as I was dismissed soon after, not by Caldwell.

Writing this, I see myself in the charabanc bound for the away
fixture with Southport College, in some way indisposed, travelling as scorer, in fact. The neck area is in question, for was I not
collarless, bandaged? I couldn't have been suffering from ton-
sillitis – even quinsies – as I did more than once in those days, for

in that case I should have been in bed. The ailment must have been a boil, I guess: the coward's boil, not the liar's quinsy.

I was happier at an earlier age, solitarily, or comparing notes only with a friend or two, playing paper cricket. I expect the procedure is still well-known. I assigned a symbol to each letter of the alphabet (e.g. 4, 2, l.b.w., caught), then opened a book at random and, following the letters on the page, played the match I had decided on. I used to alter the symbolism until reasonable verisimilitude was achieved: one couldn't have a county side, let alone England or Australia, dismissed for peanuts, half of them hit wicket. But having got a decent balance I did not stick to it, perhaps craving continual surprise. I used to keep bowling analyses, but more elaborate refinements such as county tables and Test match series were beyond my powers of application, like much else worthwhile in life. I don't think I ever descended to mingling myself, or even school heroes, with real cricketers, but I would arrange a few matches out of my head, as it were: for instance, players with names starting with 'H' v The Rest. Hobbs, Holmes, Hallows, Hendren, Hirst, Hitch, Hearne – good grief, does my memory fail so early in the list?

Some time during my boyhood the Blackpool municipality established a park, Stanley Park, in an area then behind the town. Near the park's main entrance was the ground used by the Blackpool CC. Whether it was there already or set up as part of the park's amenities I do not know. Though, like Squires Gate, always in my time a low-scoring pitch, it eventually achieved county status, no doubt helped by the promise of spectators in decent numbers from summer visitors. Perhaps a county match a season was played there, plus a week of festival cricket at the 'back end', viz. September. To many of these matches I went as a boy, later as a solicitor's articled clerk.

I have not looked up *Wisden* or other works, so in what I shall say I am sure to get things wrong, but the record will have memory's peculiar purity. In the film *Bonnie and Clyde* there is a marvellous scene of family reunion before the inevitable permanent separation, which the director shot as though it were happening in a sea-mist. That sort of sad and legendary unclarity is not quite what I am aiming for: indeed, some memories are sharp, though they resemble snapshots rather than film sequences.

Some members of the Lancashire team of the later 'twenties come first to recall. Makepeace, who opened, was a notorious slow-coach, a stonewaller and a half. Do I rightly visualise him as under medium height, gnome-like, even bow-legged? The last-named characteristic would tie in with his playing soccer for Everton, many good footballers being thus configured. Certainly his appearance and character were from a typical mould of Lancastrian, the sort of chap I might sit opposite to in the Waterhead tram, and take in, a few years before. Except when Lancashire's fate was in the balance, I was always relieved to see him go – in those days (to a degree, still) of the essentially frivolous mind that likes the *adagio* to end and the *scherzo* begin. His partner, Hallows (what divine fictioneer chose these names?), could not avoid appearing dashing by contrast, but he was in any case admirable, and, as I thought then, should have played more representative cricket. Did Ernest Tyldesley come in when Makepeace or Hallows was out, or was he at number four? Tyldesley (E.) was a great batsman, no doubt without the final polish of Hobbs, the final sparkle of Hendren, but utterly reliable, yet fluent and aesthetically satisfying. I am not sure that he, too, was not of archetypal Lancastrian breed, though possibly merely as to wearing his cap like Makepeace, at no angle at all. I had a soft spot for Farrimond, a batsman-wicketkeeper usually kept from better things by Duckworth, England's and Lancashire's regular 'keeper. I suppose his name stimulated my liking, especially as against the common-sounding Duckworth: Farrimond – aristocratic syllables. But I must add, in the manner of Dr Johnson about his cat Hodge, Duckworth was a good wicket-keeper, too.

Tyldesley was usually pronounced in Blackpool 'Tiddlesy'. The inhabitants of the town were deficient in elocutionary prowess. Very nearly as famous as Ernest was Dick Tyldesley: perhaps had been so. In my day he was extremely stout, thus must have been past his best, though that was not the impression given. I believe his white flannels were held up by a necktie: if so, that would be a habit from an earlier epoch. He was a slow right-arm bowler, bringing his arm from behind his waist (or, rather, where that once had been) in a fashion that initially seemed amateurish, a schoolboy's action. All he did was interesting, though flight of great daring was his hallmark. When he came in, low down in the order, his bat seemed fragile, wielded somewhere below his stomach, but he slogged effectively.

I saw – didn't I? – McDonald in Warwick Armstrong's Australian side before he played for Lancashire. Even in my nonage I realised he was a beautiful bowler, an adjective sometimes loosely used today – 'Buggins bowled beautifully' meaning no more perhaps than kept the run-rate down. In McDonald's case it was strictly deserved. His run-up was long but compact, the slightly flapping black hair the untidiest part of the business. He was very much sideways on when his arm started to come over, and how it came over was the perpetual mystery, the chief constituent of the pulchritude. It must have been high, like Hayes's, yet at some point it seemed to bend, as though following the most economical orbit, a moment of suppleness and grace that nevertheless one felt was adding power to the delivery.

The action of Cecil Parkin, fast-medium, was at the opposite pole. His run-up was long-striding, spiderlike, both arms held away from the body. 'Parkin,' I might announce during playground cricket, and do a fair imitation of the action if not the result. I think he also bowled slower stuff, of an eccentric nature, like Caldwell's. On the field he provided pretty continuous comedy (or, at the least, diversion), probably a man of pessimism or secret sorrow. I verily believe he was the originator of that flip of the boot that brings a ball travelling on the ground conveniently into the bowler's hand. The trick – almost a novelty – was expected by the crowd, but he did not always satisfy expectations, feigning to miss the ball with his boot, or even not to see it. Similarly, he would occasionally pretend to misfield or, what was more effective, pretend *not* to have misfielded, throwing a merely imaginary ball to the wicketkeeper. He batted perhaps as low as number ten; always hit out extravagantly, and was quite capable of making runs. I once saw him given out l.b.w. and, his being the tenth wicket down, the innings closed – the umpires removing the bails, everyone starting to walk off. Except Parkin, who with extreme naturalness affected not to have seen the umpire's finger go up, and took careful guard for the next ball. When he found himself alone at the wicket, he gave a start of surprise, and followed the players to the pavilion. The mime was rapid but explicit, absolutely not overdone.

When I went to Stanley Park as a schoolboy I expect my mother made me sandwiches for the luncheon interval. I would visit one of the refreshment tents for a ginger-beer, then to be had in stone bottles, very good. When I went as an articled clerk, probably with others from the office, we would buy pork pies and ginger-beer shandies. The pies were also very good – oval, deep, fresh, peppery. Inside the refreshment tent was gloom after the summer outdoors, the strange grass floor mostly trampled down, the walls sometimes flapping like McDonald's hair, abandoned scorecards littering the ground, a constant ebb and flow of male customers. 'I had not thought death had undone so many,' I might have quoted, had I known the verse, then not long written.

Again of early apprehension in connection with cricket was the incongruity of reality and history (or literature), a sense that came even more strongly from the few race-meetings I went to when an articled clerk. To experience the irrelevancies, accidents, banalities and tediums of actuality through the subjective vision, and then to see the rich and contradictory process in the newspaper the next day subsumed in the bare, brief list of scores (e.g. 'O'Connor l.b.w. 43') made one speculate on the nature of experience. I carried into my early fictive efforts – probably went on doing so – an obsession with the problems of naturalism and formality, so well exemplified by cricket and its records: the *Ulysses* complex, one might call it, after the novel that in my earliest cricketing days had, like *The Waste Land*, been only fairly recently completed.

In the festival cricket at Stanley Park when the season proper was over, I watched a good many players, some legendary, but mere enumeration would be superfluous. I didn't in the least mind that the matches were in essence as meaningless as those of my paper-cricket – Lancashire v Mr A. E. R. Gilligan's XI, North v South. One was sustained by the procession of characters, the perennial promise of extraordinary action, and, above all, the fleshing out of fable. One actually saw Root bowling his 'leg-theory' – short, low-trajectory balls well on the leg-side, a good few of which were ignored. Boring after a bit, but it must be remembered that curiosity about the great or notorious was then only to be properly satisfied at first-hand, newsreels (for years silent ones) and photographs merely tantalising. Good looks, the angle of a cap – such adventitious things often attracted my especial allegiance and interest, as in the case of O'Connor of Essex, before-mentioned, who at last did play for England, as I earnestly hoped he would. I remember an early appearance of Kenneth Farnes, also of Essex, then at Cambridge or (as will be seen) more likely about to go up, his exotic cap and amateur's initials giving a first impression of effeteness, quickly dissipated when he came on to bowl with super-Caldwellian speed. One got to know the Essex players, and those of Northants and Glamorgan, for Stanley Park was allowed only to entertain the less glamorous counties.

Farnes was killed in the War. One is tempted to think of 1939 as marking the end of the best epoch of one's absorption in cricket, but really the terminal date was earlier. For one thing, I never played after I left school in 1928. For another, in youth and adolescence cricket-watching, like many another activity, held promise of adventure on the side, not strictly connected with the game yet by no means making the experience of it impure.

Chronology has misted up, like that scene in *Bonnie and Clyde*. In 1938 I saw Bradman squatting in the outfield at Lord's, plucking a blade of grass to chew, humming to himself. My thought was: I must remember this for posterity. But here I am at sixty-eight, Bradman still alive – reported in *The Times* this very morning as saying that Vivian Richards is the best on-side player he has ever seen. Was it before or after the War I saw a Lancashire League poster proclaiming (on separate lines) 'Nelson with Constantine' versus some team or other – the 'Nelson with' in tiny letters, the 'Constantine' huge? Before the War, I believe – yet I almost overlapped with the great man on the BBC Board of Governors in the 'seventies. Perhaps this is the place (if there *is* any place for such an unchronological addendum) to say that, despite my previous statement, I did look in the London Library to try to check the death of Farnes, feeling that memory alone ought not to kill off one so young and so endowed – and accidentally found his book, *Tours and Tests*, published in 1940. It is a work still readable, containing some interesting opinions and observations, and of a Stendhalian self-deprecation. Typical of its modesty is the frontispiece photograph bearing the legend 'H.M. King George V examining Wyatt's thumb'. Farnes himself is in the background, recognisable by his great height. To my chagrin I found his description of McDonald far better than mine. Strangely enough, it occurs in his account of a match Essex played against Lancashire in 1930, at Blackpool (one of several county matches he appeared in *before* his university days). Undoubtedly I was there! Here is the passage:

He was then about thirty-eight years old, yet he was still fast, and still preserved that beautiful action – the most nearly perfect possible. He took quite a long run, working up easily to a maximum speed at the moment of delivery. As he reached the crease his left arm straightened sharply and pointed straight above him. The whole thing with the follow-through was extremely graceful and rhythmic, a 'grooved' action, seemingly effortless. Yet the ball became a thing of vivid life as it left his hand. McDonald, Duckworth has told me, had very long arms and amazingly supple shoulders; he could put both arms over his head and clasp his hands under his chin. He could use the full width of the crease, and so was able to avoid any holes caused by the bowling which inconvenience most bowlers. And in spite of his speed, he was so light that he could have bowled in dancing pumps.

That my novel, *The Ruined Boys* (1959), included a school cricket match is an indication of abiding interest. The scene (passionate but farcical, like much in sport) is invented, though the idea of the player Wilkes came from Caldwell. I altered the description of Wilkes to avoid identification, why I do not now recall. There is a bit of business about the scoring, which I would regard as generally interesting, in the same, fundamentally odd, way as my chance-produced paper-cricket figures used to interest me. Only the numeration relevant to the nub of the game is given (my novels usually stick to the matter in hand), but had I been more indulgent I would have assumed a willingness on the reader's part to be told, for instance, Wilkes's bowling analysis for the season to date. Statistics, physical appearance, physical action translated into figures of superiority and inferiority, with time acting on all these – such are the main elements in the game's fascination.

There is also sentiment. During the First World War, the musicologist Edward J. Dent said that 'people like George Robey make me feel patriotic'. One knows precisely what he meant – and it could be said of rather more cricketers than comedians. E. V. Lucas (I read in *The Lyttleton – Hart-Davis Letters*) 'was chary of seeing the greatest of all jugglers, Cinquevalli, because he always made him cry'. I once saw Hendren take a low catch close-in from a fierce hit, all so quickly done the ball seemed for a few moments to vanish; and simultaneously there came to mind a previously read opinion that Hendren was the greatest short-leg in the world. Brimmed a Cinquevallian tear. Both cricket's skill and Englishness are capable of touching on a high level a great audience of varying class and intellect.

But cricket also, perhaps chiefly, so leisurely is its time-scale, lavish its cast and arithmetic, moves us in retrospect. We are nostalgic for the game's past, as well as our own. Some day, I suppose, some will look fondly back on boozy, can-rattling spectators, players' rude and self-congratulatory gestures, shirts proper to squash not cricket, helmets less appropriate to Lord's than to Squires Gate.

# Twelfth Man

JACKY GILLOTT

It was annoying not to be a boy.

*Annoying!* It was more than annoying. It was, in the feeling lingo of the early fifties, damnably tragic.

After all, brimful of unrealised ambitions as I was, most of my fancies – to sing Orpheus like Kathleen Ferrier, to outclass Colonel Llewellyn over show jumps, to swim the Channel against the tide: both ways – were sweet enough to dream of. They fell, however distantly, within the bounds of reality. But to be a *boy* . . . It seemed (before I'd heard tell of that magic city, Morocco) an insuperability.

*Thews*, I wanted. Where I had got the word, heaven knows, but thews were the thing I most coveted. Gleaming bands of strength to rehouse the inert girl carcase of which I seemed, mistakenly, to be tenant.

On the grassy bank that divided the playing fields of the two schools the boys sat, jeering at the feeble lolloping and panting that characterised girls' games. Or girls' poor execution of boys' games. To belong to the sex that missed catches and squeaked if inadvertently struck by nothing more injurious than a tennis-ball was a humiliation. And the way girls ran! Even in gymslips and plimsolls they somehow contrived to run as if wearing high heels and carrying a handbag. Their elbows stuck out in the silliest possible fashion and they wasted valuable breath as they failed to reach some critical white line. I had the impression that girls *wanted* to lose, to be out as swiftly as possible in order to rejoin their friends in dumpy circles of gossip.

Surly and contemptuous, I sat alone sucking the juicy end of plucked grasses, dreaming of thews and watching the Misses Barlow and Babstock in admiration. Miss Barlow was swarthy as a gipsy with a shadow of moustache arching her upper lip as she blew on a whistle gripped permanently between her teeth. Miss Babstock was fair and freckled, a little disabled by powerful round spectacles that steamed up in the changing rooms when she made us run through the showers, ticking off each yelping body in her register. The soppiest of the girls wore plastic shower caps to protect their Toni home perms.

The Misses Barlow and Babstock had beautiful thews, handsomely revealed by the pleated shorts they habitually wore both indoors and out. Miss Barlow's shorts were navy, Miss Babstock's grey. Their short-sleeved Aertex shirts were faded by considerable washing. The need for regular laundering was doubtless brought about by the excessive effort they had to put into the physical education of girls, strenuously heaving the reluctant things over a wooden horse in the gym or trying to generate energy into some particularly sluggish hockey match – darting up and down the field in studded black boots, roaring 'Pass!' or *'Shoot!'* at a girl dribbling ineptly towards her opponent in the hope of having the ball, and thus all responsibility, taken from her.

I formed a programme for achieving massy thews and becoming a member of as many school teams as were open to me. The idea was to become as large, heavy and powerful as possible. Exercise and over-eating. At six every morning I rose and ran along sands left firm by a departed tide: a good, hard, flat landscape, silent save for the sound of gulls and my drumming, ambitious feet.

My eating became a daily spectacle of some wonder. I could polish off twenty school potatoes at a single sitting. Those on my table passed their pastry crusts, spotted dick and cubes of stodge down to me and stared with grateful amazement as all vanished. One wasn't allowed to leave the table without showing a clean plate.

Each new term and half-term's gym session started with a weigh-in and soon I was creeping up on Caroline Broderick's

hitherto unchallenged weight . . . Ten stone . . . Ten stone three . . .
At ten-and-a-half stone I had passed her and could pack a pretty
punch. Julia Fazackerly sustained a black eye from my well-
directed right. (She'd had it coming for five years, ever since – in
my first term, at the age of nine not yet accustomed to the ruling
that one was not to be excused in class – I had disgraced myself
and Julia Fazackerly, seated behind me, had drawn attention to
the fact by laying a large sheet of pink blotting-paper on the
floor.)

In another pleasing hockey game I broke Rhona Gomersall's
front teeth and split her lip open. My father, who wished me – as
his only child – to carry on the family business (factory catering),
would occasionally come to watch hockey matches in which I
played for the school to see how I was shaping up. What I lacked
in skill I made up in terrorist tactics, crashing headlong into un-
decided knots of girls and making off with the ball. I hope he was
proud of me.

Alas, I lacked not only skill but team spirit. The aggregate score
of my team mattered not a hoot to me unless I was principal
scorer. For this reason I was more truly attracted to summer sports,
to tennis and cricket where one could star more conspicuously. I
wanted that sneering ridge of boys to fall silent as my ace service
made the chalk spit from the mown court, as wickets fell apart
under the punishing balls I despatched from the bowling end.

Tennis, however, was a frustration to me. It was the one game
in which several girls excelled and my ace service never really
recovered form after a horse fell on top of me and cracked my
collar bone. Since I was too erratic for regular inclusion in the
team, the charabanc departed for other schools on Saturdays
without me more often than I liked, so cricket became the chief
focus for my ambitions. This, for a number of reasons, was
wisely judged. Most girls were rotten at it and lay about the
field sunbathing when not actually required to do anything more
active. And when called upon, they lumped around asking in
loud, truculent voices what silly mid-on could possibly *mean*. It
was noticeable the way in which, during the course of the game, the

fielders retreated further and further from the sacred distance
between the two wickets and had repeatedly to be summoned
back by a magisterial Miss Barlow or Miss Babstock.

My father, whose information couldn't always be relied upon
(he'd told me he had been a champion member of the Tooting
Bec cycling team), did have something of a cricketing record prior
to his war wound. (A knee-cap had been twisted rather badly
jumping from a truck in the desert.) He had played at the Oval.
He had played with – for years I thought he was referring to a
well-known chemist – somebody called Pothecary. He had
played with Jim Laker and captained an All-Services team against
New Zealand. So there was a modest family tradition. It boded
well. And I didn't run like a startled hen. I could throw further
than anyone else. I had tremendous biceps. All my thews, indeed,
were coming along nicely.

Every lunchtime I practised at the nets hoping Miss Babstock
would witness my dedication and the amount of wood I managed
to splinter. As well as my early morning run I went round and
round the playing fields at break leaving behind me floppy girls
with puce faces who made a great show of holding their sides in
pain. In the mirror I studied, not my complexion as they appeared
to, but my thews. In profile – flexed, bent and defined them with
a deepening satisfaction.

What gave me particular pleasure were cricket pads. They
were kept in a shed that smelt of sweat and linseed oil. Once
strapped up, it was impossible to walk like a girl. Legs stoutly
apart, one *strode* with a faint clink of buckles. I enjoyed the
theatrical business of this striding towards the wicket, flourishing one's bat, moving at an unhurried but purposeful pace. At
the crease there was more opportunity for theatre. A pause to
check it, a few preliminary blocking movements with the bat
shifting the body weight carefully this way, then that, a poem of
fluency and fearlessness. Then, after a terse nod of readiness, the
performance would be faintly spoiled by some daft underarmer
tripping towards me with a pitiful lob that one followed with a
derisive eye as it went either several feet wide of the wicket or

failed to reach it at all, dwindling to a halt a yard or so from one's feet.

There was a measure of joy in standing immobile as the wicket-keeper stumbled round to retrieve such a ball and chuck it, just as inaccurately, back to the bowler. But nothing to the joy of the occasional ball that came sufficiently close to swipe. Crack! Out to the boundary between a channel of girls ducking and clutching their heads for protection. My God, they were awful. The *waits*, while one of them dawdled off to ferret among the long grass and then, having found the ball, roll it to the person nearest rather than to the bowler! Sometimes the ball would thus pass between three, even four people before returning to the one for whom it was intended. Although my partner would groan audibly at the need to keep running while this pantomime went on, the dilatory level of fielding did make it terribly easy to knock up impressive scores. As did the terror of catching. Personally, I longed for the dramatic catch, for the Angela Brazil moment of running, judging, squinting, reaching and then rolling to the ground, that crimson treasure clasped triumphantly to the ribcage. I practised the movements with an imaginary ball in my bedroom. But no other girl, it seemed, shared this vision. Some hapless creature, having done a careful manicure during break and seeing the ball drop towards her from the sky, would raise both arms more in supplication than determination, then let it plop between her arms preferring to be damned than break her nicely fashioned nails. Some didn't even have the decency to pretend the sun had dazzled them. They just grinned cheerfully and went back to the business of acquiring a tan.

In white overalls and panamas the Misses Barlow and Babstock did their honest best to dignify this farce. Given the competition, my chances of being in the First XI seemed excellent. I developed a spin on the ball. In my run-up I went from a crouch to a spring at a terrific pace, lamming the ball at invisible speed towards whichever ninny stood with her knees pinned together at the wicket end.

Whether it was the damage that wretched horse had done or a

major defect in my eyesight (of which I was then unaware) which makes it very difficult for me to judge distance of any kind, the fact slowly and unhappily began to dawn on me that for all my crouching, sprinting, hurling and grunting the pitch was quite simply not long enough for my fearsome spins – any more than the tennis court had been for my service. Since there was a clear reluctance to adapt the distance to meet my talents, hours were spent in the arms of Miss Babstock, who ran in a crab-like partnership with me, guiding my over-arm and yelling at me to keep my eye on the wicket. Of course, keeping *my* eye – with its idiosyncratic spatial grasp – on the wicket wasn't the least use. Swinging Miss Babstock off the ground I would watch the departure of my stunning ball only to see it speeding at ear-level way past the wicketkeeper and on towards the bank dividing the boys from the girls.

Great effort was expended on trying to modify my athletically performed and perfectly useless bowling until sadly it was suggested by Miss Babstock that since I could *throw* further than anyone else, I had best field.

My heart still set on a place in the team, I accepted the new position with concealed ill-grace. Even in the slips my throwing just went too far, flying beyond the new, usurper bowler and compelling more unenthusiastic runs from the batting side. I was set further back. And further. Until it was deemed that even my magnificent throw could not possibly exceed the requisite distance. By this time I was in the long grasses. And bored. But because I still yearned beyond anything to clamber on that bus, bat under my arm, cap on my head, I forced myself to concentrate. Every now and then concentration wandered. To the boys who stuck their heads above the bank hooting and dodging down again. It was at one such lapsed moment I heard my name bawled. And Good Lord, there was that legendary catch zooming downwards towards me. I ran to meet it bold and full of Angela Brazil inspiration. I would leap, reach, cup it to my chest, roll on the ground. Hold on.

I think I did all of these things but what I remember most

sharply is that my chest *hurt*. Returning the ball casually, I bit my lip against tears and, turning my back on the Aunt Sally of boys, rubbed the place where it hurt. Then two palms I placed furtively across the area, pretending to soothe the stinging in my hands. It was a chest no longer. I had, instead, *chests*.

Two days before the match, the list went up. I sauntered towards the board. My eye ran down the names. Ran right down, to the bottom. In front of my schoolfellows, I flushed.

*Twelfth man!*

'Thank heavens for that,' I said loudly to no one in particular. 'At least I can get in a decent sunbathe.'

So I took a book and read it showily, tilting my head back against the deck-chair occasionally to receive the full benefit of the sun. 'Who won?' I enquired, yawning, as my team trooped off the field.

Next term, because it was expected of me, I played in the hockey team. My father, who came to watch, declared himself shocked. 'What on earth had you got on?' he exclaimed.

It took a minute or two to figure out what he meant.

'When you fell over . . .' he said.

'Oh-ah . . . Mm.' I nodded.

'I thought you had to wear regulation brown,' he went on. Then: 'Make sure you do. Bloody embarrassing.'

He wouldn't explain himself to my mother and I wasn't going to admit I'd pinched a pair of her green, see-through nylon knickers.

I was dropped from the team. Not because of the knickers, I think. I had lost, Miss Barlow explained sorrowfully, pursing those moustachioed lips, my sense of attack.

I didn't care. At the time I truly didn't. I gave up potatoes and took up watching local rugger matches, idling up and down the sidelines with my girl-friends joining in whorish gossip about what I continued, lasciviously, to call thews.

But it was a short-lived, unsteady progress. Exams beckoned. A career in factory catering. On the list of taboos, potatoes were joined by bread, milk, cakes, butter, chocolate, meat . . in short, food. By next summer term's weighing-in I recorded less than seven stone on the scales. I was lean, flat, freed from menstruation. But when I tried to run towards the far wicket, I fainted. Something had gone wrong.

Not until two summers later did the odd perspectives gradually sort themselves out. We moved house. The new one faced on to the local cricket pitch. My mother was a social member, my father played an occasional valiant, middle-aged game. Efforts were made to involve me, if only to liberate others from my morose and silent presence. Scoring I did with such consummate lack of interest that mythic centuries were won and twenty wickets fell at a single swoop. In retrospect, I'm amazed by the good nature of those whose performances I so misrepresented. Instead, I was given team teas to prepare, bridge rolls with a stripe of paste or sandwich spread, but this was feeble, woman's stuff so I reverted to the sullen, solitary watching of years before, shifting my deck-chair away from the others and closing my eyes on the game. Every now and then a surge of admiration or amusement drove those stubborn eyelids to flicker open. I caught myself smiling when my father, reaching into a privet to retrieve the ball, extracted instead a wonderfully large, flesh-coloured bra.

Then came the day of the great match against a boastful neighbouring village team. They were first in to bat. Three wickets went down disastrously fast to our side's joy. On came the village saviour, a big, swaggering chap confident of rescuing honour. He flexed his wrists, heeled the crease a bit and squared up smugly to our oncoming pygmy bowler. The ball – it has to be said – was an easy one. The village saviour took a swing. In fact he swung so hard he flung himself flat on his bottom and having been so imprudent as to keep his Swan Vestas in his back pocket, burst into flames.

We all ran to remove his trousers. And amidst our side's laughter, their side's mortification and one man's lifelong discomfiture, I had a sudden unexpected glimpse of a grassy bank topped by superior boys. Upended, they were. Humpty-dumpties, the lot of them. Irreparably unstuck.

I hesitate to say this of a sport regarded as one of life's gravest mysteries by some, but I have cricket to thank for the healing knowledge that nothing in this world lacks a comic profile and that it is more pleasurable to laugh in company than it is to laugh alone.

Thus armoured, one can overcome the hurt and disappointment of many a thing – not least the monstrous injustice of being twelfth man.

# The Ivanhoe

ROBERT GITTINGS

In the year 1973, that admirable actress Irene Worth gave a performance in Tchekov's *The Seagull*, directed by Jonathan Miller in the Chichester Festival Theatre's summer season. As Madame Arkadina she was electrifying, and her interpretation of the part was in many ways quite new. She was a tigress. She stalked her charming but weak-willed lover, the novelist Trigorin, like a beast of prey with every possible stratagem. In the crucial scene, where she is really making sure of him for herself, she gave a reading of the character which was theatrically unique. When she finally overcame his vacillating will, she hurled herself literally on top of him, and shouted exultantly, 'He's mine!' The tigress had captured its prey.

Now, what in the world has this to do with cricket? Well, in that same summer of 1973, the Ivanhoe Cricket Club of Chichester was celebrating the fiftieth aniversary of the Club's foundation. Though only fifty years old, no age in this part of England, legend already was at work on its history: conflicting and intriguing stories of its origins had already got about, and were variously discussed and argued in the charming and gossip-loving cathedral city of Chichester. One prevalent story anticipated both a kind of class-struggle and the inroads of the generation-gap. There was, it was said, fifty years before, a local team run in a doctrinaire and high-handed way. The older members used to put down the younger. Bright young fast bowlers were sent back to the pavilion if their laces were unorthodoxly tied, or even if they committed the sin of wearing a heavy but coloured sock over their turn-ups to minimise the pounding of their run-

up on the hard turf. In the newly permissive 1920s it was unwise
to push the young too far. There was a secession, a break-away, a
youthful splinter-group. They formed a club of their own, whose
average age was in the late teens. There came the question of a
name for the new team. Most of the youthful members had just
enjoyed or endured, according to ability or to temperament, the
novels of Sir Walter Scott as set books for what was then known
as the Higher Certificate or Oxford and Cambridge Locals.
(Nowadays Scott is out; *Lord of the Flies* in.) It was decided to
call the new club the Ivanhoe.

A pretty and a literary legend: but there is another and a quite
different one. According to this, it arises from the Southdowns,
that race of prime sheep, cultivated on the hills above Chichester,
the market-town where the cattle-market until recent times used
to spread all along East Street, now very effectively converted
into a pedestrian precinct. As in Thomas Hardy's Dorchester,
the lives of the inhabitants were connected with the rearing of
sheep, so well described in the downland essays and sketches of the
naturalist W. H. Hudson. Here is the alternative legend. A
Chichester man had failed financially. Bankruptcies were oddly
frequent in this prosperous city of family businesses. To retrieve
his fortunes, he emigrated to Australia, to New South Wales,
where eventually he made good and became owner of a small
sheep-run on the famous Ivanhoe sheep-range, celebrated by
Australian ballad-writers, such as 'Banjo' Paterson, the best of all,
in wry, Aussie songs of the outback. The new chum from
Chichester celebrated his new start by helping to found a cricket-
team in his adopted country, the Ivanhoe. He wrote back to a pal
in Chichester to tell him of his retrieved fortunes and of the
newly-founded team. The Chichester friend (possibly here is
where the two legends got mixed) was in the process of in-
augurating a new team himself. He decided to make it a twin of
the New South Wales one. He gave it the name Ivanhoe.

Round about the year 1953, when the Club had been going for
thirty years, I joined it. I had come to live in and near Chichester
a few years before, and was struck by the many clubs in the area.

Every spare piece of grass seemed to be occupied every week-end and early closing day (Thursday). Ivanhoe had announced themselves short of playing members, and indeed put an advertisement in the local paper. I joined and played. I still play, though I am what is called a Saturday-morning-phone cricketer. If by eleven o'clock on a Saturday morning the captain is still one short, he rings me up to complete his team. I often wonder if he might not do better to play one short. Predestined now to No. 11, I seldom bat and only pray I do not make too many mistakes in the field. If, at my age, I turned an arm over to bowl, that arm would probably come off at the shoulder. With great kindness and tact, they have made me the Chairman of Ivanhoe, a nominal post only functioning once a year at the Annual General Meeting. This, however, does lead me back to Irene Worth.

When the Ivanhoe Club, whatever its origins, was 50, the AGM decided that the occasion should be marked in some way. We were to notify past members, we were to hold a dinner dance. I suggested I should raise a scratch team, a Chairman's Eleven, and play the last home fixture in August against Ivanhoe itself. The suggestion caught on. It was also suggested the match should be started in some way by some celebrity. A few years before, there was an appeal to save the fabric of the house in which Keats had died in Rome; I had found myself directing a charity performance to raise funds. The cast, all giving their services free, was the most distinguished I had ever handled. It consisted of Sir John Gielgud, Sir Ralph Richardson, Irene Worth, and, incredibly, Tito Gobbi. With the two knights I had worked in minor ways before. Gobbi needed no direction. He simply went round snapping his fingers loudly and smartly to test the acoustic of the hall where we were performing. Irene Worth was sympathetic and magnificent. Reading Joseph Severn's account of Keats's death-bed, she made us all cry, even the Italian ambassador, putting in a duty appearance. That she would be playing in Chichester at the time of the Ivanhoe anniversary match seemed the finger of Providence: even more that she did not have a matinée that Saturday afternoon. I asked;

she accepted to bowl the first ball. She put on a highly fetching pair of white duck trousers. She disdained to bowl under-arm, but made a full fast bowler's run-up to the wicket, and brought her arm over in a manner that recalled the great fast bowlers of any age. It was a shame it was only a token opening, since she almost bowled the Ivanhoe captain.

This was the high spot of the game, but there were plenty of others nearly as good. When the AGM came up again the following February, I was unanimously asked to provide an annual event. I should explain that the idea behind picking my scratch team was that its composition should be roughly literary, but that it should only contain people who knew what they were doing on the cricket field. One poet, who needlessly ran himself out in this first, drawn game, laughing light-heartedly, was not asked again. If in doubt, cricket not literature was to be the criterion. In any case, I always have had a horror of the J. C. Squire type of joke match, useful as it was to provide comedy for A. G. Macdonell's *England, Their England*. It was only fair to a respectable club like Ivanhoe to provide respectable opposition. Likewise we looked for a leading lady who could clout or hurl down the first ball in some style. We found one the next year in Dorothy Tutin. She, by chance, was playing another Russian part at the Festival Theatre, Natalia Petrovna in Turgeniev's *A Month in the Country*, one of her most enchanting performances, which later transferred to the West End. Dorothy came from one particular corner of Yorkshire, from which the Tutins all spring. That alone determined her status as an opening bat, which was what she decided to be. After some serious practice, in the spirit of dedication which she brings to every part she plays, she advanced to the crease to face the bowling of her delightful actor-husband, Derek Waring. Derek, taking a very long run, bowled her a slow half-volley, which she hit with firm precision to cover-point. She retired from the field triumphantly, waving in one hand the bat and in the other the bottle of wine which my wife had brought from the direction of square-leg. It was a glorious day, and Dottie's sunny personality was matched by the weather, though the Chairman's XI unfortunately lost: a lack of really fast bowlers.

The great luck-bringer to my scratch side next year was Joan Sims. Chichester Festival Theatre is a firm favourite with actors or actresses who want to escape the cramping tentacles of type-casting in film or television. Joan was keen to break out of the 'Carry On' image. Possessed of a beautiful true soprano voice, she appeared, singing and acting in a revue about the Kings and Queens of England – a sort of updated *1066 and All That* – in which she portrayed, among others, very funnily, poor, dead Queen Anne. I managed to persuade her that on the cricket-field no one would associate her with her ruder film characters. Since this was more or less why she had come to Chichester in the first place, she was grateful. Besides, she had actually learnt to play cricket at school. This was evident when she smacked the first ball, and by no means a bad one either, firmly past mid-off to the boundary, the first four by a leading lady. This provided a good omen – I had also provided some better cricketers – and after a fine struggle the Chairman's XI won by two wickets.

There followed a gap, as regards actresses, of two years, one through lack of organisation – I had been lecturing in America – and the other through an untoward outbreak of mumps – mumps! – in the Festival Theatre Company of that year. Also, we became the victims, I think, of a trend in theatre habits and the nature of modern audiences. To ensure a full house, manage-ments, it now appears, have to pack a play with TV stars. The critics have pointed this out often enough, and applied it to Chichester more than once. TV cameras seem to miniaturise acting, and the exuberant expansion of playing to a live audience applies equally to the cricket-field. One could not, however, fault on these grounds the latest recruit to our ceremony, Gemma (*Duchess of Duke Street*) Jones. She took to the wicket as readily as she had taken to Shakespeare as Beatrice in *Much Ado*, and if she did not actually manage to hit the ball – a half-volley bowled this time by myself – she made a brave and spirited gesture, and carried off her non-vintage champagne.

So there we are. Who will perform in 1981 and in future years? My casting depends, as it must each season, on that of the theatre, and there is now a new director. I am hoping, in a sense, to read his mind. He has a penchant for Thomas Hardy. Perhaps he will try an adaptation of one of the novels, and some healthy outdoor-looking actress, who is the perfect casting for Fancy Day and Tess, will step out on our pitch. Of course, I have personally to put up with a certain amount of what may be called locker-room humour on this topic. The match is played in the same public park which provides the idyllic setting of the Chichester Theatre. The fanfares, which recall audiences after intervals, blare out over the cricket ground. 'Do you mind asking your friends to be quiet? Can't hear ourselves appeal' is a standard Saturday afternoon witticism. But thanks, I hope, to a movement to which our little opening ceremony has perhaps contributed, cricket is beginning to lose its male chauvinism. Some older members still may regard our opening event as so much time wasted from the serious business of the game, but the skill and professional attitude of a succession of leading ladies has gone far to overcome prejudice. What I want even more than a new leading lady is always a proper fast bowler to make an early breakthrough when the ceremony is over, the bottle presented, and my wife has seen the representative of the dramatic art back to the pavilion. As for the bowler, though poet, novelist, critic or publisher would be doubly welcome, what I am looking for is a real quickie, to shake, if possible, the sturdy Sussex imperturbables of the Ivanhoe Cricket Club.

# Memories of Lopez

## SIMON GRAY

I'd been batting with my usual fluency against the faster bowlers, including the fifteen-year-old who was already reputed to be the fastest bowler in the school, and had rattled up an easy twenty or so runs. The fastest bowler in the school, who I think was called Kemp, and who I know was exceptionally tall and thin, with a long, fearsome and gangly run-up, took himself off after I'd scored three successive fours by simply playing the ball gently and almost, but not quite, straight back at him. I felt pretty good. In those days, until a few minutes later that day, I always felt pretty good when I was batting; and was generally able to attribute my downfall, when I gave the matter any thought, to an act of negligence, unconstrained violence, or to a ball that somehow and unaccountably got through. I was always completely in, in fact, until the moment when I was suddenly out, and that was that. But then the bowlers I always faced simply bowled as fast and as straight as they could, Kemp-like.

So Kemp, who was also the captain, replaced himself with a chap I'd vaguely seen around the school and had heard was something of a bowler, but apart from reputation and a certain foreignness of appearance, was not in the slightest worrying to a boy who'd never been worried at the crease. His name was Lopez (Lopez!) and at fifteen he was slightly balding, and he was sallow. I looked forward to his first ball.

I spent quite a time looking forward to it, because it was quite a time coming. Not that he had much of a run-up, Lopez. There was a short amble from behind the umpire, a stutter of feet as his left elbow came up, and all the time in the world to watch his right arm come over. And then more time as the ball rolled gently through the air, and fell within easy reach of my bat, somewhere just outside the line of my off-stump. As I'd located it so early, I myself had lots of time to gather myself up before scampering powerfully out to smash it where I would. My bat curved through the air, there was a scuffling and a shuffling from behind the stumps, and if the wicketkeeper hadn't made as much of a hash of it as I had, he could have stumped me three times over.

I decided I'd better watch Lopez's next more carefully. This time I took in that actually he was coming from the wrong side of the umpire – i.e. bowling around the wicket – and this piece of information, which I hadn't bothered to register when he'd bowled his first ball, lodged like a piece of grit in my mind all through the ball's flight, and indeed long after it had passed my bat and was being tossed from fielder to fielder back to Lopez. I pondered the implications as he appeared yet again, raised his elbow, stuttered his feet, brought his right arm over, etc; then turned his back, not even bothering to watch as I picked myself up out of the tangle I'd made of myself just inside the crease.

Nothing like this, I must repeat, had ever happened to me before. I can understand now, having first watched and then listened to Jim Laker on television, that Lopez was a precociously expert bowler of off-spin, with no doubt a master-plan for each over and a separate policy for each ball, along with a shrewd insight into the psychology of each incoming batsman, even if he'd never seen him before, and by the time he bowled his fourth ball I had at least grasped that his action was so casual only because it was so accomplished. But the real devastation, of which Lopez was only the efficient cause, was the result of my seeing myself suddenly and for the first time in a different light. It was as if my feet had swollen, my pads grown almost to my chin, and my bat become both so heavy that I could scarcely lift it and too small to make contact with a ball that strayed wilfully in and out of my line of vision, without seeming at any moment to hurry itself. I survived to the end of the over, ran my partner out in the next over, and was out – I can't remember the details, but I have a clear impression – presumably a moral one – that I was l.b.w., caught, bowled, stumped, and made to hit wicket all at once – off the first ball of Lopez's next. For the first time ever, I welcomed my end.

I went to the boundary, some distance away from where the Junior Colts had dumped the pads and the scorer, and watched a chap of no known class – he'd only been picked twice for the team that term – attempt to cope with Lopez. He did somewhat better than I, eventually perishing nobly in ·the covers off a stroke that at least looked like a stroke. Some of the later batsmen, including one of the tail-enders, actually knocked Lopez about a bit. But then they probably had no idea what they were up against.

Those seven balls from Lopez marked a change in my life. From then on I never faced a half-way decent slow bowler with anything like composure. The ball ceased to be something I hit, and became a revolving tangle of contradictory opportunities – play forward; play back; get to the pitch; smother; *hit him off his length!*; use your pads; get your pads out of the way – that were invariably not taken or taken simultaneously, and either way left me stretched in some ignominious posture astraddle the crease. I think it is true to say that post-Lopez, though I continued to love cricket, I never enjoyed playing it again.

Nevertheless, by application – I took to wearing a cap, the peak of which I jerked before the bowler began his run-up – I managed to make it in due course to the school's First XI, as an opening bat. I survived there for a while because I could still usually see off the fast bowlers, but it was eventually noticed by the captain and the sportsmaster that my departure invariably followed the first bowling change. 'It's a matter of your feet, Gray old chap,' the sportsmaster explained quite sympathetically, as he pinned up the Second XI list, with my name on it. He was quite wrong. My feet were perfectly nimble. It was my mind that it was a matter of.

My slide into the Second XI was the first stage of my slide out of cricket altogether. Having been defeated by thought (my own, or Lopez's) at the wicket, I began to take it up in the classroom, and was thus able to claim that the demands made on me by essays on existentialism, *The Republic*, the French Revolution, and such, made it impossible for me to fritter my afternoons away on a cricket field. I withdrew into the library, emerging only on the occasional golden afternoon as a supercilious spectator who had outgrown even memories of the game, and I made sure always to take a book (Kafka, perhaps) with me, to help me make a telling image on a distant boundary.

Some years later, after periods in Canada and in France, I became, by a process too subterranean for me to be able to mark its stages, a cricket-addict again – but only as a spectator, naturally. I spent almost as many hours as I do now watching to or listening to the Test matches. Any game in a park, even between squabbling children, would bring me to a long halt, and I read the news-papers mainly for the county scores. I also had opinions, strong ones, on Test selection, and must have composed at least five hundred unsent telegrams to the selectors, all of them abusive. My interests became known to my students – I was supervising at Cambridge – and one of them invited me to a knock-about at the College nets. I refused, of course, with just the right amount of flirtatious shyness, until properly persuaded; and one evening proceeded, in the manner of a chap bent on humouring his juniors, to an evening session.

It was as if I went straight back to a time before Lopez and other disappointments had touched my life; or rather as if I'd really spent those seemingly drab years somewhere where I'd discovered a far more skilful cricketing self. I had, for one thing, mastered a curious but effective top spin, holding the ball in a grip that must have come from imagination or pre-natal memory, and by flicking my wrist and twisting my fingers at the arm's arc, at different points of the arm's varying arc, I became my own kind of Lopez to the best batsmen in the College's Third or was it Fourth XI? Furthermore, within minutes of my starting to bat a small group had gathered around my net to note my off-drive (and its follow-through), my on-drive (a stroke I'd found un-playable during my immature prime) and my wristy little turn to leg. At the end of the session I was invited to play in next week's game. Flushed with success, or the folly that frequently follows it, I accepted.

I was put on to bowl first change, the two opening batsmen proving efficient and stubborn accumulators, though not actually dangerous – at least, until confronted with my flickering wrist, twisting fingers and my arm's varying arc. The captain, in whom a spirit of scientific curiosity, or perhaps mere good manners, at that stage prevailed, kept me on for three overs in all, and so was as responsible as I was for changing the course of the game. In one of my resting overs I also managed to drop a catch; a slightly more difficult one than the catch I dropped almost immediately after I was taken off.

My batting was worse because it lasted longer. I played immaculately down the line of the fastish, fastish-medium, and mediumish, so tapping the ball straight back to the bowler, or in the direction of fielders it just lacked the power to reach; or in the case of the slow bowlers either missed the ball completely in my innate style, or had it skid off the bat's base to slips, third bounce. This little swine of an innings – or lengthy swine of a little innings – was complicated by my complete inability to judge a run, which meant that I remained moribund in my crease while my partner, every time he hit the ball, spurted yelping a few yards from his, only to be checked by my imperiously raised hand, and dignified instructions to no, go back. I eventually adopted a bit of a limp, to explain the inexplicable, and tried to deafen my ears to the perturbations from around the pavilion, and the increasingly hysterical gestures from a captain now no longer scientific or polite. I decided to settle for an honourable draw. As long as the next eight men could hold up the other end, I could hold up mine. But the man currently at the other end summoned me to a mid-wicket conference, in which he laid out certain facts hitherto (so I still believe) kept from me. This was a limited-over match, in the new-fangled mode. There was either victory or defeat, with nothing except a tie in between. 'But a cricket game,' I attempted to philosophise, 'that couldn't end in a draw was scarcely a game of cricket. For one thing –' 'Look,' he said, 'you've either got to run or to get out.' With my concentration thus disturbed, I was bowled a mere four overs later, which even so wasn't quite soon enough to prevent our having to concede the game through a series of suicidal run-outs and scything blows that were taken both adeptly and fumblingly on the boundary; with two wickets still standing.

This game, played some seventeen years ago, and some fourteen years after the Lopez match, ended my career as a practising cricketer. I draw no conclusions from either game, or even from both taken in relation to each other, except to affirm that for me, I now realise, cricket has been too much life itself ever to serve as a metaphor for it. Just as Lopez's off-spins altered my development at school, so did that last innings lead, and not too indirectly, to a bizarre outburst at a Cambridge literary party that blighted several delicately forming (in the Cambridge manner) friendships and love affairs. I have a fairly recurrent day-dream, though, in which I replay my last innings with a full swing of the bat, in the cavalier spirit that was my own true self, I know, before Lopez robbed me of it; and another in which Lopez himself, still balding, sallow and fifteen years old, appears from behind the umpire, around the wicket, and I dance down to cover-drive him off his length – a dream that I can revive almost at will, even though I've long known that Lopez died by his own hand shortly after leaving school, a victim of depression and, I suppose, circumstance.

# First Hero

RONALD HARWOOD

I wrote to him suggesting lunch. I had it in mind to do a profile of him and wanted to ask, tactfully of course, about his life now and his life then: did he look back often to Olympus? Did he on cold winter days remember some glorious innings, a dazzling leg-sweep at least, a wicket taken, a blinder held? Did he curse the passage of time that makes of cricketers old men at 35? How did he fill his days now? And I wanted to look at him to see if I could marry in my mind the batsman who walked so jauntily to the wicket with the middle-aged man grown portly and grey. Would I, I wondered, recapture a twinge of schoolboy excitement talking to, actually talking to the hero of my youth? I received no reply to my letter. And I remember trying to take a photograph of him trotting up the back steps of the pavilion at Newlands in Cape Town: he posed for me, his finger pointing like a gun at the camera; it would have been a fine photograph but it never came out. Of all the snaps on that roll of film – most of them taken from the boundary so that the players appeared absurdly small and totally unrecognisable – that one of him was black.

Twice I had seen him in the flesh since his great days. The first time was in a London restaurant after a long lunch. A little the worse for wear, I embraced him warmly. 'The greatest cricketer I ever saw,' I announced. No one minded. The other customers were all in similar condition to mine. He gave an embarrassed smile but was, I thought, nevertheless pleased by the compliment. 'What about that 300 in a day at Benoni?' I continued. 'Yes,' he said, 'that was fun.' Some years later I saw him at Lord's during a break for rain. By chance I sheltered with him under a roof near the Warner Stand. 'What about that 5 for 70 in the Third Test against South Africa?' I asked. 'Yes,' he said, 'that was fun.'

Compton D. C. S., Middlesex and England, visited South Africa as a member of George Mann's team in 1948-9, and I saw him for the first time on the afternoon of 2 January 1949 in Cape Town. I write so portentously of these events because Compton D. C. S., Middlesex and England, had, for the previous eighteen months, invaded my imagination and taken possession of that inner world to which young boys escape and where fantasy runs riot. It is the world of gods and heroes where the mythology allows for Harwood R. and Compton D. C. S. to bat together, to break records and be enshrined together in the Pantheon. Heroes, it seems to me, are the expression of ourselves in faultless form. Jonathan Swift wrote: 'Who'er excels in what we prize/ Appears a hero in our eyes'. Compton D. C. S. was my first hero: he represented ability, flair, talent, brilliance, courage and daring, the very qualities I lacked but to which I aspired when I took a cricket bat in my hand and asked for middle-and-leg.

He was at the height of his fame and power. The English summer of 1947 was Compton's summer. The South Africans were the touring side that year and he made six centuries against them and eighteen centuries in all that season, beating Jack Hobbs's record by two. He passed Tom Hayward's aggregate of 3,518 runs in a season although, surprisingly, he started badly, scoring only 353 runs in May; but then, on his own admission, he was a warm-weather player. He and Bill Edrich were dubbed 'the Middlesex Twins' and together they seemed to dispel the weariness of those grey years after the war.

Far away in Cape Town I used to watch the newsreels of those great innings. I see Compton now dropping on to one knee to sweep, running half-way down the pitch to play the spinners, raising his bat and smiling to acknowledge applause. And I can still recall the particular exuberance of the Gaumont-British commentator, stridently crowing, 'Watch out, Aussies! Compton's bang on form!'

The statistics of Compton's cricket are not what set him apart from others in my mind. My imagination was captured by his natural ability, inventiveness and his evident enjoyment of every moment he was out in the middle. To me, his vitality was irresistible: he had energy as a cricketer, a quality common to all stars whatever their chosen field of play. The other day I read again his autobiography, endearingly entitled *End of an Innings*, and found this passage about that summer of 1947:

At the Oval, for Middlesex against The Rest, I got 210 runs, and it remains in my memory as one of the best innings I ever played. Right from the start I played my shots and everything I attempted succeeded, even the most wildly unorthodox strokes, including the four I scored when falling forward. If I wanted a thing to happen it seemed to happen – just like that. It was the happiest and most exhilarating of sensations. I felt I could have batted with a stump.

In 1948 he headed the English Test averages against the Australians captained by Bradman. I remember a blackboard placed outside the swimming-pool I used to visit on which a cricket-loving attendant wrote the latest score and a cryptic message: 'England 42 for 3 but Compton still in' or some such. Like no other cricketer of the period, Compton supplied brightness at a time of gloom. In contrast to Hutton, a great batsman and superb stroke-player, Compton seemed to proclaim enthusiasm and pleasure; he wore his professionalism carelessly. He was a buccaneer, an innovator, a magician. That he officiated at my baptism of watching first-class cricket was to my everlasting good fortune. The Third Test Match in Cape Town and his part in it somehow combined to demonstrate the first-class game: high expectations, disappointment, involvement, fascination and interest over an extended period. It was not a great match but it was the first I saw and Compton was the magnet. As I have said the game took place in the January of 1949. In anticipation I began to use Brylcreme.

Sunday 2 January was hot and bright. I woke at dawn, counted down the minutes until it was decent to rise and, with my cousin, set off across the Cape Peninsula to the ground. In those days the journey to Newlands from where I lived in Sea Point involved a bus, a train and a fair walk. As one neared the turnstiles, excitement rising, one joined a sort of procession, an insouciant regiment of cricket-lovers, and one could hear all around talk of the impending contest. England had won the First Test and drawn the Second. This Third Test at Cape Town was South Africa's chance to level the series. Compton had been batting splendidly in all the tourists' matches. As I entered the ground I remember hoping that I would see him bat rather than field on that first day.

Newlands, so the *cognoscenti* say, is the most beautiful cricket ground in the world. The backdrop is Table Mountain, grey-blue and majestic in the light of mid-morning; the green of the grass is rich and comforting and one boundary is fringed by oak trees under whose shade spectators sit, out of the glare and heat of the sun. This was the setting for the drama.

The wait for the blazered captains to toss the coin was interminable and when at last they did appear I prayed that whoever won would put England in first: I was now determined to see Compton bat. I cannot remember who won the toss but England did bat first and out to the wicket strode Len Hutton and Cyril Washbrook to begin the first day's cricket. Hutton and Washbrook could, I knew, be stumbling blocks to my desire to see Compton. In the First Test at Johannesburg their opening partnership of 359 was a record for all Test cricket, and in Cape Town they looked as if they would perform a similar feat. Old-timers seated nearby told us not to panic: the Newlands pitch, they said, was, surprisingly, a little green and the bowlers could expect some help. The bowlers, like me, were in for a disappointment. Hutton and Washbrook batted all morning and were still there at lunch. Then, shortly after play resumed, an astonishing thing happened. Hutton, who had made 41, pushed a ball past mid-off and called Washbrook for an easy single. The batsmen had just crossed when Hutton tripped and fell flat on his face. He was run out. I am ashamed to admit I was extremely pleased. I was one wicket nearer to seeing Compton. Jack Crapp batted next. Somehow, I think because of the jokes his name prompted, one didn't take him too seriously. On the day he scored 35 and prolonged my agony. Towards tea-time he was out and my great moment had arrived.

Compton was cheered to the crease. He was rather slight and of average height. I was surprised that his hair was not slicked down as one had seen it in the Brylcreem adverts. But he had a wonderfully eccentric walk, as though double-jointed, which added to the aura of pleasure he brought with him. I could hardly breathe. He took guard and ran one off the first ball he faced. I said to my cousin, 'I think he's set for a lot of runs today.' Two balls later Athol Rowan bowled him. Compton walked eccentrically back to the pavilion. The partisans cheered. Compton was out for one.

I don't remember much of what followed that day. I see from the score card that England made 308. Washbrook was top scorer with 74 and George Mann missed his half-century by six runs. I returned home disappointed and gloomy. On the second day Compton was brought on to bowl much to the amusement of the spectators. They, like the South African batsmen, were in for a surprise. He took five wickets for 32 runs that day, including one spectacular caught-and-bowled to dismiss Dudley Nourse who had made 112. In those days the fielders did not crowd round a successful colleague as they do now for the television cameras, but I remember George Mann patting Compton on the back as they changed ends, and I also remember Compton grinning with pleasure. It was his sense of pleasure, I think, which compensated for my disappointment of the previous day and which allowed me to look forward to what remained of the game with hopefulness.

South Africa continued their innings on the third day. They scored 356, Compton finishing with 5 for 70. Hutton and Washbrook opened England's second innings and quickly whittled away the 48-run lead. I realise now, though I did not know it then, that a draw was inevitable. The players, of course, quickly appreciated that the pressure was off so scored freely and confidently. Hutton made 87 and Compton a sparkling 51 not out.

A little later in the tour against North-Eastern Transvaal at

Benoni he made his famous 300 in 181 minutes, the fastest triple century in history, sixty-six minutes for the first hundred, seventy-eight for the second, thirty-seven minutes for the third. One six, I remember from the newsreels, he hit holding the bat in one hand, using it like a tennis racket. He averaged 133 runs for the tour, and just over 50 in the Tests.

Never ever did I see him make a lot of runs. By the time I came to England in 1951, his knee was troubling him and his playing days were numbered. I went to Lord's for his last appearance for Middlesex against Worcestershire, who batted first, and when Middlesex took the field the applause for Compton started inside the pavilion and carried him all the way to the middle. I wasn't the only one to blink back tears.

'I have loved and had joy all my life from the game of cricket,' he wrote, and his love and joy were, in my case, infectious and long-lasting. His participation in a match guaranteed excitement and he bestowed on cricket a rare dash which kindled one's own delight and pleasure in the game. I still hope, after all these months, to receive a reply to my letter. To take him to lunch would be an inadequate recompense.

# Not Cricket

MICHAEL HOLROYD

Some people use sheep: I bowl. Along the years, lying in my bed, I must have sent down hundreds of overs – leg-breaks, mostly, mixed with my own version of the googly. If I am rarely successful, either at taking wickets or at inducing sleep, this does not make me feel wretched. I enjoy the rhythm, persistent, floating ... and since everything can be contained in the reading of a wicket, my thoughts are seldom pierced by dark knives in the night. Like so much else, it is largely a question of re-reading; of whether to re-live or re-write the past. With a poor memory there need be few discrepancies. Many an old man's dream, I suspect, is lit up by white-flannelled figures on a field of glorious green: and then rained off by his crying failure, at the age of eighteen, to make the team. So deep are these regrets for some they overshadow everything.

But not for me. When very young I seemed hedged with such momentous promise as to incapacitate me from doing anything at all. I seldom spoke or was seen to take any initiative, but there was an air (or so I later assumed) of miracles to come: and it was on the cricket pitch that I brought this promise to its tightest knot of suspense. At my private school I was the secret weapon of our First XI – a weapon so secret that few of our opponents could decipher me. It was not (good heavens!) that I scored boundaries or flourished the bat in any stylish way; my bowling, oscillating haphazardly between fast and slow, was seldom called upon; my fielding already showed the resentment I felt for the hardness of the ball. My contribution was independent of all this activity. I stood. As opening batsman, my favourite score at the culmination of the match was nought-not-out. I was still standing. Fast bowlers, it was said, broke their hearts against me.

My conservatism as a batsman had a complicated history. I had been sent to the same school as my father, and his brother before him. But there was a difference. In the interval the family had run out of money. As a result, though appearances were to be kept up, they could not afford all the equipment I needed. I never had, for example, proper pads or a bat. Instead I made do with my uncle's – the bat and pads he had employed with moderate success at university in the 1920s. The pads were deeply yellow and reached almost to my shoulders. I peeped out from them unafraid. The bat was a mature instrument, well-bound and fully-seasoned, giving out a deep note when struck, like a groan. I admired that bat – but I could not lift it. I was ten or twelve: the bat was more than a quarter-of-a-century old. Dressed like some odd laboratory assistant, I would drag it to the crease and then, as it were, leave it there. As I took guard, there occurred a total eclipse of the stumps. The bowler had not even a bail to aim at – no wonder I was so disheartening. After that, there was in effect no more to be done and I was the very person to do it. I had, so to speak, made my statement and there was little refuting it. We stood there, my uncle's bat and I, keeping our end up, while runs flowed and wickets fell at the other end. I had a good eye and would watch the balls swinging my way with great keenness, making lightning decisions as to what shots I could play. But I never played them except in my imagination. If I tried anything, it invariably led to my being given out either hit-wicket or leg-before-wicket – depending on which, the umpire decided, had happened first.

Occasionally, over the seasons, the ball would glance the edge of my uncle's bat and flutter into the slips bringing me a run. But it had to go far to enable me to reach the other end in those pads. In the slips I began to notice a curious figure among one of the teams we played regularly from schools nearby. He merited my attention since it was through his feet that most of my meagre totals would come. He was a large crouching boy, with a round face, hawk-like nose, hanging arms and curiously intent brown eyes. Though he appeared to miss nothing that was going on, he nevertheless also appeared to take no part in any of it. His expression was alert, yet blank, and he looked like a perpetual twelfth man. He was the only other player, I observed, who regularly scored nought-not-out. This was because he went in last and, whatever the circumstances, never received a ball, though he would prod the pitch expertly and swish his bat about a bit from the non-striking end, indicating his keenness. Everything considered, this keenness seemed remarkable and had earned him, I felt, his place in the team. He would blunder on to the field first, ahead of his captain, whirl his arms around and reach the slips long before everyone else arrived at their positions. Then he would wait. He did as much waiting as I did standing. Of course we never really spoke to each other, just nodded; but I warmed to him when, during one of the tea intervals, he put aside his cake for a moment and addressed a few words to my uncle's bat, as one might encourage a dog or cat. You could see it had set him thinking. The blankness of his expression intensified, and he wandered off.

I don't think there was any question of my deliberately steering the ball towards this figure in the slips: I was incapable of such refinements. But I observed, during my last summer at this school, how the bowlers, desperate to get past my uncle's bat, were tending to aim the ball at its very edge – from which it would slump off, with a thunderous groan, towards the slips. There were two consequences to this. It brought that strange hanging figure into the game as he had never been before. Often at the end of an over he would be left with the ball. It was from him therefore that the next bowler had to receive it; or via him that the captain was obliged to indicate a change of bowler. From all this hubbub I learnt his name, which I shall call Philipps. To spectators who did not know the game but might be watching it from the boundary, Philipps must have seemed the most important person on the field. If they knew no one else, they knew him. Sometimes, too, I noticed that he actually despatched the ball to the next bowler by bowling it along himself, as if to suggest something. I think he appreciated his new prominence in the team and I felt gratified that my uncle's bat had been instrumental in bringing him into it. I noticed, too, a peculiar smile sometimes stretch across his oval face. It gave him an odd look: almost ironic.

The second consequence of this constant edging of the ball seemed much more grave. My uncle's bat, like an old ship after a tempest, was beginning to break up. Splinters would fly off like sparks, scattering the fielders and adding to my already legendary reputation. The wound, it appeared, was a deep one and no amount of the bandaging, glueing and patching I applied could long delay the end. I felt the pathos. If only, I thought, it could have held out another five or ten years. I would have grown into it and then all those miracles-to-come might actually have burst forth. But it was a great-hearted bat and somehow it survived to the end of the season, its off-side edge like a cliff face.

Next year I went to Eton. My father had been there, and his brother before him. Unlike them I went there on a double mortgage – but without the bat. To prepare me for school my father had invited a local grocer to give me a few evening nets. There were just the two of us, the grocer and I, in a large field at evening when the bat finally cracked up. The pads, too, by that time were sprouting various materials: it seemed sensible to lay them to rest at the same time. So we hoisted the lot on to a rubbish dump, gave up and went home.

My father was anxious that I do well at Eton. A robust chap now of forty, he had been delicate in his 'teens, and lay for part of this time in Switzerland, recovering. All that he had missed then took hold of his imagination: it seemed that things like success had been somewhere else while he lay breathing in Switzerland. When had he ever heard applause, been thumped on the back, won anything? He had breasted no tapes; catapulted over no crossbars; above all he had scored no centuries. I was his second chance. He had had me padded up when I was three or four, and out on the lawn practising regardless of my aunt's

flowerbeds. We were interrupted somewhat by the Second World
War, I remember, but my grandmother was under instructions
to push the ball at me through those years, though her terrier
seemed to gain more from this exercise than I.

I went to Eton not long after the war had ended and my
father returned. He had done his bit and now settled down to see
me do mine, using some of his demobilisation pay to buy me a
bright new bat, gleaming pads, dazzling gloves: everything a
chap could want. It was now up to me.

On the first afternoon at Eton the new boys in our house were
given tea. Our parents came, joked with one another, then
slunk guiltily and gratefully off, leaving us alone with our housemaster, 'Purple' Parr. It was then that someone suddenly said
something to me. I jumped, not being used to such attention
(indeed, having gone a long way in a dozen years to avoid it),
then saw that it was Philipps, the round-faced crouching boy in
the slips. He had some cake still in his hand and was asking me
about my uncle's bat. I told him; he understood at once; and we
got to talking. I knew rather a lot about cricket, but Philipps
knew more. He knew everything. His command of bowling
analyses, going back years, was extraordinarily impressive.
Batting, in this respect, was also no problem to him. He threw
off wicketkeeping statistics too as if he had been the wicket-
keeper in Calcutta or Melbourne himself. I don't think I ever
caught him out with a question – I would have backed him against
anyone in a quiz. But his information was never dull. When he
spoke, these figures danced, sang, lived for him. He spoke with a
passion that touched even tennis players and oarsmen. It was as if
all the striving, hope, enjoyment, pain of life had been ritualised
and fitted into the rhythms and processions of a cricket match.
Life might shrink a little, but the game expanded.

Philipps knew about cricket, but cricketers did not know about
Philipps. They knew about me. In Surrey, Berkshire, even parts
of Middlesex, Stonewall Holroyd and his uncle's bat had been
spoken of. I was a useful man to have on the losing side – I might
even force a draw. So, while Philipps was despatched to some

obscure pitch on the periphery of the school, I went straight to the top game. But I went without my uncle's bat – and without that I was lost. Approaching the crease in my blinding new gear I seemed to be walking on air. Where was my ballast, my anchor? Taking guard, I felt absurdly exposed to the fast bowlers. I had never realised what a dangerous sport cricket could be. My new bat wouldn't keep still. It sent the first ball I received for an astonishing four through the covers. I felt like apologising. After all, I had done no more than contemplate a cover-drive: the bat had done the rest. To the second ball it offered a leg-glance, and I walked back with it off the field while the wicketkeeper righted my leg-stump.

People, I realised, were angry with me. I had acted completely out of character and they felt cheated. I was dropped from the top game and, after a couple of attempted sixes over the bowler's head, fell from the second to the third. In that top game cricket had been played with frightful earnestness. To excel here was the principal ambition of many boys, and the *raison d'être* of their school careers – they had not come to learn algebra. They dreamed of being capped and their emotional energy revolved round the glamour, the aesthetic brilliance of the white flannels and pristine blazer trimmed with blue. Really, nothing mattered after that.

I put away my new bat and took to leg-breaks and my own version of the googly. This, I can now reveal, consisted of 'presenting' the batsman with another monstrously obvious leg-break – then reversing my wrist at the last moment and hoping he wouldn't spot it. It seemed easier than bringing the ball out of the back of the hand – a risky business at best and a danger to the umpire. I was trained at the nets by the head of our house and captain of games, a tall thin boy who later compensated for having narrowly missed the First XI by becoming a top dog at Sotheby's. My bowling was unusual, but no legend adhered to it as it had to my uncle's bat. Nobody used leg-breaks and there was no place for such bowlers in most teams. They were expensive; they were unfashionable; they were perpetually almost getting wickets while in the intervals being regularly hit for four or six. For more

than a decade it used to be said of England's leg-break 'merchant'
D. V. P. Wright that he was the unluckiest bowler alive. I could
well believe it. The head of our house, I reckon, was the second
most unlucky; then there was me. Technically, we were fascinating: but people wanted to win their matches. As no one could
demonstrate better than Philipps, D. V. P. Wright had got
amazingly far; the head of our house even made Eton's Second XI
(or 'twenty-two' as it was called); I gave up.

But Philipps did not give up. His keenness was never blunted
by the continual drudgery of his experiences. While I sweated at
those special nets, it now shames me to remember, he volunteered
to come up and field the balls clouted over my head. We used to
talk on our way up (not so much going back) and he told me that
his parents were divorced. One of the results of this, it appeared,
was that he did not own a pair of cricket boots. It did not matter
in the sort of games he played. Nothing mattered. They were less
cricket matches than exhibitions of anarchy. Gym shoes would
do as well as any other. No one bothered if you turned up or
didn't. Philipps always turned up early. Sometimes he had to
wait almost an hour before enough people ambled along to make
up a couple of scratch teams. In the evenings he tuned his bat
against the day when he would be invited to use it.

I do not think I can be claiming too much when I say that
'Purple' Parr's was by far the worst house in the school when
Philipps and I were its stars. For two years I was its captain of
games despite the fact that I had given up cricket and did no
rowing. I had taken savagely to non-team games such as squash.
I would have played racquets too if my family could have afforded
it; I would have played tennis if I could have found the courts.
As it was, I settled for squash and as Keeper of Squash walked the
streets wearing a dark blue cap with minute crossed rackets in
gold that mystified everyone. Mystery had become my form of
glamour, and elusiveness my publicity. For the players (it seems
probable) cricket is a game; for literary gentlemen it becomes a
metaphor. Like chess, it later absorbed much of my interest. But
I play neither. That way I do not get too agitated. I am remorse-

lessly involved but, at the same time, detached. I participate as a
spectator.

Philipps took his role as spectator on to the centre of the field.
He knew more than anyone there and he remained there, year
after year, waiting to use his knowledge. I would see him in the
summer afternoons setting off to the fields like clockwork, and I
would think of Sisyphus and his stone. Possibly because of his
divorced parents, he never got a new bat or pads or anything else
during his five years at Eton. In a sense they weren't needed.
Everything looked new: but smaller. By his last year all this
miniature paraphernalia with which he stood waiting to try his
luck looked Lilliputian.

My father had done all he could to conceal his disappointment
in me, despite my having no Swiss alibi. Squash was all right of
course; but it was not (he pointed out) cricket. This worried him.
It even worried 'Purple' Parr, who came to my room one evening
to explain the ridicule that attached to him personally for having
a captain of games in his house who played no games. I felt sorry
(it was the least I could feel) but I could do little about it. 'Purple'
Parr himself did nothing, which was often his way; but my father
found a devious means of keeping his vicarious hopes alive – he
transferred them to Philipps. He had met him once or twice at tea
and, like many before him, been moved by his statistics. Soon he
began to press me with questions, often unanswerable. I remember how irritated I would be by his habit of getting my friend's
name wrong. 'How's your friend Frobisher?' he would suddenly
demand. 'Playing much is he?' Or: 'Potter scored any runs yet?'
If there was any pathos here I was not susceptible to it. But
although I felt irritated, I also felt guilty and used to go up now
and then to watch Philipps in the hope of providing my father
with something nourishing to chew over. It wasn't easy. I may
even have invented a little. But I did note a small change in
Philipps's field manners. Whenever he had the ball, he liked to
send it back to the bowler with a short fizzing action that spun it
fiercely off the ground and out of the bowler's pleading fingers.
That was all. He said nothing; his gestures revealed nothing; and

I had nothing to report. But my father's curiosity persisted and, grateful to see it diverted from me in this way, I did my best to squeeze some drops of interest from that succession of dryly uneventful afternoons. I felt as if Philipps had in some way become my alter ego.

By our last year 'Purple' Parr had given us all up and retired to drink and geometry in his study. We were a hopeless generation of which Philipps, it seemed, was our finest representative. But my father's instinct probed deeper and was spectacularly rewarded. At the end of that last summer at Eton a special match had been arranged – rather a grand matter it was, peopled largely by First and Second XI players. Philipps had somehow secured the job of scorer. This was something he did well, and it came as a surprise to me that he had been asked to do it. That reflected my opinion, I dare say, of school cricket. The match took place on our last full day and shortly before it was due to start, Philipps blundered up to me with a curious request. Would I take his place as scorer? Someone had fallen out of the game, and he had been accepted as the replacement providing he could find someone to score. So, if I took his place, he would be playing that afternoon, he added matter-of-factly.

I scored. Philipps's side fielded first. It was not supposed to be a wholly serious game – more an exhibition of some of the school's most talented players. I was scoring quietly, sharpening the pencils, lining up the rubbers, humming a little, when all at once the captain threw the ball to Philipps. It must have been pure end-of-season intoxication: or a mistake. In any event there was no chance of changing his mind. Philipps thundered like a steam engine to the wicket, rubbing the ball as he'd seen everyone else do. I could not imagine what he felt. I found it difficult to decipher my own feelings and did not trust myself to write down his name until after he had sent down his first ball. He bowled off-cutters and almost bagged a wicket with this first ball. After that he was played with puzzled caution. His action looked innocent enough: not a long run (he did not have time for that) but with something of the swaying indecision of a rocking-horse –

then the delivery, rather sudden at almost medium pace and given little air. His first over was a maiden so there was no option but to keep him on. By the end of the innings he had bowled some twenty tight overs, taken three wickets and conceded only about fifteen runs. There was, I appreciated, a hoard of hidden learning behind that bowling. Years of close observation, years of studying *Wisden* went into each delivery. It was concentrated scholarship we were witnessing and a triumph of theory over experience. Batsmen got out through the impertinence of trying to score off him. They did not realise what a studious attack was being aimed at them: and it was an *attack*.

Philipps's expression was buoyantly blank when he came off the field. No one who did not know him well could have told anything from it. Certainly there was no aspect of surprise there. I was astonished. But there was an even greater shock to come. Philipps had replaced an opening batsman. Instead of shifting up the whole order and establishing him in his normal place at the end, the captain simply asked Philipps to go in first. The world had gone topsy-turvy.

Had I not been scorer, I would have left then. I had seen his success: there were enough marvels here to repeat to my father for years. I wished 'Purple' Parr had been able to see them: but as usual he had not arrived. Like the Ancient Mariner's wedding guest, I was held there to act as witness for all: I could not choose but look.

I saw, with sinking heart, Philipps walk out with that midget bat and ridiculous pads. He actually tripped over on his way to the crease. I wrote his name down: and then it began. The first ball missed his bat, missed the wicket, the wicketkeeper's gloves and went for four byes. It appeared to have gone through everything, and so fast I could not tell whether Philipps realised what had happened. The next ball also shot to the boundary, this time from the top of Philipps's bat and over the heads of the slips. Four runs – to the best of my knowledge his best score that decade. That he had luck I think there was no doubt. But then he was owed luck. For the next hour-and-a-half, he *hammered* the bowling; he crashed the ball between them, above them, beyond them all. He seemed to be teasing the fielders. At first these champion bowlers with their gleaming flannels and hyphenated names may not have taken this onslaught so seriously; but before long they were trying all they knew to remove him. He kept them continually on the run. God knows how he did it. I had never seen anything like it before and never have again. But then I knew the years of frustration and inactivity behind it. A number of people stopped to watch, conscious that something unusual was happening. Philipps did not score a century, about seventy-five was his total and it easily won the game. We stood up, the few of us there, gave a dry cheer and clapped raggedly as he came out. He looked severe and sphinx-like sitting down to unstrap his pads; then for a moment that peculiar smile stretched silently across his face and seemed to engulf him.

Next day we left school. His parents being divorced, Philipps did not go up to university and nor did I. I never saw him play another game, though I would meet him from time to time and he would pass items of cricketing news my way – some record from New Zealand perhaps or curiosity from Canada. Once I reminded him of his schoolboy romance in that last match. He listened with what appeared deep pleasure to the story before rebuking me for having exaggerated everything. So perhaps, after all, I am re-writing rather than re-living the past. Anyway, it's the story my father likes to hear.

Shortly after he married, Philipps remarked to me that he was thinking of raising a complete eleven. Most of his children, it turned out, were girls. I don't think this mattered. In a few years, I predict, his name will be terrible to the women cricketers of Australia. And I shall have something new to tell my father.

# Sunstruck

TED HUGHES

The freedom of Saturday afternoons
Starched to cricket dazzle, nagged at a theorem –
Shaggy valley parapets
Pending like thunder, narrowing the spin-bowler's angle.

The click, disconnected, might have escaped –
A six! And the ball slammed flat!
And the bat in flinders! The heart soaring!
And everybody jumping up and running –

Fleeing after the ball, stampeding
Through the sudden hole in Saturday – but
Already clapped into hands and the trap-shout
The ball jerked back to the stumper on its elastic.

Everything collapsed that bit deeper
Towards Monday.

Misery of the brassy sycamores!
Misery of the swans and the hard ripple!

Then again Yes Yes a wild YES –
The bat flashed round the neck in a tight coil,
The stretched shout snatching for the North Sea –
But it fell far short, even of Midgeley.

And the legs running for dear life, twinkling white
In the cage of wickets

Were cornered again by the ball, pinned to the crease,
Chained to the green and white pavilion.

Cross-eyed, mid-stump, sun-descending headache!
Brains sewn into the ball's hide
Hammering at four corners of abstraction
And caught and flung back, and caught, and again caught

To be bounced on baked earth, to be clubbed
Toward the wage-mirage sparkle of mills
Toward Lord Savile's heather
Toward the veto of the poisonous Calder

Till the eyes, glad of anything, dropped
From the bails
Into the bottom of a teacup,
To sandwich crusts for the canal cygnets.

The bowler had flogged himself to a dishclout.
And the burned batsmen returned, with changed faces,
Like men returned from a far journey,
Under the long glare walls of evening

To the cool sheet and the black slot of home.

# A Straight Bat

HAMMOND INNES

I like a man who slashes about him with wild abandon, raises hell
and doesn't give a damn – even if he does come out for a duck. I
was trained as a kid, you see, on the straight-bat principle, having
a headmaster who had played for his county.

I was trained so well that for the summer term cricket became
the be-all and end-all of my small existence – the feel of the leather
as I bowled a carefully off-spun ball, the commanding sense as I
made the long walk out to the distant wicket, all eyes upon me
(at least that was the conviction), the ceremonious middle-and-
leg, the feeling of power as I mastered the bowling and began to
score – slowly, carefully, straight bat and short-running.

Once a year we had an afternoon of joyous levity. I don't know
how many fathers in how many modern schools slog away at their
sons' bowling with a slender wand of a bat only two inches wide,
but that's what our dads had to do. Every year we had a Fathers'
Match. They were pretty good, too. But the minuscule width of
the bats they were given, and the fact that they had to bowl
underarm, evened things up, so that it was quite a match – one
we all looked forward to. And what googlies they slung at us
underarm! What mighty swipes they made, hitting thin air!
And the ball beating the outfield to the boundary because we were
all laughing so much!

But mostly I think we took our cricket far too seriously. I
certainly did, which may have been something to do with the
subconscious. When I was a very small boy we lived in the
Causeway, in Horsham where I was born. It was a lovely old
street of trees and pleasant houses that led nowhere, only to the

church. Beyond the church was the river and there was a little wooden footbridge leading into meadows that were mown to a flat grass oval, and there were men in white with gaily coloured peaked caps and sweaters with coloured patterns at the neck. I can't remember that we ever paid to watch the cricket.

County matches were played there and I suppose that one time or another I must have seen most of the great cricketers of the day. But I've no recollection of them. My recollections are all of a scooter I had and hurtling through the graveyard down to the bridge. Men in white on the greensward were purely incidental, part of the decoration, like the kingcups and the waterlilies. Then my interest centred on the girl next door. She had a bike, which I borrowed.

Only at Eastbourne was I conscious of cricket as something important. My mother's family were from Eastbourne. We took our holidays there and when we visited my uncle we could hear the sound of willow hitting leather and the clapping from behind the high wall that blocked any free view of the Saffrons cricket ground.

Leveson Gower was a great name in cricket then. He toured a crack country-house team and sometimes he was at Eastbourne when we were there. My father would go and once he took me, but I must have been too young for I was bored by the slow walking back and forth at the change of overs, the long wait for anything to happen. Daylight fireworks in Devonshire Park, with thunderous bangs and pigs in the sky, was more in my line.

But I did once play stool ball, which is an odd game. At one time it was thought to have been the origin of cricket, but now it is believed that the two games were unconnected – simply growing up side by side. The bat is rather like a larger and heavier table-tennis bat, and the ball, which was originally soft, is now, I believe, hard. I cannot now remember where, or when, I played this old game, but I have a vivid recollection of seeing it played at Alfriston in the downs above Eastbourne. They were playing it in the meadow between the church and the Cuckmere river. I wonder if they still play stool ball in that lovely downland country?

One's reaction to any game changes, of course, once one ceases to be a spectator and becomes a participator. The instant I began learning to keep a straight bat I was no longer bored, not even by endless practice at the nets. I developed very quickly that sense of satisfaction, of power even, at the solid *clonk* as the ball connected with the centre of the bat and I drove it to cover. And bowling, too – there was that feeling of delight as arm and ball and eye became so totally co-ordinated that the flight of the ball was like an invisible thread connecting with the wicket. And my first bat – not borrowing now from the school store, my very own. The hours spent stroking the willow with oil till the surface was a rich, warm, lemony yellow, and as smooth as silk. And when the cracks of hard use appeared, then binding it with tape. The point at which taping was seen to be necessary was like a long-service medal.

A veteran now, master of the game and captain of the side.

And then, suddenly, everything changed. I went on to an old Elizabethan grammar school and was instantly cut down to size by their total lack of interest in my well-trained prowess. I switched to shooting, which took me away to Bisley, the scent of bell-tented turf, of gun oil and cordite, a form of travel the cricketers came to envy. And incidentally, an activity that totally cured me of any desire to shoot to kill (either pheasant or human), so that when war came I avoided small arms and went into the impersonal long-range killing business, a gunner shooting at aircraft. And the next time I played cricket was at Tewfik on the shores of the Red Sea.

We were waiting to embark for the invasion of Sicily. The pitch was sand and somebody had dug up an old bat and some tennis balls. I can't remember what we used for a wicket – rifles or bayonets, something like that. And afterwards we would wade out naked through acres of hot salt water scummed with oil from the refinery and effluent from the gathering convoy.

And when the shooting was over, and I had earned some

money, I didn't revert to cricket for my recreation, or to any other ball game, or even to target shooting; I bought a boat and started sailing, which if you get the right sort of boat does take you somewhere.

My work as a writer was taking me to some very strange places anyway. I was all round the coasts of Arabia, in the Empty Quarter and into Buraimi when Sheikh Zaid was just a local Bedou chieftain. All this was for a book called *The Doomed Oasis* – I think perhaps the most fantastic and colourful of all my journeys – and we played cricket, I remember, before setting out for the islands of the Persian Gulf and those fantastic inlets on the south side of the Straits of Hormuz. The two sides were made up from the crew of one of HM frigates. She had just come in from a pirate-catching exercise and was awaiting orders for an Arabian cruise. I can't remember anything about that match, who scored what or who won, only that we played it on the shore within sight of the ship and sailed shortly afterwards, eventually to pick up the Sultan of Oman and become involved in an oil landing – this was before anybody had drilled a well in the Trucial Oman.

Sometimes I wonder why I was born in England, where drowsy summers echoed to the sound of leather on wood and the slow march of the seasons was a country idyll marked by progression from one game to the next. I blink my eyes and the hedges are half gone, the lanes poisoned by exhaust fumes, the meadows unending vistas of sprayed corn or laid concrete. But sometimes from a car, or a train window, I see those once-familiar figures in white, standing still and peaceful on mown grass swards waiting for something to happen. It is a tableau that is essentially a part of the summer of my youth.

I don't envy them now, those figures in white with time on their hands; I don't want to take part.

I just don't want them to disappear.

# The Mystery of Cricket

P. J. KAVANAGH

I nearly put 'The Mystery of My Interest in Cricket' at the head of this, because it is odd that a non-athletic person like myself should be so dotingly fascinated by a game. I mean – what is it? An absurd business that goes on far too long. Yet it has held me, as nothing except sexuality has held me, and with something of the same involuntary fascination, since I first heard the clink of pad-buckles in a cricket-bag.

Incidentally, this interest has nothing to do with imitation, is not an attempt to impress others. Those who do not see the point of cricket (perhaps there is none) often suspect that we fanatics, enquiring of each other the latest Test score, are hopelessly conventional, Basil Radfords and Naunton Waynes playing at a dream of vanished Empire. How little they know us, and what a mixed batch we are. I have spent afternoons in Lord's Taverns with a loquacious pair of Pakistani brothers who knew the second-innings scores of obscure county games that had been played before they were born. They were an extreme case but there were plenty of us to argue with them. No, our passion is self-generated, not social. I doubt, for instance, if my father even knew the rules, and at school my interest in cricket, if noticed at all, impressed nobody.

Perhaps it was indeed those pads, the kit, that first caught my imagination: the look a batsman has of being armoured for the joust; his lonely heroism walking out, his even greater loneliness walking back, peeling off his sausage gloves, or his gloves spiked in rubber, black or green, and his bat, that beautifully coloured and discoloured piece of wood, spicily redolent of putty, sticking out from under the sleeve of his billowing white shirt.

I was never much good, so I did not have the incitement of talent.

I am trying to find my way back to where it all started. Cigarette cards? Those neatly open-shirted figures in braided blazers I stuck in the dun-coloured book provided? Kenneth Farnes, Hedley Verity, W. Voce: pre-War faces to be seen again (or not seen) once the War was over – that distant treat, birthday and Christmas combined, promised by grown-ups, when everything would somehow be different, and better. The name Don Bradman stuck in my eight-year-old mind, the 'Don' sounding especially romantic, like Don John of Austria in Chesterton's poem that someone had read to me.

Perhaps it was the first real cricket match I saw that made the infection bite deep into my mind. It is still the best. It was at Lord's, in 1945, I think, a gathering of servicemen, a 'Victory' Test. Learie Constantine leapt towards a ball as though his legs were a pair of compasses, infinitely extendable, and his arms stretched as though unattached to his shoulders to seize balls apparently far out of reach, to throw them at the stumps in one movement, his body almost horizontal and on-balance. Hammond scored a century, going down on one knee with the final flick of his off-drive, and Keith Miller hit a six to the top level of the stand near the pavilion. There was also a bowler with the memorable name of D. V. P. Wright, whose face, like Hammond's, had been on those cigarette cards, and he kangaroo-hopped to the wicket beating both batsman and stumps almost every other delivery . . . But this is not nostalgia. It is the astonished recognition that these memories are more vivid to me than almost any other memory of any kind. Why? Why do I remember those figures from such a long time ago, and so many others, their movements, mannerisms, even the way E. R. T. Holmes knotted a white handkerchief round his neck? Who on earth was E. R. T. Holmes that I should remember him when I have forgotten so much else? Or R. W. V. Robins, or Laurie Fishlock, or Long

Jim Sims or, most cherished of all, the two Langridges, John and Jas.? I was besotted. I still am. A Sussex supporter, I was distraught when S. C. Griffith lost his place as England's wicket-keeper to an upstart called T. G. Evans. But when, years later, I stood next to Godfrey Evans at a bar, I stared, entranced, at his hammered, mis-shapen hands.

As soon as I could, at school, I set myself to learn to bowl. This is where my belief that cricket lends itself to certain kinds of obsessives, and is not a particularly 'English' game at all, receives confirmation.

My nightly companion at the corner of the playing-field, coat for a bowling-mark, oil-drum for a wicket, was a Pole, Karol Bystram. He was as fanatical as I was. We were both determined to learn the game. Every night of the summer term, *every* night, we bowled at each other till it was dark. We must have bowled tens of thousands of deliveries. In the end I think I could pitch a ball on the wicket and reasonably near the right spot with my eyes shut, and I still can. I even made the school team – just; third-change bowler never, as far as I remember, asked to bowl and always so terrified of getting out first ball that I usually did. Once, first ball, I was given the dream opportunity: a full toss on the leg. I smote it for four, the watching school broke into cheers which faded to silence as they saw me on the way back to the pavilion. In my eager swing my pad had brushed the wicket and knocked off the bail. I can hardly remember a keener disappoint-ment. The headmaster – an ex-county player himself and much admired by me – murmured as I passed him, 'You're not a cricketer, Kavanagh, you're a comedian,' and I pretended to join in the sycophantic laughter. So it always was, a chapter of dis-asters, never playing the one good game I felt I had it in me to play and now I have played what I reckon is my last game and that was a disaster too. What a sad tale it is!

One odd thing is that after I left school I never played or thought of playing for another ten years. Perhaps I was ashamed of my interest. Admittedly I was abroad most of the time but I am fairly certain that I thought cricket should play no part in the life of an aspirant writer who, to save his soul, must draw a firm line between himself and the Hearties. What snobbishness! It was only when I was old enough to recognise and admit my true enthusiasms that I allowed myself to play again – in Java, of all places. In Djakarta there was, perhaps there still is, a superb cricket club called, appropriately, The Box. There, with Australians, Indians and even the occasional Dutchman, I played again, not caring about the turbanned waiters, the absurd fag-end of Imperialism it all represented, or did not represent; absolved of guilt and self-consciousness I played and gloried in it. Without success, of course. But, I fancy, with just enough stylishness sketched while the cognoscenti were looking to ensure that I was asked again.

Back in England I played once or twice in Battersea Park where as umpire I gave an l.b.w. decision against the art critic, David Sylvester. The ball was entirely white with blanco from his perfect pads but as he strode scowling past me he hissed that he had hit the ball and therefore was not out and I recognised a fellow-dreamer, and the shattered dream.

I even for a time flirted with village cricket, that fiercely competitive cauldron, but I played for a team that consisted almost entirely of relations, indeed seven of the team bore the same surname; the two fast bowlers took all the wickets, the two openers scored all the runs, and I grew tired of fielding at long leg.

Then came the great day, a game under a captain who detected my passion. I was invited to play for the magazine *Private Eye* by William Rushton, on the beautiful ground near the house of the editor. I was thrown the ball by the kindly Willie and those long summer evenings with Bystram at last bore fruit. I had not bowled for years and I took a wicket. Indeed, I took four. Incoming batsmen conferred with outgoing batsmen to discover what I was 'doing'. I was doing nothing at all except bowling with the suddenly released enthusiasm of a lifetime and enjoying myself beyond reason. This game became for me an annual event, greatly looked forward to.

Sometimes there came from the magazine less understanding

captains than Willie, bearded exposers of corruption in high places, less sensitive to the subsonic bleeps of yearning, electric emanations from the figure ageing year by year in the deep field. But there were high-spots still, for me, until the year of the last game. After four years' absence I went out to face a new demon-bowler on a hat-trick. The first one hit the middle of my bat, so did the second. Was this the innings I had been waiting to play since I was nine years old? I was sure it was, confidence welled within me. Playing forward fearlessly to the third ball – had not David Steele saved England by doing just this? – I was knocked flat in a welter of blood and stars: Retd. hurt o. Looking up through a penumbra of small boys' faces – thrilled at the sight of blood – a doctor's face loomed, his Sunday afternoon ruined. He drove to his hospital in Reading to get materials to stick my face together and, lying on a rug in the car park being attended to, hopelessly embarrassed, I acknowledged to myself that a career was over – one that had never begun. I had *watched* that ball rising towards my face, waited for my body to take avoiding action which a year a two before it would have done instinctively. Nothing had happened. I was too slow. I was too old.

It is a strange moment to arrive at: the knowledge that an ambition would never be achieved; salutary, I suppose. But the passion does not fade. I write this against the background of the Test commentary on radio. Woolmer is in trouble on his return to Test cricket. I feel for him, but I still do not know why I feel so much. The loneliness of it, of course, the uncertainty and yet the clarity of a game that makes it impossible for a man to fudge, cheat, pretend; and the smallest instinctive movement seals his fate as a hero, or as an also-ran.

Those who write about cricket are often tempted into grandiose analogies but as a game it really is rather like the writing of a poem. What you do either works or does not and no one can tell you precisely wherein you have failed, nor can you know for certain if you will ever succeed, or, if you have succeeded, that you will ever do so again. The failure is in you, it is you that is getting in your own way.

The solitariness has a tang of the heroic about it, and round the great player an aura settles. The first cricket match to which I took my son he spent the whole afternoon collecting empty Coca-Cola cans from underneath the stand while I watched the now portly Cowdrey proceed to a stately 50. When we passed the pavilion he was taking off his boots and for some reason he looked up and gave us a smile. I said, 'You'll always be lucky now, you've been smiled on by Colin Cowdrey,' and I was only three-quarters joking. Like poets, cricketers spend unimaginable numbers of hours doing something as near pointless as possible, trying to dig an elusive perfection out of themselves in the face of an infinite number of variables, and as a result a large proportion of their lives belongs to the realm of the mystical. Like poets' their faces are deeply engraved by introspection – all cricketers seem prematurely lined – because they are as deeply locked in a struggle with themselves as they are with the opposition. But they look happier than poets.

# Wilfred Rhodes

HARRY KEMP

When the Almighty fashioned Wilfred Rhodes
He breathed upon the clay:

'Thou'lt be left-hander, and play for Yorkshire;
And be perennial thorn to the Red Rose.
With brass stud at thy shirt-collar
Thou'lt bowl all day from Kirkstall Lane end.'

Then so far forgot Himself to mutter:
'And God help bloody batsman at the other!'

# The Cyclical Supremacy of Australia in World Cricket

## THOMAS KENEALLY

We may be a small and callow race but there is a divinity to our cricket. There are profound social and cultural reasons for it. As late as the 1950s, the curriculum in Australian schools was identical to that of an English grammar school. Poetry cut out at Tennyson. The only history was European history. When we spoke of literary figures, we spoke of Englishmen. But when we spoke of cricket, we spoke of our own. We couldn't make it in literature because we had none of the right seasons, the plants laughed at European botany, the absurd animals had no mythology behind them. But cricket was possible! We knew why it was. We had more sunshine, we ate more protein, we washed more regularly than the Poms! In the manner in which soccer is the great way up for children from the economic sumps of Brazil, so cricket was the great way out of Australian cultural ignominy. No Australian had written *Paradise Lost*, but Bradman had made 100 before lunch at Lord's.

About the age of ten therefore I had my cultural aspirations irretrievably tangled with my lust to be opening batsman for Australia. At that stage I played a game which I believe was common throughout the British Empire – it was played with two hexagonal strips of metal or wood. On each face of one of the pieces was marked a number – 1, 2, 3, 4, 6 – and on the sixth face was printed *Howzat!* On the other piece the various ways you can lose your wicket were listed – bowled, l.b.w, caught, etc., with on the sixth side the most exalted and exalting words ever spoken, *NOT OUT*.

I spent most of the waking hours of my pre-adolescence

playing this game with two imaginary cricket teams composed of the world's greatest writers and the world's greatest composers. I remember that Tolstoy went in at first wicket down for the writers. Thomas Hardy was always high in the batting order yet for one whole summer managed a batting average of only about 11. H. G. Wells was twelfth man for a long time and at one stage was even dropped back to play Sheffield Shield for New South Wales. Handel and Bach, despite their paunches and their progenitive urges, were the stars of the composers' line-up, and I remember that Borodin – though a Russian and low in the batting order – sometimes scored a century at eighth wicket down.

The realities of cricket were more painful than this delightful and private game. Thursday afternoon, we put on our creams under the brazen sky and set off in a crocodile line to some parched suburban pitch. At the head of the line strode a lanky religious brother, possibly Irish but always a fanatic for this British game. Behind him, carrying the blanched cricket bag, two of the best cricketers in the class walked, chatting to him about field placements and test innings which, already in a young life, they had seen plenty of. From the bag came a delicious smell of leather, linseed oil, sweat, padding. And they walked in the midst of it, high on it, as acolytes should be. To us butterfingers further back in the line, as to the unbeliever and unworthy at the back of the temple, only the faintest tang reached. You knew that the two bag-carriers were going to be the captains of the day's cricket and you sent messages to them up the line, begging each of them indiscriminately to pick you in his team. It was a humiliation to be picked ninth or lower. If someone had made me the right offer, I would have sold my soul to be picked fifth.

There were certain glamour field placements too. Point, cover, silly mid-on, square leg and slips were the placings of glory, and I was torn between them and the fear of that fierce six-stitcher ball with a bullet at its heart. The worst insult was to be put somewhere out of trouble, on the grounds that even if you stopped a ball, your return would be so wide and erratic that over-throws and similar disasters would result. I had a curly-headed

Byronic friend who was always placed at deep fine leg, a point to which very few Australian schoolboys of that era ever walloped the ball. Sometimes he would forget to change position at the ends of overs, or when a left-hander was in. The others would forget him and he would stay out there dreaming, oblivious of all the passion at the central pitch. Occasionally a wild hook would send one his way. He would not have seen the stroke. He would not be aware that the red pellet was diving at him out of the sun. Then, having shaken his head and returned to reality to see the brother, gentle *confrère* of Christ, glaring at him from the umpire's position at the bowler's end, he looked to the sky from which he knew the threat was coming and was struck in both eyes by the fierce sun. So that while the ball hung in its easy trajectory, the fielders closer in, the bearers of the aromatic bag loudest of all, would begin to mourn the inevitable dropped catch. 'Geez, ees gunna drop it. Stroik a loight, Viney, keep yer bloody eyes on it.'

A look of focused intelligence would now come to Viney's features, his hands would be raised like an Ethiopian's in prayer and the ball would bounce on his shoulder and so hit the grass. 'Geez, yor 'is mate, Keneally. Some mate 'e is. Geez, bloody drongo, that Viney.' And the wicketkeeper would be standing with gloves on his hips, shaking his head and saying, 'Geez, bloody drongo.'

From such disasters I came to understand that one watched the ball, never let it out of one's sight. There was no other way to social success in the antipodes. And in fact there was no other way to deification – even today, there are few other ways.

I am proud to say that out of some instinct I stuck to Viney – I knew that ultimately he was playing a more serious kind of cricket in his head, even as the ball lobbed on his shoulder, even as it refused to fall into the sensitive web of his fingers. But I was a more social animal than Viney. Therefore, I had to come to terms with the leather orb.

Nature is always profligate, and the rule is that when you have a few million children all under a national onus to catch, bowl, bat, then you have to produce some good'uns. But Australian society has become more sophisticated since then. There *are* one or two writers and even a historian who are revered. We have found that it *is* possible for Australians to have literary ideas about the place, that Australia is not outside the aesthetic universe. In short, Australia – which used to have one unifying rite, cricket – has now become pluralist. I cannot but predict it will be a disaster for Australian cricket.

Recently I played in a game between Australian writers (and yes, all you Aussie-bashers, we were able to find eleven!) and Australian Actors' Equity. It was a brilliant Sydney day, the sun coruscating off the harbour, and we striding around inspecting a pitch on which Victor Trumper had played. The actors' team looked impressive. They were all angular Australian Adonises, stars from the Australian soapies which you see, as an alternative to the Carson show, in Californian motels at 10.30 at night. They looked like the sort of lads who in my generation would not have been permitted not to be brilliant cricketers. In truth they were frightful. We had them out before the wives, mistresses and small party of devotees had the lunch ready or the beer cold. We noticed that there were no recriminations, that they took a cavalier attitude towards their ducks and run-outs. Later, in the field, they commiserated with each other over dropped catches. There was no one there to stiffen them with the appropriate chants of, 'Geez, no bloody hoper drongo!'

And because of that there was no exultation to the game. I played a stroke over mid-on which would, in the old days when cricket counted, have won me a week's social grace and a nod from the fierce Christian Brother at the stumps. Now, all the urgency and all the ecstasy were gone. Even Kerry Packer, who avenged some forgotten school cricket-team slight by buying the game for himself, must be aware of this. That despite the big money, cricket in Australia has become merely a game. And when that happens, we're in trouble.

# Hill Cricket

LAURIE LEE

I come from a country of hill-cricket, where for decades the village players have been great toilers on the slopes and have developed a whole range of off-the-level techniques. Indeed, in those steep valleys running away through the Cotswold escarpment it was well-nigh impossible to find a level space for a wicket, and the most we could hope for, when we were boys, was some well-trodden goat-path winding among the tussocks.

One of the most unbalanced, yet beautiful, of cricket fields in my local district is the one that stands high on its hill above the village of Sheepscombe. Its general contour is that of a pony's back, with head held erect – the pavilion built somewhere between the ears, then the pitch itself starting halfway down the neck, levelling off for a bit along the saddle then plunging down the hind-quarters and away to the boundary. A straight drive from one end runs slap into the hill, and after trickling for a few yards, stops dead; while from the other end it soars out and disappears over the brow of the hill, and then the players get lost for a while, or sit around in the grass, till the ball is returned by some passing cowman.

A lasting memory of this ground is of sitting on the pavilion porch and watching Frank Mansell – Sheepscombe's demon bowler – come racing up the hill to deliver. At first only the outfield was visible, then you'd see the top of Frank's cap, then his flushed face and great heaving shoulders, till gradually, like a galleon, he'd come billowing into view and loose his fast one like a shot from a cannon.

Some time during the late twenties I bicycled from our hills down into Cheltenham to see Gloucestershire play the visiting Australians. I remember Arthur Mailey and others in their huge cloth caps – strange bottle-faced men from the other side of the world who laughed sharply and spoke a kind of scrambled Cockney.

Watching the fierceness of their game on that green English ground, I began to speculate about the country they came from, and how they played cricket in their own home towns, and what their pitches were like 15,000 miles down through the bulk of the world.

Later, I began to hear tales of 'The Hill' at Sydney, and what with hills being so much a part of our local game, I started to wonder about this too. One day, I swore, I'd go there and see them at it. I'd sit on The Hill at Sydney, and feel at home.

A few years ago I arranged this at last while staying with my brother, who lives near the cricket ground at Sydney. It was Christmas-summer, the time of a Test series against New Zealand, and we dressed up one afternoon and went to see the game. Our destination, it seemed, was the Members' Pavilion, but I asked for The Hill instead. This was reluctantly agreed to, and together with another friend – one of the many sons of an ex-Archbishop of Canterbury – we picked our way carefully towards that legendary place.

It was a bright hot day, with tiny clouds in the sky and a keen air smelling of freshly picked oysters. This was soon enriched by the smell of freshly pricked beer-cans as several thousand cricket-watchers settled down to the game. They were a striking lot, many half-naked, with thin wiry legs supporting huge muscled torsos. Each wore round his middle, like a Lonsdale belt, the sacred pot of the dedicated beer-drinker. And almost everyone had beside him, to accompany the afternoon's play, several dozen beer cans or bottles packed in great portable ice-boxes. As one for whom a normal afternoon at Lord's might have absorbed at most a couple of long-held pints, the sight and quantity of each man's supply struck me as another dimension of cricket altogether.

New Zealand was batting that afternoon, and doing rather well. The chaste pavilions appeared not to notice. But The Hill around us was already rolling with noise, with cries of protest, throaty advice and challenge.

Having picked a comparatively bare spot half-way up the slope, it soon became clear to us that we were in a sort of no-man's-land between two opposing forces – New Zealand supporters below, Australians above. Each run from New Zealand would send up a tidal cheer from their men to meet a counter-jeer crashing down from behind.

About a quarter of an hour before stumps, trouble began. The afternoon had been long and hot. The New Zealand side had done rather too well; and worse, supplies of beer had run out. Every man was now squatting on a cairn of crumpled empties, his face sweating with thirst and emotion. Suddenly they all got to their feet, picked up their cans and bottles, and began hurling them spitefully at one another.

'Don't like the look of this,' said my brother to the Arch-bishop's son, and they put their heads down between their knees. Missiles were now whistling in all directions, and tinkling and thumping on the ground all round.

Caught as we were in mid-fire, I felt in a favoured position, and began to watch the battle with my head well up. Barrage and counter-barrage criss-crossed above me, seeming to go in waves as the men gathered fresh ammunition.

Then looking down for a moment I saw large drops of blood falling on to my 'Somerset-Maugham' white tropical suiting. 'That's rich-looking blood,' I thought; then realised it was my own. I'd been clobbered on the head by a beer bottle.

I felt no pain, but from this small flesh wound I bled like a slaughtered calf. No one around me seemed to have been similarly damaged, so I lay back and made the most of it. My white suit showed up the blood to some advantage, and I was soon surrounded by an admiring crowd. 'Now see what you've done. Hell, he looks bad, don't 'e? Reckon he's dyin'? Better call a doctor.'

The battle was over, and the cricket-watchers calmed down. The sight of blood made them contrite as children. There was anxious sympathy all round, and maybe I overdid it, for suddenly I was being given the kiss of life by a policeman. I broke free from this and fell into the soft cotton-clothed arms of some young student nurses from Adelaide, who held my wound closed with their long scented fingers till the more proper bandages arrived.

Getting blooded on The Hill at Sydney cricket ground has always struck me as something of a rare privilege for a foreigner. It was a badge of both the passion and remorse of the cricket-watching fraternity of Sydney, and later made me many friends in bars of that city.

# The Moon Match

## BERNARD LOVELL

The village cricket ground was almost exactly two miles north of the telescope at Jodrell Bank. Nothing particular about that, you may think; yet for me it is inextricably linked with one of the great dramas of the space age, played out over a weekend in September 1959. For five seasons I had looked eagerly from the ground southwards searching for any sign that the massive structure of steel would be visible above the intervening trees. Always the tensions and the nearly destructive problems of the week vanished in the sunshine on that lovely ground – to the extent that one eminent American visitor, dragged reluctantly to the match one Saturday afternoon, remarked that he could not understand the cricket but he understood why Lovell was able to survive.

On 12 September 1959 some of those problems were solved; at least the telescope was finished and had been working for nearly two years. In that season I was the captain of the First XI. Everything had gone splendidly and we were unbeaten. Indeed we fielded a strong team, for as soon as some of the regular members became preoccupied with the harvest or holidays we gathered in two Etonians and a Harrovian, who had recently done battle at Lord's, as well as our local MP. Also we owned a very fast bowler (by village-pitch standards) who, for some reason that I cannot now remember, always played for us on Saturday afternoons, although he was a nominal member of one of the Lancashire or Cheshire league clubs.

On that Saturday morning I awoke with one anxiety and determination – with only a few games to play, to preserve our unbeaten record for the season. The weather was no problem, our ground was on sand, and unless a thunderstorm was in progress we could always play. In any event the sun was shining. The morning at Jodrell was quiet and uneventful. At that time we had quite a team of Americans working with us. A year earlier I had been visited by a high-ranking officer of the United States Air Force. Stung by American failures in space and the succession of Soviet successes they planned to use the rocket of an Atlas inter-continental missile to send a probe to the moon. Odd though it may seem nowadays they had no radio telescope with which to track it, neither did anyone else in the West except Jodrell. Of course I agreed to help and soon we had a line of USAF trailers linked to our control room near the telescope. Already they had made four attempts and every one had failed. More launchings were planned and so the Americans remained with us patiently waiting, testing their equipment with their telex machines and telephones permanently linked to Washington and Los Angeles. On that Saturday morning they were there in their air-conditioned trailers as usual – and as usual I called in to talk about the weather or whatever subject might be relevant. 'We shall stay around until they wake up in Washington and then go away for the weekend.' And what, they asked, would be my plans? 'Playing cricket, a key match, neighbouring village. See you on Monday.'

So I returned home for an early lunch. I lived in a village two miles the other side of the telescope from the cricket ground. According to the old maps there was a cricket ground in my village earlier in the century but it was no longer large enough to sustain a team. Our matches began at 2.30 and as usual on that Saturday I threw my bag into the car about half-past one to be in good time. But I had reckoned without the Russians. Our house has two entrances from the lane. The one we always use is the longer and goes over a cattle grid into the lane. Turning left at that point after a few hundred yards we pass the other shorter entrance to the rear of the house. A favourite game for the young after waving a visitor goodbye was to dash through the house and courtyard and confront the departing visitor with a second wave at this point. No reason to do this with me on a Saturday afternoon, but a child was there – and this was a halt signal, not a cheerful wave: 'You must come back, you're wanted very urgently on the phone.' My leisurely contemplation of the afternoon's game was shattered. In fact I was wanted urgently on two telephones. We had two different lines, one the normal private house phone and the other an extension from the Jodrell switchboard. The telephones had rung in chorus. The duty controller from Jodrell conveyed a businesslike message that the Russians had 'launched a rocket which would reach the moon on Sunday evening'. The voice on the house phone was that of an excited pressman asking what we were 'going to do about it'. My answer was brief: 'I am going to play cricket.'

I returned to the car and drove away, but I was disturbed. I passed the telescope, radiant in the sunshine, odd, I thought, that at this moment it is studying the moon by radar. Should I call in? Impossible, I would be late. We tossed; I won, we batted. Plenty of batsmen, I'll go ten or eleven. The game started, the score mounted, but for the first time ever on that ground I was finding it hard to concentrate on the cricket. I was recalling the message of the Jodrell duty controller that the Russians had announced that their rocket would reach the moon on Sunday evening. Why could they be so certain that they were able to make such an unambiguous announcement? It would be a colossal achievement, a precision of launching and guidance hitherto unapproached. The Americans had already failed four times and the Russians had tried and failed nine months ago (2 January 1959).

We were doing well, already thirty-odd for no wicket; 150 would be a winning score with our bowling array. Yes, it was that affair of the first Russian attempt, Lunik I, that was bothering me. What happened? Why was I irritated by that Lunik? The wicket was hard and dry and our openers were enjoying themselves. The legside boundary on the lane side was quite short and a full toss could easily be despatched for six. That happened now and the ball nearly hit the village phone-box, a dozen yards over the boundary. Perhaps I should telephone Jodrell and find out if there was any more information. Yes, of course, I began to remember the Lunik I story.

A year earlier in Moscow after the failure of the first American attempt I had asked the Russians if they intended to follow the USA and attempt to send a rocket to the moon. The answer was that no attempt at a lunar rocket would be made until they could do the job properly and guide the rockets precisely. In any case I did not know of any radio telescope in the Soviet Union capable of tracking a rocket to that distance. That, coupled with similar negative conversations with Soviet space scientists later in 1958, led me to the conviction that the Russians had no immediate intention of attempting this feat. It was an erroneous judgement, since Lunik I was launched early in January 1959. We were under pressure to locate the rocket so that the Soviet claims could be assessed. We failed to do so. Without knowledge of the radio frequency used by the Russians or of the trajectory, our search was equivalent to that for the proverbial needle in the haystack. I complained to the Soviet Academy of Sciences on the grounds that they had failed to provide us with the simple information enabling us to locate their rocket and verify their claims which were regarded with great suspicion in the West.

There had never been a response and I had no intention of wasting time again searching for Soviet luniks – so I was playing cricket now; but then there was something strange about that precise announcement. They never, under any circumstances, made such a claim unless they were absolutely certain of success and that it could be demonstrated. But this was a claim of an event that would happen thirty hours later. I was disturbed, and thankful that we were batting. Was this Lunik 2 in some strange way the Soviet response to my complaints and had they assumed we would collaborate and verify their claim?

I had settled, as usual, with the opposing captain that we would take the tea interval at 4.30. In September it was difficult to continue play much after 7 p.m. We ought to get enough runs to declare at tea. Nearly 4 p.m. but no sign of tea preparations. The ladies worked on a rota, week by week, and this Saturday, by chance, the task fell to my wife assisted by any of the children who were home and willing. Where were they? The least of my worries became the state of the game. If tea was late then it would be dark before we could hope to bowl out the opponents, and perhaps I really ought to get back to Jodrell at a reasonable time. Ah! here they are at last with baskets of sandwiches and buns but looking unusually bothered. Why were they so late? 'You try to get tea for twenty-two cricketers plus umpires and scorers with the phones ringing continuously and you'll soon know why we're late – you really must do something.' – 'Look, the telescope is already doing two separate jobs every day and night and I'm not going to waste time on another wild goose chase after a Russian rocket.'

As I spoke my conviction that I would do nothing began to fade. 'All right, for heaven's sake light up the boiler otherwise we'll be late for tea, and have you got some pennies?' That phone-box just over the boundary. I would go there. Stan was the vice-captain, a left-hander and powerful hitter already padded up, bat in hand, awaiting the fall of the next wicket. 'Look, Stan, it's 4.15, we've already got 130 on the board. Get a few quick ones and we'll declare at tea. I must make some telephone calls so don't wait for me.'

I phoned the controller at Jodrell; the telescope was still following the moon – but nothing to do with the Lunik. Yes, the information was still firm from Moscow that a rocket had been launched which would reach the moon on Sunday evening. 'What time?' – 'About ten I believe – and by the way the American chaps are still here, asking where they can find you – something about a message from Washington.' – 'Tell them to wait, I'll come in when we've finished the cricket match in about three hours' time.' I saw them coming in for tea. I had time for one more call. To John Davies, my senior colleague who shared my enthusiasm for the new adventures in space. If any man could locate the rocket from sparse information, then there was no one better. Could he possibly meet me at Jodrell about 7.30 to discuss the situation? Of course he would be there.

I returned to the field. We finished with 155 for 5. Yes, there was time for a cup of tea. 4.50 would give us two hours and ten minutes until 7 and then the agreed extra fifteen minutes if there was chance of a finish. A bright evening still but the light will be getting poor by 7. We really ought to paint those sightscreens during the winter. In any case they were too low, especially where the ground sloped at the south end. Still it might help now. Put on Bill with his high trajectory at that end and the ball will be in the tree line. Trouble is, though, that their blacksmith might be in form; a boundary every ball of the over from him was nothing unusual and our boundaries really were rather short.

Lucky for me that our opponents were from a neighbouring village. For us they were foreigners and always got far more vicious treatment than would have been meted out to a team from the Antipodes. So it was that evening. Long ago in my university days I was played as a fastish bowler and now generally opened with a few overs. That evening I saw no reason why I should change the habit and went on down wind and down slope at a greater pace than was, perhaps, wise for one who had just celebrated a forty-sixth birthday. However, with our league man at the other end it had the desired effect. The Etonian behind the stumps, still thinking of the well-groomed pitch at Lord's, had one or two nasty surprises and the first dozen runs on the board were all byes, but then he moved back a few yards and in my third over justified his existence by catching their number one at full stretch one-handed. The next man was a Wykehamist – the squire's son home for the hols. Nice boy, but today I did not like the look of him. He was a good bat and that summer had made a pile of runs. Neither did I like the contemptuous way he treated the last two balls of my over. Five-thirty and 30 for 1 was not my idea of how the evening should be going. Then I remembered that the squire's family and that of the Harrow boy who bowled leg-breaks were not exactly the best of friends. One of those ancient feuds that survived generation after generation.

The Harrovian, whose name was Jeremy, was a left-hander and his leg-breaks could be quite fast and nasty, especially on this roughish pitch. As he crossed over to field next to me at second slip I pulled on my sweater. 'You take over from me, Jeremy. When you get that fellow in your sights bowl him a straight one which he'll hit through the covers for four. Make the next one the most ferocious leg-break you can manage, and we'll get him in the slips.' Jeremy needed no encouragement, he had a special distaste for the Wykehamist and it was 40 for 2.

Only the blacksmith to worry about now. I wonder where that rocket is. Let me see – must have been launched about 1 p.m. our time, escape velocity 11 km per sec. – oh! why do I always remember rocket velocities in metric and the distance to the moon in miles? Six o'clock, 50 for 2, and they don't like it, they're beginning to block. Must shift this pair. Let me see, 11 km per second – that would be about 7 miles per second, 400-odd miles per minute – yes, that's right, about 25,000 miles per hour. Must already have travelled 100,000 miles and we haven't got these chaps out yet. Ah, there goes his leg stump thank heavens, it's the other opener, never did like bowling or fielding to left-handers. Still, we don't know the orbit and can't think that one out now. In any case it can't be as far from earth as that, so we ought to have ample signal strength if only we could find it. Here comes their number five: the blacksmith. Must concentrate on the cricket. He could double the score in the next half-hour if we're not careful.

Stan, the vice-captain, was in the covers. Surely he played against this fellow one night last week in some knock-out game? 'Stan, we've got to get rid of this fellow quick.' – 'Easy,' replied Stan; 'he's not in very good shape today – drank too much at a party last night and is still complaining of a hangover. We've pitched the wickets in line with that old oak where the owl's got a nest. Get Bill to give him a few slow ones as high as he can make them. What with the sun nearly in his eyes and that oak tree he won't see them.' He didn't, and my anxieties were over before they had any good reason to complain about the light.

In fact, whether they complained about the state of the pitch, the light or the oak tree I never knew. For once I escaped from the after-match drinks and post-mortem in the Arms and with no time to change (although I did get my boots off – in those days they had spikes) I made haste to the telescope. As I turned into the main road I saw the moon still in the south-eastern sky. Still twenty-seven hours from the time at which the Russians claim their rocket will reach the moon. Extraordinary! That means that, from the Soviet Union, the moon will be low in the west and becoming difficult to see, but will be nearly on our meridian and ideally placed for observations with the Jodrell telescope. To reach the control building of the telescope I had to drive past the American trailers – and the American contingent was there, in a state approaching frenzy, having been constantly harassed by voices from Washington and Los Angeles the whole afternoon demanding that they should attempt to locate the Soviet rocket. It was unfortunate for them that I was playing cricket because that was the only reply they could give – that nothing could be done until I returned. Harassed by their failures with their Atlas rocket and not wishing to believe that the Russians had this technical superiority, the voices from across the Atlantic were incredulous at our apparent indifference. However, I was unmoved by this transatlantic interest and remained in a casual frame of mind until I unlocked the office containing the telex machine. And there, with the paper streaming out on the floor, was a message from Moscow giving precise details of the frequencies of the transmitters in the Lunik and the co-ordinates for the latitude and longitude of Jodrell Bank, giving a time of lunar impact as 10 p.m. on the following evening. The message had been despatched from Moscow less than one hour after the launching of the rocket. Clearly the Russians had prepared the calculations for Jodrell Bank in advance and had an almost audacious confidence in the success of the mission.

The cricket match was over and it was time to act. The rest is history. By Sunday afternoon Jodrell was thronged by press, radio and television men correctly sensing that if the Soviets could hit the moon with a rocket then they could hit any place on earth with precision. By the evening our normally peaceful building was a place of fantasy. For the high-ranking American who insisted on telephoning to me in a state of disbelief half an hour before impact, it was only necessary for me to hold the telephone mouthpiece close to our loudspeaker. A minute after 10 p.m. the press men got their headlines – RED ROCKET HITS THE MOON. WORLD HEARS NEWS FROM JODRELL BANK. As the leader-writer in *The Times* wrote, 'The rocket, in Soviet hands, has become a precision instrument . . . a demonstration to the world of what Soviet technology can achieve – simple stark and impressive . . .'

But for the first six hours of this drama I had played cricket!

# Len, Clarrie, Will and Old Vic

LEO McKERN

I suppose that being born in Sydney in 1920 meant some almost inevitable occupation with the great game from early childhood; at school, after school, on Saturdays and Sundays; on the beach, at Sydney Cricket Ground. Or sitting glued in the early hours to the radio, and the Australian Broadcasting Commission's supposedly instant broadcasts from Lord's.

A friend of mine's first job was as messenger-tea-boy in the A.B.C. studios, and he let me into the great secret that the 'direct' broadcasts consisted in fact of an announcer reading a series of cables delivered in a sort of bucket-chain, my friend being the main link. And very important too. In many cases there was the inevitable hold-up, when the commentator invented spur-of-the moment dramas; 'Ah, I see a small dog has run onto the pitch . . . what is it . . . a fox-terrier? Yes, a small fox-terrier . . . one of the umpires is trying to get rid of it . . . some amusement in the crowd . . . etc., etc.' while waving arms and distorted face frantically signalled for the next cable. He even had a little block of wood and a tiny baton to deliver direct to the microphone the necessary 'THOK' of each stroke.

At lucky times, a Test in Sydney Cricket Ground, I invariably sat on 'The Hill', and in that particular picnic atmosphere, among the grass-root experts and basic philosophers, I wouldn't have had a stand seat if you'd paid me.

The many and diverse thrills of the Sydney Ground were always a much-treasured treat; if it wasn't cricket it was the breathtaking floodlit massed pipe bands, the dirt-track speedway racing, or the Royal Easter Show and the bags and bags of really free samples. The hot sun on the crushed grass of The Hill, the bottle of lemonade, the limp sandwiches from home, the sun-proof handkerchief around the forehead and cigarette-paper nose-shade; the great Australian roar, the spine-cold silences, the inevitable true wit with his solos.

At school I was a medium-pace spin bowler and an indifferent bat. In my class was Livingstone, a tiny boy and a marvel with the bat even at thirteen. He played State cricket I think, later, and was admired, envied, and had more eager friends than he knew what to do with. And being small, he reminded us of Bradman.

I lost an eye in 1941, which meant losing perspective vision as well, but by the early fifties I had compensated enough to play in the Stratford Memorial Theatre's team for two years, where a director, years before, used to send to London agents for such actors as 'a good fast bowler who can play Laertes'. There were four Aussies there one year; Ron Haddrick had played for a State back home, and Ray Sherry was a sinewy fast bowler, and we played surrounding villages every Sunday, enormously pleasurable. I remember bowling a particularly loose one, and even before the stroke was delivered, properly punishing, I saw is was going for a slamming four or six, and threw my arms in the air in despair; the ball was driven so hard into one palm that retention of the catch was without volition, my fingers clamped around the ball by the impact. I walked back to my mark looking, of course, as if that was exactly what I had intended. But I couldn't pick up anything for a week.

Old Len, who if not dead now must be over eighty, which would not surprise me, was a flyman at the Theatre. A very tall and stringy-tough Northcountryman who had played both cricket and football for his County. He bowled occasionally, very slow and very spinny. Just before his first over one Sunday morning he ambled over to me at cover and asked 'Canst tha catch, Leo lad?' 'Pretty well,' I said. 'Right then . . . we'll 'ave this bugger first ball.' And we did. He sent me down a hill on the village field to the boundary and his first ball was sent for a tremendous potential six. The village side's yell of delight stopped suddenly at the apogee and in a beautiful silence the little red comet descended.

If I had missed that catch, even with my Nelson excuse, I would have taken my glass eye out and jumped on it, and never looked lovely old Len in the face again. I had not moved a step from where he had fielded me.

It was while I was at Stratford that I learned at long last to move the ball in the air. When I saw it happen the first time I felt as if I had done the Indian Rope Trick, tickled pink, as my father used to say. That particular village side's number two bat was a young bespectacled man with a very good reputation and one very bad habit. Balls outside his off stump he refused to play, but how beautifully; with an extremely graceful lifting of the bat, one knee bent just so, a posture he held for a moment for the admiration of all. A pretty bat, as they say. But he certainly punished the bowling anywhere but on his off. I offered him four straight balls outside that stump, each balletically refused, and broke the fifth in onto it.

What joy these very small things give us, all the greater when one is pretty mediocre.

Licking the Poms was then, as now, a national ambition; and yet I sometimes think that, even though the game is and has been every bit as much Australian as English, the Australians could never have invented it. Indeed many in my school thought it a sissy's game; and as for tennis . . .! Rugger, yes; and they went on to develop Australian Rules. Possibly it was all part of beating the Pommies at their own games, cricket, tennis, that is very much Australian. Splendid swimmers, of course, with that incredibly beautiful coastline, and my wife is the only Australian I know who couldn't swim before she left infants' school, but then she's special in all sorts of funny ways.

I am told on good authority that the arrival of the first Australian Test team in England considerably surprised the interested population by being all white men and not beautifully ugly aborigines. Perhaps it is not so surprising, because ever since I landed in Liverpool in the late autumn of 1946 with fifty bob, enough to get to London, I have always been mildly surprised at how little is known about Australia. Harry Kippax, journalist and contemporary, who made that awful trip with me, and who is a nephew of the great Australian cricketer of that name, took one look over the side on that dismal morning and remarked, 'the quality of Mersey is not strained'. As indeed it wasn't. And still isn't. Both of us knew London as well as I knew Coogee, and Edgar Wallace and others had told me all about the English, and even the Welsh, Scots and Irish. An attenuated result of colonialism of course, and here, in 1946, though Australia ceased being a colony in 1901, it was still so in the general mind. When I spoke then, people winced; now it is an accomplishment to speak 'Strine', socially amusing.

I remember the fury body-line bowling aroused. My particular hero was Clarrie Grimmett, who could place his ball on a sixpence every time, and Larwood was a sort of monster, a nasty stratagem of the Poms because they couldn't win a straight game. And indeed he was a beginning; it is not the same game; the long grubby fingers of violence brush the twenty-two yards, and a visor in 1930 would have been an object of stunned amazement or laughter.

Inevitably, materialism has become part of the game; and as old Polonius seemed to suggest, it brings problems with it; money is a very subtle changer of attitudes, and as the tendency seems more and more to relate all human activity in terms of the stuff, it has of course affected the game. Can any player of a game be worth a million pounds? How much is a wife worth? How golden should a particular handshake be? Eventually it will become a matter of how many angels can dance on the point of a pin. A fair go for all is a reasonable attitude, but in any contract that is otherwise as tight as a drum there is always that one word that seems to stick in everyone's throat; what exactly does 'reasonable' mean?

I remember Len the flyman telling me of the benefit matches in his younger days; the particular and very famous player he watched from the slips (he had enormous hands, did Len) hit the winning six and had his cap off running for the gate and his dues from the rapidly-departing crowd before the ball hit the ground. There wasn't much money in the game then for the players, and I daresay there are many of them who would mutter, 'There isn't much now either'. Yet I can understand the rearguard, some in high places, vainly trying to stem the rising tide flooding onto the sacred fields.

In some minds the words 'Cricket' and 'Amateur' are inseparable; but in practice, with the money and facilities of whole countries behind their people on the track or in the field, how long can that attitude be practical? But, my word, to see a gold won, against the odds, and to know it was done on a budget as slim as the athlete's ankles, is very heart-warming.

And floodlit cricket seems a bit like the Giant Slalom run on polystyrene chips.

During my three years with the Old Vic Company too, our small passions on stage were more than matched in the dusty rehearsal room upstairs in games of table cricket all summer. We were without the wonderful bonus of the week-end games of Stratford, but a small group of us carefully carved out three-inch bats and flipped the overs from under the middle finger like squeezed pips. We became amazingly adroit at inswingers and backspins; and if we were lucky with an otherwise extremely hard rehearsal and playing schedule, why, the Oval is only just down the road.

I remember reading a story set in a city state somewhere in the future, of a people whose practice it was to put their malefactors to death in an ingenious and terrifying way. Immobilised in the centre of a vast stadium, alone, the wretch was subjected, in a dreadful silence, to the concentrated will of the whole populace, who stared at him in a detestation and hatred of such malevolence that he died. I wonder if Larwood ever felt a small shiver on Sydney cricket ground? Because unlike the big-ball game, I remember cricket as sometimes containing the long silences that crept the flesh as fiercely as the great roared releases of excitement. There is a deliberateness in the game that is missing from the other, and moments of great drama sometimes contain slow movement or absolute stillness that draws out the very essence of the tragedy or the triumph like a fine wire. A soft Antipodean 'Oh, GAWD!' breathed into a total silence can be almost, in effect, Shakespearean.

One of my wife's favourite 'Pears' prints (strangely enough, for she is not a cricket enthusiast) is the one of the knickerbockered turn-of-the century boy with rolled-up shirt sleeves. Chin up, straight bat, in front of the un-bailed stumps and the red geraniums, he is 'Captain of the Eleven' in some English garden. Jane collects these particular bygones, and pursued this one for four years, constantly discovering at auctions and dealers' sales that it is also prized by cricketers, and constantly just missing one. And I must say, now that she has been finally successful, and the Captain has pride of place on the kitchen wall, that it is a most gently evocative thing, charming and very companionable.

I feel a bit of a fraud, writing about cricket, being, although Australian, not exactly a tail-ender but not far from it, and not having played for many years. Although it was certainly part of my scene, as they say nowadays, I wasn't as 'into it' perhaps as much as many friends. I was simply tyro enough not to be content with watching, and like most other things in which I became interested, I had to do it. It may have something to do with being an actor. I was asked once to play a piano in a film; the director said, 'You do play, don't you?' I answered no, I couldn't, but I could act as if I could. I was on safe ground, of course, because the really clever people in films can make the actors look good with all sorts of magic; and I must say it looked pretty good in the end result.

So that I think it probable that my style promised more than my performance gave; but I had to *do* it, watching was not enough, and when I was tossed the ball for an over, it was as belly-warming as an exit round.

I have not been to a ground for a shamefully long time. Television coverage may have assisted this sloth; the one-day County matches are great watching, but the feel of that hard red ball, though far away and long ago, is still very real, and that 'thok' still the most evocative sound of all.

In the last few days, on the other side of the world (my side, I suppose, though I have been here thirty-five years) Australia has just denied New Zealand the chance of a win by delivering the last ball underhand, along the pitch. Oh, dear. The New Zealand Premier, no less, called it a cowardly act; no wonder, he said, that the Aussies wore yellow shirts. Strong stuff indeed, and many would say it isn't cricket. Or would they? Young people would fall about if that term was used in all seriousness in their hearing. It's old fashioned, and therefore funny. But everyone knew exactly what it meant; it expressed things difficult perhaps to put into other words, and covered a vast range of feelings, attitudes, standards and morals. Many of these have passed away, like the wonderful ice-cream I bought on The Hill from the white-coated man with the tray; ('Peanuts, lollies and chocs!') and when young people show amusement at the conception of it not being cricket, I wonder if there's that much to laugh at? For whatever the words meant, like the Game itself, what have they got to replace it?

# The Crooked Bat

ARTHUR MARSHALL

Crooked meaning not straight: not crooked meaning dishonest. It always seemed to me, as a schoolboy reluctantly playing cricket in the 1920s, that a straight bat, so highly prized by the experts, was in my case mere foolishness, sending the ball, when I managed to make contact with it, feebly back whence it had come. With a crooked bat there was at least a chance of deflecting the offensive weapon either to right or left and scoring a 'run'. To attempt to score anything at all may savour of self-advertisement but that was never my aim. My sights were not set on a ribboned coat or a captain's hand on my shoulder smote. The sole purpose of a run was to remove me, however briefly, from the end where the action was.

Cricket was a manly game. Manly masters spoke of 'the discipline of the hard ball'. Schools preferred manly games. Games were only manly if it was possible while playing them to be killed or drowned or, at the very least, badly maimed. Cricket could be splendidly dangerous. Tennis was not manly, and if a boy had asked permission to spend the afternoon playing croquet he would have been instantly punished for his 'general attitude'. Athletics were admitted into the charmed lethal circle as a boy could, with a little ingenuity, get impaled during the pole-vault or be decapitated by a discus and die a manly death. Fives were thought to be rather tame until one boy ran his head into a stone buttress and got concussion and another fainted dead away from heat and fatigue. Then everybody cheered up about fives. The things to aim at in games were fright and total exhaustion. It was felt that these, coupled with a diet that was only modestly calorie-laden, would keep our thoughts running along the brightest and most wholesome lines. As a plan, this was a failure.

For cricket matches against other schools, the school pavilion was much in evidence. At my preparatory school, Stirling Court on the Hampshire coast, the pavilion smelt strongly of linseed oil and disinfectant and for its construction reliance had been largely placed on corrugated iron. Within could be found cricket nets and spiders and dirty pads and spiders and old team photographs and old spiders. There was also a bat signed by Hobbs which we proudly displayed to opposing players in an unconscious spirit of gamesmanship. But despite this trophy, a sad air of failure and decay pervaded the building. From its windows innumerable cricketing disasters had been witnessed: for example, our defeat by Dumbleton Park when our total score had been eight, three of which were byes. There had been, too, the shaming afternoon when our captain, out first ball, had burst into a torrent of hysterical tears.

But cricket did have one supreme advantage over football. It could be stopped by rain. Every morning at prayers, devout cricket-haters put up a plea for a downpour. As we were in England, our prayers were quite frequently answered, but nothing, nothing but the death of the headmaster could stop football. We could hardly pray for the headmaster, a nice man, to die. In rain, sleet, hail and lightning, shivering and shuddering and soaked to the skin, we battled on. Even in dense fog we kept at it, a shining example to Dartmoor working parties. But cricket was another matter, cricket was a more sensitive affair altogether, and if, as I fear, there is cricket in heaven, there will also, please God, be rain.

When the dread moment arrived and our side went in, I found myself, low down on the list, actually at the wicket and taking guard ('Leg-stump, please'), and positively holding a bat. But held straight or crooked, sooner or later there would come the musical sound of skittling pegs and flying bails and I could remove myself and my pads and sit down. And once safely installed on a rug by the hedge and more or less out of sight, day-dreams, and usually theatrical ones, took over.

At most schools in the 'twenties there was never any question of being let off cricket. The thought of asking not to play it never entered anybody's head. If it had, the consequences, at a public school anyhow, were clearly foreseeable. Suppose, let us say, a poetically-minded boy had announced that he wished to spend the afternoon writing an ode, he would have been immediately beaten (four strokes) by the Head of the House. Poetry was unhealthy stuff. Look at Byron. If the poet had been more specific and had said that he wanted to write an Ode to the Matron ('Oh Matron, when with grizzled head half bent with care, sweet ministrant of salve and unguent, breasting thy way defiant bust worn high . . .'), he would have been beaten (six strokes) by the Housemaster, and the poor (certainly) innocent (probably) Matron would have found herself writing to the scholastic agents, Chitty and Gale, for a new situation ('. . . said to have pleasant personality . . . prepared take sole charge . . . excellent "mixer" . . .'). If the embryo Shelley had said that he wished to write an Ode to the Captain of Cricket ('Oh Dennis, when with auburn head half bent with care . . .'), expulsion would have been considered, this extreme measure being subsequently watered down, after an infinity of scowls and threats, to a beating (eight strokes) by the Headmaster. These ceremonies used to take place at 9 p.m., the Headmaster sporting a dinner-jacket and being freshly vitamin-charged. The beatings were done, as usual, in the spirit of this hurts me more than you, which was said to be plenty. . . .

Though a crooked bat was frowned upon, to use the wrong, two-sides-of-a-triangle side was considered definitely illegal. Following my ingenious plan of deflecting the ball to one side or the other and then getting the hell out of it, I once made use of this wrong side of the bat and brought down upon myself a stream of abuse. The myth that this was, somehow, a dishonest practice, was one of many myths then current in schools:

—If you had a cracked lip and drank from a chipped cup, you would at once catch a disease that was as unmentionable as it was difficult to spell.

—The Eton College Officers' Training Corps was not allowed to wear the King's regulation khaki uniform as they had once, at an OTC camp, bayoneted a boy to death. On Field Days didn't they turn out and turn up in a slightly outré pinkish material of their own devising? Well, then!

—Cold water came to the boil more quickly than hot water.

—Any actress employed upon the musical-comedy stage could be employed in a more private role for a sum of not less than fifty pounds. Didn't this vast extra intake of money explain those sumptu-ous-looking country houses in the soggier sections of the Thames Valley, and the photographs that went with them ('Off duty! Bimbo and self redesigning the bog garden.')?

At cricket there was never any thought of excusing those unfortunate enough to wear glasses. It was pre-contact lens days and short-sighted boys left their spectacles in their blazers in the pavilion. They stood, when batting, blinded by the sun and enfeebled by cruel Nature, peering uncertainly up the pitch in a hopeless attempt to see whence Nemesis was coming. They had to rely heavily on their other senses. Their sense of hearing supplied the thud and thunder of the bowler's cricketing boots, the wicket-keeper's heavy breathing (now coming from a lower angle as he crouched down in readiness) and the disagreeable whistling sound of the ball itself which indicated that it had been released and was on its way. Their sense of smell supplied the wind-borne unpleasantnesses of hot flannel, hot sock, hot boy, all of minimal value as directional guides. And their sense of touch told them, sharply and painfully, that the ball had arrived.

And here there was an unfairness. The boys in the First and Second XIs, fully sighted and well able to protect themselves, were provided with a contraption called a 'box', a snug and reinforced padded leather compartment worn about the crutch and into which they tucked, I assume, whatever came most easily

to hand. It would have been considered a gross impertinence for
any lesser player to plead for this protection. In the lower eche-
lons, our genitals were expendable.

Fashions in cricket change like any others. At Stirling Court
the important thing was what the ball would do when it struck
the ground. It could go right or go left. It could do nothing
special, or it could hit a tuft and shoot sharply upwards, a most
unnerving ball. I understand, however, that nowadays the only
matter of interest is what the ball does in the air. It seems that
it 'swings' this way or that, though I cannot, alas, bring myself
greatly to care.

It is sad but true that most of the best schoolboy cricketers of
my day paid for their ephemeral glories with a lifetime of
mediocrity. Cricketing fame can be fleeting. Who, for example,
still remembers that Amy Johnson had one of her front teeth
broken by a cricket ball and that she was the only girl at the
Boulevard Secondary School, Hull, who could bowl over-arm?

Nothing was stranger at preparatory schools in the 1920s than
the way in which a sudden spree was visited on the inmates.
Without a word of warning, everybody up-anchored and shot
off to somewhere else. At Stirling Court one summer's
day a special treat was announced. We were all to go by charabanc, as a bus was then called, to watch a professional cricket
match at Portsmouth. The outing meant, at least, no school
work and even the more anti-cricket boys were in merry mood
as we clambered on board. Williamson and I, deep in chat as
was our custom, settled ourselves in. We were only mildly
surprised to observe that the expedition was not being led by
the games master but by a strangely-scented rotundity who
taught Latin, was said to debauch the maids and pawn con-
fiscated penknives, and survived but one shaky term. Off we
went and on reaching the ground it was apparent that the game
had been in progress for some time. Philip Mead, of whom even
I had heard, was batting.

When we had found our seats, our first concern, after the

hour's drive, was to make for the lavatory, an open-air and rather whiffy square construction of brick, conveniently close. As we hastened in, a solitary figure drew all eyes. In a corner, and facing outwards, an aged and decrepit clergyman was standing, smiling encouragement and wildly waggling. At our fairly tender years this was a startling spectacle and one hardly knew where to look. Where not to look was plain to all. Subsequent visits found him, hope on hope ever, still there and still at it. Not a cricket-lover, evidently.

In the charabanc *en route* for home, Mead's leg-glides gave place as a subject of conversation to our thoughts and views on the muddled divine. Could he have been, we charitably asked ourselves, quite right in the head? Unhinged in some way? Instinct told us not to discuss the matter with Matron when, that evening at bed-time, she inspected our toe-nails and indulged herself, after her lonely hours, with a few swift snippings.

Further astonishments completed a remarkable day. We were given two fried eggs each for supper, perched on a mound of sauté potatoes. This sumptuousness was without precedent and so entranced the school that the head boy automatically jumped up and gave three cheers for Mrs Macdonald, the headmaster's deaf and remote wife, whose Buff Orpingtons had strained away to produce the main item of the feast.

While we were munching the eggs and discussing, naturally, the Reverend Whosit, the door burst open and the games master entered. Respectful silence fell. His lips could be seen to be trembling. He gulped. 'I want you all to know,' he said, 'that I alone was responsible for the charabanc starting so late this morning and for your missing part of the match. I can only apologise and ask for your forgiveness.' Silence continued; even I had stopped eating. 'But, although you may find it in your hearts to forgive me, I can never forgive myself.' Pressing a handkerchief to his wobbling mouth, he hurried out.

There now! What an exciting emotional outburst to round off the day! As it happened, neither Williamson nor I had noticed that the charabanc had started late. Happily seated in the very front of the conveyance, after shrieks of 'bags I!', we had been discussing the charms of Dorothy Dickson and he had at last agreed to swop his signed photograph of her for some rather pretty and ingenious cogwheels from my Number 4 Meccano set. As far as we were concerned, the charabanc need never have left at all. . . .

At school the best cricket players were loaded with honours and privileges throughout their brief years of glory, not the least of which was to see their names in print (a thrill at that age). The school magazine dutifully recorded their successes and faults.

*Characters of the XI*

H. R. J. VEREKER. Has 'skippered' excellently. His googlies were cleverly flighted and he has an outstanding action. His decision to promote G. J. B. Eyebright from the 'Colts' was fully justified.

G. J. B. EYEBRIGHT. An attractive bat who fully justified his promotion from the 'Colts'.

N. C. DE B. GASCOYNE. It is time he learnt not to nibble at off balls. Alert at silly mid-on but goes down rather sluggishly. Must use his head more.

Every cricket match, however dreary or disastrous, was fully reported. One dreadful term at Stirling Court when summer influenza had filled the dormitories and emptied the pavilion, we could only provide an XI to play against Dumbleton Park by pressing into service the eleven boys still on their feet. I had avoided summer influenza.

*v*. Dumbleton Park
Played at Stirling Court on 3 July
Lost by nine wickets

'. . . . and was quickly "yorked" for 2. Marshall, playing a little tentatively on 0, failed to survive a confident appeal for l.b.w. and assisted in the side's rapid collapse . . .'

A rather unfortunate humorous occurrence took place at Dumbleton Park, whither we had had to walk (two miles) in a surly, shuffling crocodile to watch yet another cricket match. A large, non-playing Dumbletonian, a well-known wag called Montefiore, politely sought to divert the visitors. He was wearing a tight white sweater and up inside it he inserted two cricket balls where a woman's breasts would, in his opinion, be. Looking very improbable, he then paraded mincingly up and down before our section of the spectators. He was a huge success. Our delighted laughter rang out, and some of us even applauded. As a spectacle, the cricket didn't stand an earthly.

At the close of play we scuffed our way back to Stirling Court and were just beginning our supper when the headmaster appeared, looking very far from genial. 'Which of you laughed at Montefiore and his disgusting exhibition?' There was a long, frightened silence. 'Stand up any boy who laughed at Montefiore!' More silence, and then a single victim courageously rose from his seat. It was Williamson, *noblesse oblige*. The rest of us, cowards to a boy, strove to look as though we had been deeply shocked by Montefiore.

Williamson was beaten just before evening prayers. By the time the summons came for him to go to the headmaster's study, he had transformed himself into the tragic person of Charles I going forth to his execution. Nothing could have been more regal as he strode from the room, patting a head here, a cheek there. 'Grieve ye not, good my peoples,' he said, passing solemnly through the door, 'and when I am gone, pray you, look to the Queen.' When he returned shortly after, rather pink in the face, Charles I had been forgotten. 'Only three, and they didn't hurt a bit.' It was characteristic of his generous nature to bear us no grudge for not owning up with him. . . .

I estimate that during my passage through the 1920s, 2,000 hours, or about eighty-four days and nights, or twelve whole weeks of my life were spent, longing to be elsewhere, in flannelled gloom in the middle of a field. But no, I am wrong. Luckily enough it was not always in the middle of the field but more towards the side of it. Having, at Stirling Court, proved myself a butterfingers at anything calling for speedy action and initiative near the batsman and wicket, I spent a comparatively peaceful two years in a position well known at preparatory schools but without, I feel, any official recognition. I refer to the key post of Long Stop. It is to be found immediately behind the wicket-keeper (at Stirling Court, the wicket was kept, naturally, by Williamson) towards the boundary of the field of play and it has much to recommend it.

Socially it was agreeable as it allowed you to pass the time of day with friends enjoying nougat nearby, but its chief charm lay in the fact that there was only one chance in five of you ever being drawn into the unlovely cricketing picture. The ball when bowled might hit the batsman, the batsman might hit it, it might hit the wicket, it might hit the wicketkeeper. When it missed all these hazards and came rolling towards you, you found yourself in the very thick of the game. Old hands like myself, however, felt no need to panic. The grass in the out-field was by nature long and lush and if it had not recently been mown, there was a good chance of the ball coming to a halt before it even reached you. No point in meeting trouble half-way. Ignoring unmannerly shouts to run, you waited for the ball to come to rest and then, hurrying briskly forward, you picked it up and threw it in, thus skilfully preventing the batsmen from crossing for the fifth time.

At school we faced the tyranny of cricket, and of all games, in the same uncomplaining way that we faced surds, fractions, Canada's exports, Euclid, Tasmania's imports and the Hundred Years' War. It was all part of the scholastic merry-go-round, part of Life's rich pattern. Daily we put on those hot and un-suitable cricketing togs, the bags supported by a school belt with snake clasp. On our heads we placed those enormous shapeless grey felt bonnets without which small boys were thought to succumb instantly from sunstroke, and out on to the field we trooped for a generous three hours of the national game.

Beneath a tree stood the visible scoring apparatus, a selection of white numbers on sheets of black tin hung on a discarded blackboard and mysteriously known as the Tallywag. The boys who worked this were a sort of walking wounded, boys recovering from boils or headaches or lunch or asthmatic attacks and they had behind them a long tradition of indolence and lack of cooperation. They lay on their stomachs chewing wine-gums and reading another chapter of *The Black Gang*. When they tired of that, they would just aimlessly hit each other for five minutes or so. From time to time, a despairing cry of 'TALLYWAG' would reach them from the pitch, and they would then reluctantly change the tin plates to a score that was possibly accurate to the nearest ten. At the end of play, they were allowed by old custom to leave the Tallywag showing a somewhat improbable result to the game (999 for 1, last man 998). . . .

The admirable length of the summer holidays prevented one from thinking very much about the forthcoming winter term and what lay ahead in the form of rugby football. But rugby football did have one small silver lining – you could occasionally lie down and take a short rest. Of course, it wasn't called lying down and resting. It was known as 'falling on the ball' to stop the opposing forwards dribbling it, and it was an entirely brave and praiseworthy action. It usually caused a loose scrum to be formed over your inert body and so your resting period was sometimes quite prolonged. The ground might be damp but exertion was momentarily over. Pleasantly relaxed and outstretched, one could ponder on this and that – the universe, the eternal mysteries, or which delicacy was being prepared for house supper at 7 p.m. I did a lot of falling on the ball. 'Well fallen, Marshall,' a kindly captain would cry, drawing attention to my selfless pluck. While lying down one sometimes got a football boot in the face but then everything here below has its price.

In the summer holidays there were still a lot of games. Parents tended to think that juvenile social life could not move happily forward without games. And so out of doors we played tennis and croquet and golf and badminton, and indoors there was bridge, bezique, halma, chess, happy families, mah-jongg and a pencil-and-paper game called Consequences which provided pleasurable fantasies such as 'Stanley Baldwin met Gladys Cooper in the Taj Mahal'.

I rather enjoyed the tennis parties. For these the sun seemed always to shine. They began at 3 p.m. and everybody was dressed entirely in white, though ladies were permitted a coloured Suzanne Lenglen bandeau to keep their shingles in position, and the belts that supported the gentlemen's flannels could, at a pinch, be dark blue. On the very tick of three, you alighted from your bicycle, shook hands with your hostess ('*How* you've shot up, Arthur! School seems to suit you!') and then, with the other guests, you stood gazing at the tennis court which old Hawker had freshly marked out with wavering hand and tottering feet.

In those days, the tennis posts were not such reliable contrivances as they are now and on really damp courts (vicarage ones were, for some reason, especially sodden) the softness of the earth and the tension of the net caused the posts to lean amorously towards each other. Geometrically, this lowers the height of the net. Here there was no question of a white band in the middle to keep the net down. The whole problem was how to keep it up and it was quite in order to prop the centre of the net with a sort of metal prong. If there were no prong, an agonised and embarrassed daughter of the house might sometimes whisper to her mother that she thought the net was sagging. The reply was firm and simple: 'Erica, it is *not* sagging. Now, hurry up all of you, you're wasting precious sunlight.'

If you were fortunate, you would find upon the tennis court six tennis balls, never one more, and frequently one less. They had been in service since the beginning of the season and were now dark green in colour and, though light in weight from constant use, were strangely reluctant to bounce very high. Sometimes they had been smeared with tennis-shoe whitening so that the first few shots covered you with exciting explosions of white dust. Then they went dark green again. On a table in a shady spot (under the cedar, if cedar there were) stood the refreshment, a large jug of home-made lemonade, than which there is nothing nicer, covered with a piece of butter-muslin to discourage flies and hemmed with beads to keep it in place. There were deck chairs scattered about and a rug or two (a large bundle of rugs sometimes turned out to contain an elderly relation, wheezing encouragement), and some of those old-fashioned racquet presses that look like mediaeval contraptions for helping reluctant persons to speak up.

The number of players for one court was usually ten, so you had to get as fond of sitting down and talking as of playing. When the main body of guests had arrived ('I think poor old Gregory must have got a puncture'), and the hostess had made mention of what a lovely day they had brought with them, she would then say, 'Now, how will you play? Who'll start?' This was the cue for everybody to put on a condemned look and shout simultaneously, 'Oh no, I'd much rather sit out. Please, Mrs Bancroft, truly.' In the end, four players were chivvied on to the court, where they all set up a wailing moan of 'Well, I must be given the best player because I'm absolutely putrid, no really I am.'

The tennis-playing itself was a sort of ritual. It bristled with ceremony and complications and observances and rules of behaviour. For example, if you did a particularly good service, what one might gaily call an 'ace', the accepted thing was to assume that your opponent wasn't looking and hadn't prepared himself. 'I say, were you ready?' you called, to which the invariable answer was 'Yes, but not for that!' Merry chuckles. If a ball came down the centre of the court, or anywhere near it, you and your partner both screeched 'Yours, partner' and then leapt away from the ball as though it were a hand grenade just fizzing to a conclusion. To rush towards such a ball would have been to lay yourself open to the serious charge of 'poaching'. Poaching wasn't popular; poachers' names became known and then poachers weren't asked again.

Shots that looked as though they had fallen just out of court had to be sportingly announced as having fallen just in ('No, honestly Helen, I'm quite sure'). Not a moment passed without some sort of comment from somebody and the air rang with 'Good shot', 'Hard luck', 'Well tried' and 'Oh I say, *I* didn't think it was coming over either'. If there was a spirited rally, with the ball changing sides as often as five or six times, somebody was sure to give a jolly cry of 'Why go to Wimbledon?' Shots of unintentional brilliance, such as a dazzling backhand sliced smash off the racquet handle and part of one's thumb, had to be apologised for for minutes on end. When a ball was carelessly struck and flew out of court and into the flowers, that was the signal for all the spectators to rise, to say in unison 'All right, I'll get it', and then to move off in a sort of mass migration and start trampling down the lupins.

Play halted during this manœuvre while all the players gathered at the nearest point behind the stop-netting and yelled conflicting instructions: 'Further in, Cyril', '*Much* more to your right', 'Now, Muriel, walk straight towards me'. If a ball was lost during the last hour of play, the hostess would say 'Never mind, we'll look for it later', which explains why there were sometimes five balls instead of six.

The first set after tea (home-made cakes, huge slices of wafer-thin bread-and-butter, ginger snaps, Earl Grey) was always a men's four, the ladies being thought to be too distended with macaroons to be able to move with any ease or pleasure. So they sat out and dabbed their mouths with the handkerchiefs that had been tucked into the gold bangles which they wore just above the left elbow.

Later on, the master of the house would sometimes return from work and could occasionally be coaxed by his wife into taking part: 'I think that if we spoke *really* nicely to Herbert he might be persuaded to join you in a final set.' Loyal cries of 'Hooray!' from the guests, and ten minutes or so later the genial and beflannelled host would reappear from the house shouting something comical such as 'Lead on, Macduff', or 'Will one of you young chaps lend me a bat?' And then, after his efforts had turned him a deep and rather worrying purple colour, and despite everybody's cooperation he had lost the set 6–0, there would start up the usual preparations for goodbye – 'Just look at the time', 'I must really fly: we've got Aunt Honor coming to dinner'. And in a flurry of thank-yous, it was on to one's bicycle and away. And if one hadn't poached, there would probably be another tennis party the very next day.

Even the most high-spirited boys experienced a feeling of wretchedness and doom when returning to Stirling Court for the winter term. We were as dejected as Mrs Macdonald's Michaelmas daisies which by now were covered in cobwebs and sea-mist and general dankness and were the only one of Nature's vegetable wonders currently visible from the classroom windows. . . .

When the first endless fortnight had come to a close, it was only the beginning of October, with two full months and most of December still to go. Life was a drab procession of dreadful Latin and French irregular verbs (among them, poor old *ouïr*, of which so little seemed to exist). The French sentences we translated were always either full of unreality ('This rake is mine but whose hoes are those?') or non-sequiturs ('My hands are very sore but I am richer than you think').

Still, there were always the new boys to persecute and bombard with cricketing riddles:

> Who was the first cricketer in the Bible?
> Don't know.
> St Peter.
> Why?
> He stood up before the eleven and was bold.
> Oh.
>
> Who bowled fewest balls in the Bible?
> Don't know.
> The eunuchs.
> Why?
> They hadn't any.
> Oh.

To savour more fully the pleasure of not having to play cricket, we would often run over the high points of the summer season. One year the sports master had been removed, not for any of the usual reasons but with appendicitis. His replacement seemed not to care for cricket and to do nothing but sit in the shade and read and this withdrawal gave a boy called Mould a chance to shine. He was very small and rather weasel-like and he had become an expert bowler of high-speed sneaks, varying them with those balls of alarmingly high trajectory that come dropping out of the sky like a bomb. Neither of these deliveries is recommended by the cognoscenti, but then neither of them is actually illegal and as the gentleman in the shade seemed neither to notice nor mind, Mould opened our bowling for a full six weeks. Success was immediate. To stop the sneaks (it was impossible to score from them), the very bottom of the bat had to be used. This frequently sent a painful, stinging tremor up the bat and the batsman's arms, in which case Mould would bowl the next ball instantly, usually capturing a valuable wicket. On dazzlingly sunny days, Mould's bombs took fine toll of the blinded batsmen, either in wickets or in injuries. In this manner, we had been able to trounce our dreaded rivals, Dumbleton Park, both 'at home' and 'away', while Westcliff went down like ninepins (a total of 7, and three boys in tears).

And in addition to Mould, there was always Williamson, who went in first wicket down and whose regal deportment with the bat constantly demoralised opposing bowlers. His haughty mien put one in mind of Henry VIII and it was his habit, while the bowler was thundering down for his first ball, to cry out 'just one moment, please', and then effect a small adjustment to his clothing. But alas, when the sports' master returned, minus appendix, all was discovered, we were reprimanded for unsporting behaviour, and poor Mould was demoted to the second eleven.

One evening, during a winter term, something took place that, unknown to me at the time, was to give an unusual purpose to my life. The headmaster announced that there was to be a school debate. What a debate was had to be explained to most of us. The motion before us was something to do with public transport. The debate began. Masters spoke. Boys droned on about this and that. Probably mishearing some debating point, or idiotically misunderstanding it, I got up and said something or other, and everybody laughed, and laughed really quite loudly. I blushed, thinking I had been stupid, but I was very far from being displeased. Golly, what an *agreeable* sound, I thought, and I had, however unwittingly, caused it. I had suddenly become consciously aware of laughter and since that day I have always tried to go where laughter was, to seek laughter out, to impede laughter as little as possible, to have as friends people who could make me laugh (they have been extremely kind), to read books that provoke, either intentionally or otherwise, laughter, to see plays intended to provide laughter. I am aware that as a major aim in life this has been frivolous and petty and, maybe, rather contemptible and that I should have been worrying about the state of the world, the human condition, and poverty and famine and misery. But I am afraid that I haven't been and, I must confess, it's been great fun.

# Heroes and Others

MICHAEL MEYER

My great-uncle Ted Marsden played a few times for Middlesex around the turn of the century as a quick left-hand bowler – Alec Waugh remembers missing a catch off him on the Hampstead ground shortly after the 1914 war – and in 1930 he took me to Lord's to watch the Test Trial, England v the Rest. Larwood and Tate opened the bowling to Jardine and G. T. S. Stevens; Stevens was soon caught by Chapman and Duleepsinhji square-cut his first ball from Larwood for four. Then someone tried a short run to the left of cover and the fieldsman, moving very fast, picked up and threw in underhand in the same movement and just failed to achieve a run-out. 'Who was that?' I asked, and Uncle Ted replied: 'Jack Hobbs.' What giants were arrayed before me! The Rest (Wyatt, Ames, Leyland, J. C. White and the like) could make only 138, Walter Robins and George Geary each taking four wickets. Then Sutcliffe went early, and Hobbs, in his forty-eighth year, and the young Hammond added a hundred before rain stopped play. Not a bad introduction to the game.

I was not quite nine, but my interest in cricket must already have been keen, for I remember, after an hour of Hobbs and Hammond, wishing that one of them would get out so that my hero Frank Woolley, next on the card, could bat. I first saw him two years later at the Oval, for the Rest of England against the Champion County, Yorkshire. He pulled Bill Bowes for five boundaries with that lazily murderous swing; then a sixth, whereupon he mysteriously strolled towards the pavilion. 'He's not out,' Uncle Ted assured me, but he was; he had hit his wicket. I was miserable for – how long? An hour, five minutes? I don't remember.

A child needs heroes, and mine were cricketers. I collected their likenesses on cigarette cards. Though born north of the river, only a few hundred yards from Lord's in Hamilton Terrace (on the first day of the 1921 Lord's Test v Australia, when Woolley scored 95 out of an England total of 187), I supported Surrey, because my nurse came from Wonersh. She was the most important person in my life, my mother having died when I was very small, and although we still lived near Lord's in Portland Place I faithfully made the long Tube journey to the Oval and watched most of my early cricket there. Three years later I saw Hobbs, then over fifty, hit the West Indian bowlers for a double-century in a day.

My father loved furniture and Dutch paintings, boxing and rugger, but was bored by cricket; but when we were on holiday I sometimes persuaded him, or some other adult in the seaside hotel, to take me to a game, and later in that first cricket-watching summer of 1930 I saw Tate take six Australian wickets for 18 before lunch at Hove, including Ponsford clean bowled second ball of the match. That, too, was a day to remember, for Alan Kippax scored the most graceful century and the last pair, Hurwood and Hornibrook, added 100 – to my rage, for they left no time for me to see Duleepsinhji bat. I saw Lionel Tennyson, huge and ponderous, at Southampton, and heard the professionals address him as milord; but mostly, we stayed at Hythe, and in the late thirties I watched many games at Canterbury, Dover and Folkestone. Woolley was then in the twilight of his career, but he was still in wonderful form – he had been recalled, albeit unsuccessfully, to the England side in 1934 at the age of 47 – and whenever I saw him bat he made runs, except once, and even that day was to be gloriously redeemed.

None of my many heroes, then or since, has matched Woolley for excitement and romance. To describe him in terms of modern batsmen, he combined the grace of Graveney with the power of Dexter – or, if you are too young to have seen them, the grace of Gower with the power of Botham. Once, as he waited to bat at Canterbury, I saw him dozing in a deckchair in the sun; a wicket fell, the applause aroused him, and out he strolled with that awkward, stiff-legged stride. There was an extraordinary negligence about his batting, as though his thoughts were elsewhere, but what terrible things he did to bowlers! In my memory he is continually lofting the ball, though lofting is a poor description of those blistering low-trajectory drives, straight or over extra-cover, seeming to gather pace as they skimmed first-bounce into the crowd.

My late agent, David Higham, told me how one lunchtime in 1911 he hesitated whether to spend the afternoon on the beach or at the county ground, chose the latter and saw Alletson of Notts hit 142 out of 152 for the last wicket in forty minutes. I was almost as lucky, for in 1937 I witnessed every ball of the famous Kent v Gloucestershire match at Dover. Charles Barnett hit 70 in the first half-hour, G. W. Parker scored a double-century in four hours, and Gloucestershire ended with 434. Woolley, just past his fiftieth birthday, bowled 24 overs of left-arm spin and took 3 for 82, including Hammond caught at slip for 3. Next day Kent replied with 399, Woolley 100 in two hours. No hope of a result, we thought, but along we went on the final day – after all, Barnett and Hammond would be batting, and one might catch another glimpse of Woolley. Gloucestershire were all out for 182 (Hammond 52), leaving Kent to score 218 in under two hours. We sat resignedly to watch the match peter into a draw, but Kent got the runs in 71 minutes. Woolley hit 44 out of 68 in 25 minutes, Ames 70 out of 100 in 26 minutes, including a direct hit on a uniformed constable, and Watt 39 of the last 51 in 10 minutes. Ashdown, the anchor man, was left 62 not out. Gloucestershire, to their credit, bowled 23·2 overs in that time; would any side have done the same today? Poor Tom Goddard, that great off-spinner, was clouted for 98 in 8·2 overs.

In 1938 Woolley played his last game at Canterbury. It was against Bradman's Australians, and Australia batted all the first day for 479. Next morning, before a huge crowd, Woolley pushed the first ball of the innings a yard down the pitch and went for a short run. We all laughed happily, for there was no close fielder in front, but Walker, the wicketkeeper, somehow moved quickly enough to throw down the bowler's wicket. Surely Woolley could not be out; everyone knew, for the papers had told us, that this was to be his last appearance on his favourite ground; but the umpire's finger was raised. Never, even in the darkest hour of a Test Match, have I known such a silence settle on an English crowd. Woolley run out first ball of a lovely sunny day.

Kent crumbled quickly, and in mid-afternoon followed on. Woolley came out for his positively last innings. His second or third ball he lofted head-high dangerously close to the right of mid-on. It went for four but I remember wondering at the time whether the fieldsman tried as hard as he might have done to reach it. The next hour was as magical as any I have spent at a cricket match. The old man hit the Australian bowling all over the ground. One passage I especially remember. He drove Fleet-wood-Smith (I think) over extra-cover for four. Bradman moved the fieldsman back thirty yards and the next ball went over his head first-bounce over the ropes. Back went the fields-man to the edge, and the next ball, or was it the one after, soared high over him into the crowd. In under the hour he hit a six, a five and fifteen fours. At 81 he was brilliantly caught at deepish mid-on off a low skimming drive by, appropriately, Bradman. *Wisden* tells me that Ames scored 139 and added with Brian Valentine 95 in 45 minutes, but I don't remember that.

I had other heroes in the thirties. There were the great hitters, Barnett, Gimblett, Wellard, Fender, Eastman of Essex, who once hit the first five balls of a county match to the boundary, Jack Parsons and Jim Smith. These, like Woolley, lived dangerously, and thrilled me more than the classical batsmen such as Hobbs, Hammond, Hutton, Bradman and Headley. And I had another set of heroes, whom I had heard of but not seen: Learie Constantine, L. G. and A. M. Crawley, E. R. T. Holmes, D. J. Knight, my namesake R. J. O. Meyer and J. C. Clay. Whether my knowledge of these derived from reading or from cigarette cards I do not recall; I suspect the latter, with their often romanticised portraits. Decades later I was to play with Aidan Crawley at Vincent Square; he scored a beautiful fifty, and Bobby Simpson, his partner, said he had never seen a straighter bat. W. T. S. Stallybrass, who presided over Oxford cricket for much of the first half of this century, once told me that of all the great Oxford batsmen he had seen he would rather watch Aidan Crawley score fifty than anyone else.

One attraction of cricket in those days was that every county side contained three or four old Test cricketers aged forty or over, batsmen or spinners. Retirement then offered little except a job as coach or groundsman, unless they had saved enough to set up as a small tobacconist or newsagent. Fred Berry, who bowled for Surrey and later coached at my school, told me what an advantage it was for a young bowler to have these wise heads close at hand. There were then, too, which one does not find now, a number of unashamedly bad fieldsmen, not always old ones; C. S. Marriott, Bill Bowes, Alf Gover and Tom Goddard would not, I think, protest at being named in this category. This added to the fun, as did the fact that many tail-enders made no pretensions to batting skill and marched in, like us unskilled admirers, only for a hopeful swipe.

I was never good enough to get near the school eleven and, on Sunday afternoons, resorted to table substitutes such as Stumpz, which Julian Symons explains elsewhere in this book, and a simple but ingenious game which my friend John Eyre, later a distinguished history teacher, invented and which I strongly recommend. We would each select a team, usually of famous players but with ourselves at number three. Then the captain of the batting side would open *Wisden* at random, and his opening bat would get the number of runs made by the opening batsman on that page, and would be out in the same manner. Thus, if 'c Ashdown b Watt', then our batsman would be caught by whichever member of the fielding side corresponded in batting order to Ashdown, off whichever bowler corresponded in the *bowling analysis* to Watt. There was one match in that year's *Wisden* in which the number three batsman had scored a double century, but it was regarded as unsporting to feel for this page. Occasionally we would pick more fanciful teams. I had one of Monsters, in which the batting was opened by Dracula and the Albert Memorial, with the German master at number three. I also once, proudly, produced a Menu XI, the batting order, with one exception, being the same as the eating order. My discovery in 'Births and Deaths' of two forgotten cricketers named Curry and Rice was a help, and in the end I had a useful team and a substantial, if indigestible, meal. Grace, Fry, Place, Partridge, Curry, Rice, Peach, Parkin, Beveridge, Paine, Crapp. The last-named cricketer, here batting unusually low down (no doubt through indisposition), provided frequent schoolboy delights, as when *The Times* solemnly reported: 'Immediately after lunch, Crapp was dropped in front of the pavilion.'

'Imaginary Headlines', too, can produce interesting teams. I don't remember the old ones, but from the 1979 first-class averages a sinister story can be disinterred:

SAVAGE FRENCH BUTCHER
ORDERS SHARP STEELE
WOOD BORE LOVE CHILDS BRAIN

Naturally, I collected autographs, and I still have my little red book with them and those of actors, some of whom later became my friends. Once I asked Bradman for his autograph as he left a net at Lord's, and was doubly snubbed, silently by him and verbally by the MCC secretary, Colonel Rait-Kerr, who threatened me with expulsion from the ground. I was slightly comforted, years afterwards, when I became a member and learned that the Colonel displayed the same imperial brusqueness towards any of us, however senior and venerable, who incurred his displeasure, which was an easy thing to do.

The coming of war meant that humble cricketers such as myself occasionally found ourselves actually playing with giants. I even had a slip catch held off me by Alan Fairfax of Australia, who had bowled Jack Hobbs on the latter's last Test appearance, and fielded out a half-century by Lord Tennyson, by then very ample indeed but still a beefy clouter. I captained a side which included Crusoe Robertson-Glasgow, most delightful of men (Harry Altham once told me he thought Crusoe the best of all cricket writers, including even Cardus), and, batting against Dulwich College for a scratch team raised by C. S. Marriott, was bowled for 0 by a lad called Trevor Bailey. There were some great contests during and just after the war, one of which caused me more agony than any I have known on a cricket field, except perhaps that Woolley run-out. In 1945, an England XI was playing the Dominions at Lord's; I had to catch a late afternoon train to Tonbridge and was forced to leave as Learie Constantine strolled negligently in to join, of all people, Keith Miller. Trains were infrequent then and I had no choice, and so missed one of the most ferocious partnerships ever seen at Lord's, 117 in 45 minutes, including the celebrated six which Miller hit into one of the pavilion turrets. Today one would simply have watched the television replay; not so then, just as, making a quick dart to the Q Stand lavatory during the 1938 Lord's Test, I missed for ever Verity's spectacular diving catch in the gully which dismissed McCabe.

Soon after the war I went to live in Sweden, and assumed that my active, if that word can be used, cricketing days were over, though I read the reports keenly and there was a cricket slot machine in an obscure alley in Stockholm where a bowler aimed underhand sneaks at a batsman who either hit them for four or was bowled. It must have made less money than any other slot machine in Scandinavia, for I never saw anyone else using it. How on earth did it get there? Occasionally some enthusiast arranged a scratch game on a disused and very exposed airfield in the city outskirts. But when I returned to England in the fifties I found myself drawn into three wandering clubs of differing though equally delightful character: the Bushmen, the Jesters and, improbably, the Old Wellingtonians.

The Bushmen, though in terms of skill the least distinguished of the three, was of formidable intellectual stature. It had been founded during the war to provide exercise for the BBC Overseas Services, then, as now, based in Bush House. When I joined them our opening batsmen were Hugh Carleton Greene and Patrick Gordon-Walker, later to become Director-General of the BBC and Foreign Secretary respectively. Both were men of commanding authority but uncertain running technique. Contradictory calls, each of a seemingly papal infallibility, would shake the welkin; my abiding memory of those games, doubtless exaggerated by time, is of those Titans standing face to face in the same crease. Edmund Blunden turned out for us frequently, Richard Crossman occasionally, as did Learie Constantine, a regular and valued broadcaster. He once hit fifty in under three overs against a Buckinghamshire village before lobbing a catch to, as he put it, the only fieldsman who looked likely to hold one.

Once, at Great Dunmow, a Swede was pressed into service. He had never even seen the game played, and indeed could not have done, for he was short-sighted to a degree. As luck would have it, he had to bat, at number eleven of course, with three runs needed and five balls to face. He was told to ask for middle and hold his bat tightly, upright and absolutely still. The bowler was big and took a long run, but luckily our Swede could not see that, let alone the ball. The first two missed everything, the third took the edge and went through the slips for four. He never played again, his average stands for ever at infinity, and the Bushmen remain, surely, the only club whose batting averages will ever be headed by a blind Swede.

On another occasion, at Great Missenden, we had totalled 99, a good score for us. The village had fielded one short, but assured us that they would bat eleven. Their ninth wicket fell at 94. The surviving batsman was a boy of perhaps ten, who had shown little ability to make contact, and now towards the wicket walked a mite of at most eight, wearing shorts and a single pad on what turned out to be his front leg. Since it was Bushman tradition to let everyone, if possible, have a go, the ball was handed to the head of the Chinese Section, an Englishman admittedly, but one who had not played since prep school several decades before. The more cowardly among us, as is the way when very young or obviously inept batsmen come in, moved close in the hope of an easy picking. The Chinese expert opened with three of the widest wides that even we Bushmen had ever seen. He was then ordered to bowl underhand. His next delivery was within reach, but of such a slowness and trajectory that even the mite was emboldened to have a go. He swung his bat bravely and lofted it vertically off the edge within easy reach of short leg, who needed to take only one pace forward to be under it. But short leg was an eminent German specialist and writer on wine, weighing many stone, who always brought a bottle of special claret or burgundy to accompany his lunch. He stood in his beret and coloured cardigan, his eyes half-closed. Our cries aroused him, surely too late. But no. His practised mind assessed the situation in a trice, he toppled forward like an Atlas felled, the ball landed in his vast hands as he hit the ground, somehow stayed there, and the match was won.

Edmund Blunden was a good cricketer, an excellent wicket-keeper whom, however, we preferred to use elsewhere in the field, since unlike the rest of us he was a keen chaser of the ball even in his fifties. For some reason he refused to wear batting gloves, and would return to the pavilion with his knuckles bleeding like a Regency prizefighter, but this seemed not to bother him. I played with him often, and also once with Siegfried Sassoon in the latter's village of Heytesbury in Wiltshire. I had written to consult him on some minor Romantic poet, and he invited me to come for the week-end 'and bring bat and pads, we play Devizes 2nd XI on Sunday'. He was 62 then, still lean and mobile; I have read that he could tie up his shoelaces without bending his knees when he was over 80. Sadly, he didn't bat that day, for we declared before he was due in. After half an hour's fielding, he walked silently towards the pavilion. Our skipper, a shepherd

(I do not lie) named Clodd, signalled to a spectator to 'take the Captain's place'. Such an unadvertised departure was evidently no uncommon occurrence. I assumed he must have left for the usual reason; instead, he stalked round the perimeter of the ground three or four times, apparently deep in thought; then, in the middle of an over, returned to his place at mid-off as silently as he had left, whereupon the spectator went back to his bench. No one commented on this; apart from everything else, Sassoon owned the field.

I have played cricket with a lot of writers and actors. Mervyn Peake, who had been wing-threequarter for Kent Schoolboys, was a beautiful fieldsman, and Nigel Balchin, the author of *The Small Back Room*, that fine novel about wartime boffins, kept wicket occasionally for Wiltshire. Trevor Howard was a class club bat, Malcolm McDowell a good off-spinner and Tom Stoppard an excellent wicketkeeper. Even Kenneth Tynan was, unexpectedly, a graceful left-hander. Once in the mid-sixties I found myself playing for a Theatre Eleven raised by Dame Peggy Ashcroft, a knowledgeable enthusiast, against the City of Stratford-upon-Avon on the ground by the river there to celebrate some centenary connected with David Garrick. Over a thousand spectators had gathered, and we took the field first. We had two distinguished Hamlets in the covers, Tom Courtenay and David Warner; Ian Carmichael at mid-on, Tom Stoppard keeping wicket and Harold Pinter in the slips. Julian Bream, the guitarist, umpired in an extraordinarily battered straw boater, like the one Bud Flanagan used to wear in the Crazy Gang shows. The City side ranged from the local MP to a police-man, who did most of the bowling.

A television personality gave a running commentary on the proceedings over a microphone, identifying each fieldsman, with facetious observations, as he stopped, or retrieved, the ball. Whenever the ball reached me, which happened rather often during the opening overs, a (welcome to most of us) silence fell. I could imagine the commentator whispering: 'Who the hell is he, anyway?' (or perhaps: 'Who the hell is Ibsen?'). After the third or fourth silence, a buzz of speculation arose from the crowd. Who was the mystery fieldsman? When, at length, my identity was proclaimed ('. . . translator of – *pause* – Ibsen – and Strindberg'), there was a groan of anti-climax, as when the manager of a theatre announces the non-appearance of a star. Julian Bream gave everyone out at the least murmur of appeal. When we batted, star after star departed l.b.w. after the briefest of stays, and when he adjudged Ian Carmichael run out before he had received a ball, Dame Peggy decided it was time to assert her authority and strode on to the field. She held a whispered discussion with Bream, or anyway addressed him (and it may not have been whispered); Carmichael was recalled (he had, in fairness, been out by several feet), and later batsmen were more fortunate.

From the mid-fifties until the end of the seventies I played every summer weekend. The Jesters were, and are, the nicest kind of wandering club, serious but not over-serious; I liked opening the innings for them, reckoning that I was no more likely to survive if I batted lower down and that, if I was dismissed early, the others might briefly suppose that there was something in the bowling or the wicket. Equally agreeable, and rather good, were the Old Wellingtonians, who, when I first turned out for them, always had a Major-General at mid-on, differing from match to match, but always, or so it seemed, a Major-General. This worthy, unless the ball went straight to him, made only a token effort to stop it, while younger fieldsmen, even sometimes myself, cried: 'All right, sir', and pursued it. That seemed to me the ideal of how to spend an afternoon, and in time I found myself (the only boy in that military school who had ever failed the OTC 'Certificate A' and, in those far-off thirties, a pacifist to boot) a kind of honorary Major-General, not expected to stop or pursue anything. Lately, I took particular pleasure in playing in the annual match against the Staff College, Camberley, where, as the most senior member of a side presumed (wrongly in fact) to have a military bias, I was tacitly supposed to be a real Major-General or something nearly as high, once by a full General who insisted that I sit next to him at lunch with Colonels and the like placed lower down.

Even pleasanter, if possible, were the matches arranged during the sixties at Vincent Square between the National Book League and an Authors' XI. We authors were always reinforced by Great Players; thus, my schoolboy fantasies were realised, for I found myself chatting easily at lunch to Douglas Jardine, throwing in to Godfrey Evans, fielding beside Richie Benaud. Dizziest height of all, I was once invited to bowl. Our captain, the then editor of *Punch*, who admitted to having downed eight gin-and-tonics before lunch, mumbled: 'Adjust your field.' The previous bowler had been quickish, so I said to cover: 'A little deeper, would you, Compton?' To a tall man at slip: 'Up close, please, Miller.' And to the quiet little man at mid-on: 'Right on the fence, if you don't mind, er – Lindwall.' And they all obeyed. I had difficulty in restraining myself from changing the field after every ball.

Now that I approach sixty, I make only a few token appearances each summer. The ground must be small, and the catering imaginative. I do not expect ever to make twenty again, or hold a catch; even as Major-Generals go, my contributions become increasingly modest. Already the umpires seem somewhat youthful. I fear it may only be a few years before I hear myself saying: 'Who's that young fellow fiddling with the bails on top of the Grand Stand?' But at least I am probably the only Ibsen translator who has hit a six in both Stockholm and the Hague.

# Mirage at Mickleham

FRANCIS MEYNELL

This country was not strange to me
Nor quite familiar grown.
I knew it not by stack and tree,
Only by wood and down.

Dazzled by dappled land and light
And scarce-transparent shadow
I thought I saw that quickening sight –
The field close-set, the men in white –
Cricketers in the meadow.

And yet no batsman takes his guard.
No ball is bowled, no hit is heard.

The haze is blown, the yew-tree stirs.
For sign of life I search the sward.
Only white stones, these cricketers –
Only white stones in the churchyard.

# G. Moore Run Out 3

GERALD MOORE

A distinguished visitor to Rossall saw the name of Thomas Beecham on the panel of the 1897 School Cricket XI and remarked: 'Same name as the conductor.' The headmaster replied: 'It is indeed the one and only Sir Thomas.' 'Well, that certainly is a surprise' – then a little later – 'He can't be such a bad chap after all.'

Musicians and actors are notorious for their love of the game. Sir Keith Falkner during his regime as Principal at the Royal College of Music had a net installed on the premises; Hervey Alan, adjudicating singers one summer afternoon and cut off from the outer world, arranged for the usher to bring him the latest Test score every half-hour; Sir Arnold Bax, one-time Master of the King's Music, Sir John Barbirolli and Solomon the pianist all were or are *aficionados*. The Australian baritone Harold Williams played for New South Wales in the Sheffield Shield competition. But it was John Christie who confirmed the relationship between the two worlds of music and cricket. He wanted Roy Henderson to sing to Fritz Busch, musical director of Glyndebourne Opera, and Carl Ebert, producer, with a view to engaging Henderson for their first season in 1934. Naturally they were happy with his voice and artistry. 'But,' they asked, 'can he act?' Christie's answer came without a moment's pause, given with quiet authority. The answer mystified the two German artists, though they nodded sagely and were completely convinced. John said: 'Of course he can act; he's a cricketer.'

It would be mock modesty were I to gloss over my prowess as a cricketer. I am of the opinion that my potential was incalculable.

Here I recognise an analogy with music when recalling the number of young hopefuls who have sung or played to me, all of them confident that they had mellifluous voices or a gift for the violin or pianoforte, and sadly, sometimes painfully, I had to make them aware that I could detect no grounds for their cherished aspirations.

Honesty compels me to confess that my only innings at school that I can remember is when I made three runs for the Lower Third second eleven. There is a reason for this recollection; it was because I was the highest scorer in the side. Only wild ambition to attain greater glory by adding an extra run to my total brought about my downfall. The run-out was a near thing, a mere matter of twelve feet.

In 1938 when I was giving summer classes at Downe House (not in cricket), Sir Thomas Armstrong, the Principal, asked me to play for the faculty in a cricket match versus the students, and 'Can you bowl?' 'Of course.' This was not true; at school I kept wicket because I had a safe pair of hands and enjoyed wearing pads and gloves, but I hardly remember having bowled. None the less I bowled two overs in the match from which fourteen runs were made and took two wickets. Not too bad perhaps. But I was taken off forthwith and sent sulking to the slips.

Quite by chance as a young man in the twenties I ran into Andrew Sandham, who for many years opened the Surrey innings with J. B. Hobbs. In 1926 they shared a famous partnership of 428 against Oxford University. He is the most modest of men and was kind enough to talk cricket with me. He told me of one occasion when 'Our wickets had been falling cheaply, Hobbs had gone, we were 6 for 101. I had been in for two-and-a-half hours and had managed to scrape 49 runs when I was joined by Fender. Mr Fender made his 50 before I did.' It was a generous acknowledgement and a creditable reflection on the professional's character. I believe P. G. H. Fender's feat was at Northampton when he made 50 in nineteen minutes and went on to make his century in thirty-five.

I reminded Sandham of the most ludicrous catch I ever saw on a cricket field. It happened in a Middlesex-Surrey match. Sir (then Mr) P. F. Warner (a most charming man who talked music to me much more knowledgably than I can talk about cricket) was the victim. He was facing the wily Fender. The first four deliveries were identical in pace, length, bounce, and each time were countered defensively with bat breast-high, immovable as a wall, straight as a ramrod; the stroke – if such it can be described – of impeccable technique and style with the ball rebounding gently from the bat and dropping disconsolately a few feet in front of the popping crease. The fifth ball was once again like the preceding four; once again it was greeted by quiescent bat; once again obeying the law of gravity it began its gentle descent. But now came a slight variation on the theme. It never reached mother earth but found itself nestling comfortably in the capacious piratical hand of first slip. This fieldsman, unobserved, had crept silently and surreptitiously forward as the bowler began his run-up, had timed his arrival at the stumps precisely as bat kissed ball, then flung himself forward and sideways as a knight moves on the chessboard – though with considerably more speed – to make the catch at full length, almost under the nose of the astonished batsman. The culprit was 'Bill' Hitch, a cricketer of personality and undoubted anticipation. Sandham remembered the incident well: 'Mr Warner was very angry,' he said.

The Surrey XI at this period had many fine players, J. B. Hobbs, P. G. H. Fender, A. Sandham, J. W. Hitch, H. A. Peach, A. Ducat and the redoubtable Herbert Strudwick who in his career dismissed close on 1,500 batsmen as wicketkeeper for England and his county. Long after his retirement he paid occasional visits, 'keeping his hand in', to A. R. Gover's indoor cricket school in Wandsworth. William Primrose, the viola player, went there as often as he could spare the time, to be coached by the Surrey bowler. He turned up one evening a little early, to find only Strudwick in attendance. Strudwick offered to send down a few balls pending Gover's arrival. Primrose asked him if he had ever bowled before, to be told that in his professional life Strudwick had bowled one solitary over in a county match. 'He bowled six balls to me,' declared Primrose, 'and hit my off-stump three times.' I estimate the famous wicketkeeper would have been in his sixties when this occurred.

When we took a house in Hamilton Terrace, a mere stone's throw from Lord's, I was in the seventh heaven. From our garden we could hear the applause when an important match drew a big crowd and I would hastily scamper round the corner to see what was happening. After nearly fifty years of happily married life I have found that my wife has but one shortcoming: she is unmoved by cricket, though of late she has taken some interest in one-day games and Test matches. A maiden over finds her attention wandering, two maidens in succession bore her to distraction. All the same she took my sudden sallies to Lord's in good part. It is necessary for one member of the family to be sane.

I rarely found myself alone when I was there and often would see Neville Cardus, bless his heart. I value my friendship with him, loved him for his devotion to music and his thraldom to cricket. His prose on each of these subjects was music in itself: I am the proud possessor of half a dozen of his books, all of them signed with affection by him. I gloat over the vignette in his autobiography of that glorious innings at the Oval in 1902, the most wonderful innings in all the annals of Test matches. G. L. Jessop was the hero. The Australians were giants, their bowlers, on a villainous pitch, unplayable and their fieldsmen impeccable. Three wickets fell for 10, five for 48 with MacLaren, Palairet, J. T. Tyldesley, Hayward, Braund, the finest batsmen, back in the pavilion. England's defeat was as inevitable as night follows day when, with his side still needing 215 runs, 'the Croucher' strode to the wicket and 'plunged the game into the realms of melodrama where virtue is always triumphant'. In a short period the cock-a-hoop Australian Titans were reduced to a rabble. Jessop scored 104 in 65 minutes and turned the Oval into utter confusion. Spectators in their hundreds, who had been leaving the ground in despair, fought their way back to their seats. Delirium prevailed. Strong men wiped tears from their eyes. Perfect strangers embraced.

If I were standing in the Long Room at Lord's on a draughty day Neville would come and talk, standing between me and the play. He obliterated my view but it was worth it; these princes of the game know when *not* to look.

His experience in a Bradford railway station could have happened nowhere but in Yorkshire or Lancashire. He was wending his way back to Manchester, having a cup of tea in the refreshment room after Lancashire had beaten Yorkshire in the early afternoon of the third day, when he was accosted by a stranger: 'Thou'll be happy at result of game, no doubt?'

'Yes, I am pleased Lancashire won.'

'Well, I hope thee has heart attack on t'way home!'

And it was in another tea-room, this time at Lord's adjoining the Tavern, that John Tillett, my agent, and I had an encounter, though not so abrasive as Neville's. Two men approached us and asked us if they might share our table; they were F. E. Woolley and K. S. Duleepsinhji. With one voice we cried 'Delighted'. It was the only word we uttered for the next fifteen minutes. We were tongue-tied.

Were I asked which batsman has given me more pleasure than any other I should name Frank Woolley. Of all his exploits, surely the most outstanding was that against W. W. Armstrong's unconquerable Australians in 1921, when he just missed his century in each innings of the Lord's Test match. I expressed this opinion to the Vice-Chancellor of Leeds University, no less. This man of mighty intellect and encyclopaedic brain casually replied, '95 in the first innings and 93 in the second.' Roy Henderson, then an impecunious student (as he described himself), stood in St John's Wood Road with a dozen or more youngsters getting a vicarious thrill by looking at the scoreboard: periodically they were moved on by a policeman and as regularly returned in a kind of tug-of-war which continued till close of play.

As for Duleep, I feel I know a lot about him as man and cricketer since George T. Beckwith, a friend of mine for fifty years, was at Cheltenham College with him and was wicketkeeper under his captaincy. Beckwith, in response to my request, wrote a tribute so eloquently and picturesquely expressed that, with his permission, I reproduce it.

In our last year we won the house cricket championship with a heterogeneous side consisting of Duleep, two other members of the College First XI and eight rabbits. The knock-out competition consisted of three rounds – all two-innings matches played to a finish. Games started on half-holidays, had to be continued after school when unfinished and were sometimes if very behind schedule played before breakfast with dew on the wicket. Sometimes we felt we were engaged on the same game every day for weeks. Duleep seemed to be on the field during the whole course of these three matches, for he opened the innings (and as far as I can remember made centuries in every match) and bowled unchanged. His leg-spinners to which he gave plenty of air were a very destructive force in school cricket. I could not always read his googly behind the stumps, so he had pity on my weakness and scratched his ear before delivering it.

Our opponents in the final had a strong batting side and were much better as a team. They won the toss and at the end of their second innings set us 240 to win: this was the highest innings of the match and rather a lot for the fourth innings of a house match. I asked Duleep what he thought of our chances and he replied: 'I don't see how we can fail to get them.'

We did get them for the fall of three wickets. Duleep's share was 175 not out. His character was as charming and balanced as his batting. I never knew him out of temper or rattled, there was no trace of conceit, just calm confidence in his own tremendous powers. As a captain in the field he never addressed a word of exhortation – certainly not of annoyance; we played twice as hard under him, impelled by his concentration and example.

Only once did he display anger in all the years I knew him. When captaining Sussex versus Kent at Canterbury he found the wicket suspiciously damp during a very dry period and Sussex were foozled out by 'Tich' Freeman. Duleep said: 'Wait till they come to Hove, I'll make a century in each innings.' In fact he made a century in the first and a double-century in the second.

George Beckwith refers to Duleep's eight rabbits, but when I recall my 'run-out 3' as the top score the Lower Third must have had eleven of them. This early promise of mine never fructified. My years in Canada from 1913 to 1920 deprived me of cricket and the MCC of a second Duleepsinjhi. I never lost my love for the game, however, and found some interest in watching baseball where the symmetry and rhythmical exactitude were fascinating. (The foremost batter in America and our leading batsman in England bore a quaint approximation in name; Cobb and Hobbs. Tyrus Cobb topped the batting average season after season; I do not need to extol our unequalled Sir Jack.) But the noise! Everybody yells; the spectators only rest their voices when chewing peanuts – it is considered *de rigueur* at baseball – and the players chew gum. 'What is that you are chewing?' bellowed some ferocious fan at an unfortunate pitcher who, having been hit all over the ball park, was being replaced, 'Is it your contract?' I think of Lord's, Hove and Canterbury and shudder. Only television has made it clear that our players have adopted the gum-chewing habit, but I concede that any man might suffer from a dry throat if he saw Botham, Lillee or Garner thundering towards him from the other end.

Despite the din, a certain ritual is observed in baseball; before or after the seventh innings (there are nine in all), I cannot remember which, there is a break in play for one or two minutes when everybody stands up. This practice led Bernard Shaw to remark that baseball reminded him of 'The Hallelujah Chorus' in Handel's *Messiah*.

Of the three stages, youth, middle-age and 'You are looking wonderful', I have arrived at the last and I find that the noises now invading our county grounds are becoming uncivilized. In America, to be fair, vocal chords are relied on to supply the cacophony, but here we have bettered the instruction and, especially in one-day matches, the horn (sounding one melancholy note over and over again), the piercing whistle and even the drum are heard. The performers of these instruments of torture are squalid nuisances to all. I suppose they cannot be barred from the ground (and in any case could still blow and bang, without the gates) but they might be induced to play *con sordino* (with mute). Similarly the shouters should employ *mezza voce*.

Had these pests been in attendance at the Oxford v Cambridge match in 1952 they would have kept me on the watch and saved me embarrassment, for, truth to tell, I was sitting in the sunshine on the Father Time stand dozing peacefully; the game, with respect, was quiet, uneventful and a little boring. Suddenly there was a mighty 'clang' under my nose as a ball hit the railing. It was a 'sixer'. I jumped out of my skin and thereafter remained awake. The Cambridge batsman who so nearly put an end to me was the present Bishop of Liverpool who, heedless that he had shattered my repose, went on to make 127. It was a close call for me. He remembered the stroke when I spoke about it some years later and was amused but not one atom concerned about the near man-slaughter. It was before he was ordained.

Another entanglement with cricket, on an occasion when I expected it least, was in Paris. I was asked to play there under the auspices of UNESCO at a concours of the International Music Council. We attended a reception and it was there that I found myself on a sticky wicket. Mme Régine Crespin, Yehudi Men-uhin, Mstislav Rostropovitch and I were grouped for a press photograph. We were posed before a huge tapestry which our hostess assured me represented a cricket match, and she then told me to explain the game of cricket 'in a few words' to these three innocents who, after all, had done nothing to offend me. The tapestry was of surpassing richness of colour, the overall design impressive and not without grandeur, but its meaning escaped me, for the implements these 'cricketers' were wielding were un-recognisable, while the protagonists, judging by their attire, were preparing for either a Ball or 'The Wars of the Roses'. 'Look this way, please', called the photographer, upon which I embarked on my explanation. Hardly had I uttered a dozen words than I could see that my friends looked ill at ease. They thought I had gone mad. What would 'cricket persons' such as Neville Cardus, Brian Johnston, E. W. Swanton have done? On the proposition that attack is the best form of defence I turned to my hostess and declared that Régine, Yehudi and Slava had been inadequately educated. I also declared the innings closed and dismissed the class.

# Test

V. S. NAIPAUL

## The First Day

At Waterloo and Trafalgar Square the Underground train begins
to fill. Young men in tweed jackets, carrying mackintoshes and
holdalls. Older men in City black, carrying umbrellas. At every
station the crowd grows. Whole families now, equipped as for a
rainy camping weekend. And more than a sprinkling of West
Indians. At Baker Street we are like a rush-hour train. It is eleven
o'clock on a Thursday morning and we are travelling north. The
train empties at St John's Wood. Buy your return ticket now, the
boards say. We will regret that we didn't. Later. Now we are in
too much of a hurry. We pass the souvenir sellers, the man selling
the West Indian newspaper, the white-coated newspaper vendors.
The newspaper posters. What billing these cricket writers get!

Then inside. It is wet. Play has not begun. A Barbadian in a blue
suit, a tall man standing behind the sightscreen, has lost his brother
in the crowd, and is worried. He has been in London for four years
and a half. He has the bearing of a student. But: 'I works. In
transport.' The groundsmen in vivid green lounge against the
wicket-covers. Someone rushes out to them with a plate of what
looks like cakes. There is applause. Few people have eaten before
such a large appreciative audience. Presently, though, there is
action. The covers are removed, the groundsmen retreat into
obscurity, and the rites begin.

Trueman bowling to Conrad Hunte. Four, through the slips.
Four, to mid-wicket. Four, past gully. Never has a Test opened
like this. A Jamaican whispers: 'I think Worrell made the right
decision.' A little later: 'It's all right now. I feel we getting on top.'

The bowling tightens. The batsmen are on the defensive, often in trouble.

'I think Conrad Hunte taking this Moral Rearmament a little too seriously. He don't want to hit the ball because the leather come from an animal.'

A chance.

The Jamaican says: 'If England have to win, they can't win now.'

I puzzle over this. Then he leans back and whispers again: 'England can't win now. *If* they have to win.'

Lunch. In front of the Tavern the middle-class West Indians. For them too this is a reunion.

'. . . and, boy, I had to leave Grenada because politics were making it too hot for me.'

'What, they have politics in Grenada?'

Laughter.

'You are lucky to be seeing me here today, let me tell you. The only thing in which I remain West Indian is cricket. Only thing.'

'. . . and when they come here, they don't even change'.

'Change? Them?'

Elsewhere:

'I hear the economic situation not too good in Trinidad these days.'

'All those damn strikes. You know our West Indian labour. Money, money. And if you say "work", they strike.'

But the cricket ever returns.

'I don't know why they pick McMorris in place of Carew. You can't have two sheet-anchors as opening batsmen. Carew would have made 16. Sixteen and out. But he wouldn't have let the bowling get on top as it is now. I feel it have a lil politics in McMorris pick, you know.'

After lunch, McMorris leg before to Trueman.

'Man, I can't say I sorry. Poke, poke.'

Hunte goes. And, 65 runs later, Sobers.

'It isn't a healthy score, is it?'

'My dear girl, I didn't know you followed cricket.'

'Man, how you could help it at home? In Barbados. And with all my brothers. It didn't look like this, though, this morning. Thirteen in the first over.'

'But that's cricket.'

A cracking drive, picked up almost on the boundary.

'Two runs only for that. So near and so far.'

'But that's life.'

'Man, you're a philosopher. It must be that advanced age of yours you've been telling me about.'

'Come, come, my dear. It isn't polite to agree with me. But seriously, what you doing up here?'

'Studying, as they say. Interior decorating. It's a hard country, boy. I came here to make money.' Chuckle.

'You should have gone somewhere else.'

In a doorway of the Tavern:

'If Collie Smith didn't dead, that boy Solomon wouldn'ta get pick, you know.'

'If Collie Smith didn't dead.'

'He used to jump out and hit Statham for six and thing, you know.'

'I not so sure that Worrell make the right decision.'

'Boy, I don't know. I had a look through binoculars. It breaking up already, you know. You didn't see the umpire stop Dexter running across the pitch?'

'Which one is Solomon? They look like twins.'

'Solomon have the cap. And Kanhai a lil fatter.'

'But how a man could get fat, eh, playing all this cricket?'

'Not getting *fat*. Just putting on a lil *weight*.'

'O Christ! He out! Kanhai.'

Afterwards, Mrs Worrell in a party at the back of the pavilion:

'Did you enjoy the cricket, Mrs Worrell?'

'All except Frank's duck.'

'A captain's privilege.'

*The Second Day*

McMorris, the West Indian opening batsman whose failure yesterday was so widely discussed by his compatriots around the ground, was this morning practising at the nets. To him, bowling, Sobers and Valentine. Beyond the stands, the match proper continues, Solomon and Murray batting, according to the transistors. But around the nets there is this group that prefers nearness to cricketers. McMorris is struck on the pads. 'How's that?' Sobers calls. 'Out! Out!' the West Indians behind the nets shout, and raise their fingers. McMorris turns. 'You don't out down the line in England.' Two Jamaicans, wearing the brimless porkpie hats recently come into fashion among West Indian workers in England, lean on each other's shoulders and stand, swaying, directly behind the stumps.

'Mac, boy,' one says, 'I cyan't tell you how I feel it yesterday when they out you. I feel it, man. Tell me, you sleep well last night? I couldn't sleep, boy.'

McMorris snicks one into the slips from Valentine. Then he hooks one from Sobers. It is his favourite shot.

'I wait for those,' he tells us.

A Jamaican sucks his teeth. 'Tcha! Him didn't bat like that yesterday.' And walks away.

The West Indian wickets in the meantime fall. Enter Wesley Hall. Trueman and he are old antagonists, and the West Indians buzz good-humouredly. During this encounter the larger interest of the match recedes. Hall drives Trueman straight back for four, the final humiliation of the fast bowler. Trueman gets his own back by hitting Hall on the ankle, and Hall clowningly exaggerates his distress. The middle-class West Indians in the Tavern are not so impressed.

'It's too un-hostile, man, to coin a word. You don't win Test matches with that attitude.'

West Indies all out for 301.

And England immediately in trouble. At ten past one Dexter comes in to face a score of 2 for 1. Twenty for one, lunch nearly due, and Griffith gets another wicket. A Jamaican, drunk on more than the bitter he is holding, talks of divine justice: Griffith's previous ball had been no-balled.

'You know, we going to see the West Indies bat again today.'

'But I want them to make some runs, though. I don't want it to be a walk-over.'

'Yes, man. I want to see some cricket on Monday.'

But then Dexter. Tall, commanding, incapable of error or gracelessness. Every shot, whatever its result, finished, decisive. Dexter hooking: the ball seeming momentarily *arrested* by the bat before being redirected. Dexter simplifying: an illusion of time, even against these very fast bowlers.

'If they going to make runs, I want to see Dexter make them.'

'It would be nice. But I don't want him to stay too long. Barrington could stay there till kingdom come. But Dexter does score too damn fast. He could demoralise any side in half an hour. Look, they scoring now at the rate of six runs an over.'

'How you would captain the side? Take off Griffith?'

Sobers comes on. And Dexter, unbelievably, goes. West Indian interest subsides.

'I trying to sell a lil insurance these days, boy. You could sell to Barbadians. Once they over here and they start putting aside the couple of pounds every week, you could sell to them. But don't talk to the Jamaicans.'

'I know. They pay three weeks' premiums, and they want to borrow three hundred pounds.'

In the Tavern:

'You know what's wrong with our West Indians? No damn discipline. Look at this business this morning. That Hall and Trueman nonsense. Kya-kya, very funny. But that is not the way the Aussies win Tests. I tell you, what we need is *conscription*. Put every one of the idlers in the army. Give them discipline.'

The score mounts. Worrell puts himself on. He wants to destroy this partnership between Parks and Titmus before the end of play. There is determination in his run, his delivery. It transmits itself to the West Indian crowd, the West Indian team. And, sad for Parks, who had shown some strokes, Worrell gets his wicket. Trueman enters. But Hall is damaged. There can be no revenge for the morning's humiliation. And matters are now too serious for clowning anyway.

West Indies 301. England 244 for 7.

Afterwards, Mrs Worrell in her party.

'You can still bowl, then, Mrs Worrell. You can still bowl.'

'Frank willed that, didn't he, Mrs Worrell?'

'Both of us willed it.'

'So, Mrs Worrell, the old man can still bowl.'

'Old man? You are referring to my father or my husband?'

### The Third Day

Lord's Ground Full, the boards said at St John's Wood station, and there was two-way traffic on Wellington Road. No one practising at the nets today. And Trueman and Titmus still batting. Hall, recovered this morning, wins his duel with Trueman by clean bowling him. But England is by no means finished. Shackleton is correct and unnervous against Hall and Griffith, Titmus regularly steals a run at the end of the over.

Titmus won't get 50; England won't make 300, won't make 301. These are the bets being made in the free seats, West Indian against West Indian. Lord's has restrained them: in the West Indies they will gamble on who will field the next ball, how many runs will be scored in the over. For them a cricket match is an unceasing drama.

Titmus gets his 50. All over the free stands money changes hands. Then England are all out for 297. More money changes hands. It has worked out fairly. Those who backed Titmus for 50 backed England for 300.

Anxiety now, as the West Indians come out for the second innings. With the scores so even, the match is beginning all over again. 'I feel we losing a wicket before lunch. And I feel that it not going to be McMorris, but Hunte. I don't know, I just have this feeling.' Hunte hits a six off a bad ball from Trueman, and alarms the West Indians. 'Trueman vex too bad now.' What opens so brightly can't end well. So it turns out. Hunte is caught by Cowdrey off Shackleton. And in comes Kanhai, at twenty past one, with ten minutes to lunch, and the score 15 for 1. How does a batsman feel at such a time?

I inquire. And, as there are few self-respecting West Indians who are not in touch with someone who is in touch with the cricketers, I am rewarded. I hear that Kanhai, before he goes in to bat, sits silent and moody, 'tensing himself up'. As soon as the first West Indian wicket falls he puts on his gloves and, without a word, goes out.

Now, however, as he appears running down the pavilion steps, bat in one hand, the other hand lifted and slightly crooked, all his tenseness, if tenseness there ever was, has disappeared. There is nothing in that elegant figure to suggest nervousness. And when he does bat he gives an impression of instant confidence.

The crowd stirs just before the luncheon break. There is movement in the stands. Trueman is bowling his last over. McMorris is out! Caught Cowdrey again. McMorris has made his last effective appearance in this match. He goes in, they all go in. Lunch.

For West Indians it is an anxious interval. Will Worrell send in Sobers after lunch? Or Butcher? Or Solomon, the steady? It is Butcher; the batting order remains unchanged. Butcher and Kanhai take the score to 50. Thereafter there is a slowing up. Kanhai is subdued, unnatural, over-cautious. It isn't the West Indians' day. Kanhai is caught in the slips, by Cowdrey again. Just as no one runs down the pavilion steps more jauntily, no one walks back more sadly. His bat is a useless implement; he peels off his gloves as though stripping himself of an undeserved badge. Gloves flapping, he walks back, head bowed. This is not the manner of Sobers. Sobers never walks so fast as when he is dismissed. It is part of his personality, almost part of the grace of his play. And this walk back is something we will soon see.

84 for four.

'You hear the latest from British Guiana?'

'What, the strike still on?'

'Things really bad out there.'

'Man, go away, eh. We facing defeat, and you want to talk politics.'

It looks like defeat. Some West Indians in the free seats withdraw from the game altogether and sit on the grass near the nets, talking over private problems, pints of bitter between their feet. No need to ask, from the shouts immediately after tea, what has happened. Applause; no hands thrown up in the air; the West Indians standing still. Silence. Fresh applause, polite, English. This has only one meaning: another wicket.

The English turn slightly partisan. A green-coated Lord's employee, a cushion-seller, says to a West Indian: 'Things not going well now?' The West Indian shrugs, and concentrates on Solomon, small, red-capped, brisk, walking back to the pavilion.

'I can sell you a good seat,' the man says. 'I am quite comfortable, thank you,' the West Indian says. He isn't. Soon he moves and joins a group of other West Indians standing just behind the sightscreen.

Enter Worrell.

'If only we make 150 we back in the game. Only 150.'

And, incredibly, in the slow hour after tea, this happens. Butcher and Worrell remain, and, remaining, grow more aggressive.

The latest of the Worrell late cuts.

'The old man still sweet to watch, you know.'

The old man is Worrell, nearly 39.

The 50 partnership.

'How much more for the old lady?' The old lady is Butcher's century, due soon. And it comes, with two fours. A West Indian jumps on some eminence behind the sightscreen and dances, holding aloft a pint of bitter. Mackintoshes are thrown up in the air; arms are raised and held in massive V-signs. Two men do an impromptu jive.

'Wait until they get 200. Then you going to hear noise.'

The noise comes. It comes again, to mark the 100 partnership. Butcher, elegant, watchful, becomes attacking, even wild.

'That is Mr Butcher! That is Mr Basil Fitzpatrick Butcher!'

And in the end the score is 214 for five.

'Boy, things was bad. Real bad. 104 for five.'

'I didn't say nothing, but, boy, I nearly faint when Solomon out.'

In the Tavern:

'This is historic. This is the first time a West Indian team has fought back. The first time.'

'But, man, where did you get to, man? I was looking for a shoulder to lean on, and when I look for you, you gone.'

Many had in fact sought comfort in privacy. Many had joined the plebeian West Indians, to draw comfort from their shouting. But now assurance returns.

'I know that Frank has got everything staked on winning this match, let me tell you. And you know what's going to happen afterwards? At Edgbaston they are going to beat Trueman into the ground. Finish him off for the season.'

Behind the pavilion, the autograph hunters, and some West Indians.

'That girl only want to see Butcher. She would die for Butcher tonight.'

'I just want to see the great Garry and the great Rohan.'

Garry is Sobers, Rohan is Kanhai. These batsmen failed today. But they remain great. West Indies 301 and 214 for five. England 297.

### The Fourth Day

After the weekend tension, farce. We are scarcely settled when the five remaining West Indian wickets fall, for 15 runs. England, as if infected, quickly lose their two opening batsmen. Hall is bowling from the pavilion end, and his long run is accompanied by a sighing cheer which reaches its climax at the moment of delivery. Pity the English batsmen. Even at Lord's, where they might have thought they were safest, they now have to face an audience which is hostile.

And Dexter is out! Dexter, of the mighty strokes, out before lunch! Three for 31.

Outside the Tavern:

'I just meet Harold. Lance Gibbs send a message.'

How often, in these West Indian matches, conspiratorial word is sent straight from the players to their friends!

'Lance say,' the messenger whispers, 'the wicket taking spin. He say it going to be all over by teatime.'

Odd, too, how the West Indians have influenced the English spectators. There, on one of the Tavern benches, something like a shouting match has gone on all morning between an English supporter and a West Indian.

'The only man who could save all–you is Graveney. And all–you ain't even pick him. You didn't see him there Thursday, standing up just next to the tea-stand in jacket and tie, with a mackintosh thrown over his arm? Why they don't pick the man? You know what? They must think Graveney is a black man.'

Simultaneously: 'Well, if Macmillan resigns I vote Socialist next election. And – I am a Tory.' The speaker is English (such distinctions are now necessary), thin, very young, with spectacles and a tweed jacket. 'And,' he repeats, as though with self-awe, 'I am a Tory.'

In spite of that message from Lance Gibbs, Barrington and Cowdrey appear to be in no trouble.

'This is just what I was afraid of. You saw how Cowdrey played that ball? If they let him get set, the match is lost.'

When Cowdrey is struck on the arm by a fast rising ball from Hall, the ground is stilled. Cowdrey retires. Hall is chastened. So too are the West Indian spectators. Close comes in. And almost immediately Barrington carts Lance Gibbs for two sixes.

'Who was the man who brought that message from Lance Gibbs?'

'Rohan Kanhai did send a message, too, remember? He was going to get a century on Saturday.'

Where has Barrington got these strokes from? This aggression? And Close, why is he so stubborn? The minutes pass, the score climbs. 'These West Indian cricketers have some mighty names, eh? *Wesley* Hall. *Garfield* Sobers. *Rohan* Kanhai.'

'What about McMorris? What is his name?' A chuckle, choking speech. 'Easton.'

Nothing about McMorris, while this match lasts, can be taken seriously.

Now there are appeals for light, and the cricket stops. The Queen arrives. She is in light pink. The players reappear in blazers, the English in dark blue, the West Indians in maroon. They line up outside the pavilion gate, and hands are shaken, to a polite clapping which is as removed from the tension of the match as these courtly, bowing figures are removed from the cricketers we have been watching for four days.

With Barrington and Close settled in, and the score at the end of play 116 for three, the match has once more swung in England's favour. Rain. The crowd waits for further play, but despairingly, and it seems that the game has been destroyed by the weather.

### The Fifth Day

And so it continued to seem today. Rain held up play for more than three hours, and the crowd was small. But what a day for the 7,000 who went! Barrington, the hero of England's first innings, out at 130, when England needed 104 to win. Parks out at 138. Then Titmus, the stayer, came in, and after tea it seemed that England, needing only 31 runs with five wickets in hand, was safely home. The match was ending in anti-climax. But one shot – May's cover-drive off Ramadhin at Edgbaston in 1957 – can change a match. And one ball. That ball now comes. Titmus is caught off Hall by – McMorris. And, next ball, Trueman goes. Only Close now remains for England, with 31 runs to get, and the clock advancing to six. Every ball holds drama. Every run narrows the gap. Hall bowls untiringly from the pavilion end. Will his strength never give out? Will Worrell have to bring on the slower bowlers – Sobers, himself or even Gibbs, whose message had reached us yesterday? Miraculously to some, shatteringly to others, it is Close who cracks. Seventy his personal score, an English victory only 15 runs away. Close pays for the adventuring which until then had brought him such reward. He is out, caught behind the wicket. However, the runs trickle in. And when, two balls before the end, Shackleton is run out any finish is still possible.

Two fours will do the trick. Or a four and a two. Or a mighty swipe for six. Or a wicket. Cowdrey comes in, his injured left arm bandaged. And this is the ridiculous public-school heroism of cricket: a man with a bandaged arm saving his side, yet without having to face a ball. It is the peculiar *style* of cricket, and its improbable appreciation links these dissimilar people – English and West Indian.

Day after day I have left Lord's emotionally drained. What other game could have stretched hope and anxiety over six days? A slow game, but there were moments when it was torment to watch, when I joined those others, equally exhausted, sitting on the grass behind the stands. And what other game can leave so little sense of triumph or defeat? The anguish and joy of a cricket match last only while the match lasts. Close was marvellous. But it didn't seem so to me while he was in. Frustration denied generosity. But now admiration is pure. This has been a match of heroes, and there have been heroes on both sides. Close, Barrington, Titmus, Shackleton, Trueman, Dexter. Butcher, Worrell, Hall, Griffith, Kanhai, Solomon. Cricket a team game? Teams play, and one team is to be willed to victory. But it is the individual who remains in the memory, he who has purged the emotions by delight and fear.

# Arthur Wellard (1902–1980)
## (Somerset, England and Gaieties)

### HAROLD PINTER

*Gaieties C.C. is a wandering side which plays club cricket in the Home Counties. It was established in 1937.*

In July 1974 Gaieties CC was engaged in an excruciatingly tense contest with Banstead. We had bowled Banstead out for 175 and had not regarded the task ahead as particularly daunting. However, we had made a terrible mess of it and when our ninth wicket fell still needed five runs to win. That we were so close was entirely due to our opening batsman, Robert East, who at that point was 96 not out. The light was appalling. Our last man was Arthur Wellard, then aged seventy-two. He wasn't at all happy about the reigning state of affairs. He had castigated us throughout the innings for our wretched performance and now objected strongly to the fact that he was compelled to bat. I can't see the bloody wicket from here, how do you expect me to see the bloody ball? As a rider, his rheumatism was killing him. (He had bowled eighteen overs for 29 runs in the Banstead innings.) He lumbered out to the wicket, cursing.

Banstead were never a sentimental crowd. The sight of an old man taking guard in no way softened their intent. Their quickie had two balls left to complete the over. He bowled them, they were pretty quick, and Arthur let both go by outside the off-stump, his bat raised high. Whether he let them go, or whether he didn't see them, was a question of some debate, but something told us that he had seen them, clearly, and allowed them to pass.

East drove the first ball of the next over straight for four, bringing up his hundred and leaving us with one run to win. The next five balls he struck to the deep-set field. There were clear singles for the asking in these shots but Arthur in each case declined the invitation, with an uplifted hand. He was past the age, his hand asserted, when running singles was anything else but a mug's game.

So Arthur prepared to face what we knew had to be the last over, with one run to win. The Gaieties side, to a man, stood, smoked, walked in circles outside the pavilion, peering out at the pitch through the gloom. It appeared to be night, but we could discern Arthur standing erect, waiting for the ball. The quickie raced in and bowled. We saw Arthur's left leg go down the wicket, the bat sweep, and were suddenly aware that the ball had gone miles, in the long-on area, over the boundary for four. We had won.

In the bar he pronounced himself well pleased. No trouble, he said. He tried to get me with a yorker. Where's the boy who made the ton? He did well. Tell him he can buy me a pint.

Arthur played his last game for Gaieties in 1975. By this time his arm was low and discernibly crooked and his bowling was accompanied by a remarkable range of grunts. He was also, naturally, slow, but his variation of length still asked questions of the batsman and he could still move one away, late. But he could now be hit and he could no longer see the ball quickly enough to catch it. He retired from the field at the age of seventy-three and became our umpire. He had been playing cricket for some fifty years.

What was Hammond like, Arthur, in his prime? Hammond? I used to bowl against Hammond at Taunton. Jack White set two rings on the off-side, an inner ring and an outer ring. Old Wally banged them through both rings. Off the back foot. Nobody could stop him. Never anyone to touch old Wally on the off-side, off the back foot. What was he like on the front foot, Arthur? He was bloody useful on the front foot, too.

What about Larwood, Arthur? How fast was he? Larwood? He was a bit quick, Larwood. Quickest thing I ever saw. First time I faced him was at Trent Bridge, that was my first season with Somerset. Who's this Larwood? I said, supposed to be a bit pacey, is he? I didn't reckon the stories. He's a bit quick, they said. A bit quick? I said. We'll see about that. I'd faced a few quickies in

Kent. Well, I went out there and I got four balls from Larwood
and I didn't see any of them. The first I knew about them was
Bert Lilley throwing them back. The fifth ball knocked my hob
over and I didn't see that one either. I'll tell you, he was a bit
quick, Harold Larwood.

*Wisden* supports this: May 1929. Trent Bridge. Notts v Somerset. A. W. Wellard b Larwood o. What Arthur didn't mention
was that in the Notts innings we read: H. Larwood b Wellard o.

Did I ever tell you the story about Harry Smith of Leicester?
Arthur went on. He had a stutter. One day they went out into
the field against Notts. Harry likes the look of the wicket, he
thinks it'll suit him. I'll tell you what, S-s-skip, he says to his
skipper, I think I'll b-b-bounce one or two. Wait a minute, says
the skip, you know who they've got on the other side? They've
got Larwood and Voce. I'll just b-b-bounce one or two, says
Harry. So he bounces one or two and Notts don't like it much.
Anyway, Leicestershire go in before the end of the day and
Larwood and Voce knock them over like tin soldiers and suddenly
old Harry finds he's at the wicket. Larwood and Voce go for him.
Harry's never seen so many balls around his ears. He thinks
they're going to kill him. Suddenly he gets a touch and Sam
Staples dives at first slip and it looks as though he's caught it.
Harry takes off his gloves and walks. Wait a minute, Harry, says
Sam, it was a bump ball, I didn't catch it. Yes, you f-f-f-fucking-
well did, says Harry, and he's back in the pavilion before you can
say Jack Robinson.

Arthur would roar at that one but he never missed what was
going on in the middle. Even side-on to the pitch and not apparently paying any attention he could see what the ball was
doing. She popped, he would say, he wasn't forward enough. It's
no good half-arsing about, it's no good playing half-cock on a
wicket like this, it's not the bloody Oval. What he wants to do,
he wants to get his front foot right forward, see what I mean,
get to the pitch of it. Then he stands a chance. The batsman was
caught at slip. It was inevitable, said Arthur. Inevitable. He was
half-arsing about.

Once, on a beautiful wicket at Eastbourne I suddenly played a cover drive for four, probably the best shot I ever played in my life. A few overs later I was clean bowled. Arthur was waiting for me in front of the pavilion. What do you think you're doing? he asked. What do you mean? I said. What do you think you're doing, playing back to a pitched-up ball? Was it pitched-up? I said. I thought it was short of a length. Short of a length! he exploded. You must be going blind. You made it into a yorker! Oh, I said. Well, anyway, Arthur, what did you think of that cover drive? Never mind the cover drive, Arthur said. Just stop all that playing back to full-length balls. You had a fifty there for the asking. Sorry, Arthur, I said.

Arthur was a stern critic of my batting and with good reason. My skills were limited. There were only two things I could do well. I possessed quite a gritty defence and I could hit straight for six – sometimes, oddly enough, off the back foot. But I didn't do either of these things very often. I had little concentration, patience or, the most important thing of all, true relaxation. And my judgement was distinctly less than impeccable. Listen, son, Arthur would say, you've got a good pair of forearms but just because you give one ball the charge and get away with it doesn't mean you can go out and give the next ball the charge, does it? Be sensible. What do you think the bowler's doing? He's thinking, son, thinking, he's thinking how to get you out. And if he sees you're going to give him the charge every ball he's got you for breakfast. You're supposed to be an intelligent man. Use your intelligence. Sorry, Arthur, I said.

Occasionally I would perform respectably, under Arthur's scrutiny. Once, when we were in terrible trouble, 40 for five or something, against Hook and Southborough, I managed to get my head down and stayed at the wicket for an hour and a quarter, for some twenty-five runs; thus, with my partner, warding off disaster. On my return to the pavilion Arthur looked at me steadily and said: I was proud of you. I don't suppose any words said to me have given me greater pleasure.

As is well known, Arthur (until Sobers beat it) held the record for hitting the most sixes in an over; five – off Armstrong of Derbyshire in 1936. He did the same thing in 1938, off Woolley. During his professional career he scored over twelve thousand runs, of which three thousand were in sixes. (He also took over sixteen hundred wickets.) He agreed that he was seeing the ball well against Armstrong and Woolley but the six he remembered above all was one he hit off Amar Singh at Bombay on Lord Tennyson's Indian tour of 1938.

He wasn't a bad bowler, Amar Singh. He moved it about a bit. He dug it in. You had to watch yourself. Anyway, he suddenly let one go, it was well up and swinging. I could see it all the way and I hit it. Well, they've got these stands in Bombay, one on top of the other, and I saw this ball, she was still climbing when she hit the top of the top stand. I was aiming for that river they've got over there. The Ganges. If it hadn't been for that bloody top stand I'd have had it in the Ganges. That wasn't a bad blow, that one.

To do with the same tour, Arthur told us the story about Joe Hardstaff and the Maharajah, the night before the game at Madras. This Maharajah was a big drinker, you see, so he invited a few of us over for a drinking competition one night. Well, I was there and old George Pope and one or two others, but we couldn't take the pace, so we dropped out, round about midnight. Well, this Maharajah, he had everything on the table: whisky, brandy, gin, the lot, and it was left to him and Joe, and Joe had to go with him, glass for glass. Well, Joe went with him, Joe could take a few in those days, and they went at it until five o'clock in the morning and the Maharajah is still standing and Joe suddenly goes out like a light. Amazing man, that Maharajah, can't remember his name. Anyway, we take Joe home, get him into his bed, he's still not uttering, he's as good as dead, and, my word of honour, we think, Christ, old Joe's gone too far this time. Next day he goes out to bat before lunch, he stays there all day and he makes two hundred. Sweated it all out, you see.

*Wisden* confirms the innings, at least: Lord Tennyson's Team v Madras. January 1938. J. Hardstaff c Gopalan b Parthasarathi 213.

(Hardstaff never appeared in trouble, according to *Wisden*, and, batting five hours, he hit twenty-four fours.)

As an umpire Arthur was strictly impartial, by the highest standards, but didn't see the giving of advice to his side as straying from the moral obligations his role imposed. The batsman would grope forward, snick a single through the slips, run, and find Arthur staring at him at the bowler's end. Where's your feet? Arthur would say out of the side of his mouth. You've got feet, haven't you? Use them. You're playing cricket, son, not poker. To our off-break bowler he would mutter: Go round the wicket and bring up another short leg, put him round the corner, give it some air, make the most of it, she's turning, son, she's turning. Or to me, the captain of the day: What are you doing with a silly mid-off on a wicket like this? Put him out to extra cover. Let the lad have a go. See what I mean? Pretend you're frightened of him. He'll fall for it.

Once, when I was the silly mid-off in question, having declined his advice, I dived and made a catch. As the batsman was retreating, Arthur called me over. Good catch, he said. Except it wasn't a catch. It was a bump ball. Bump ball? I said. It was a clean catch. Cunning bugger, said Arthur. That was a bump ball. The trouble was the man walked. If he'd have stayed where he was and you'd have appealed I'd have given him not out. Anyway, he's out, I said. He's out all right, said Arthur. But I didn't give him out.

He umpired for Gaieties for four years. He never gave a Gaieties batsman not out when he thought him to be out. Nor did he ever give opposition batsmen out when he considered them to be not out. No chance, he would retort to our lbw appeals, not in the same parish, you must be joking.

Compton and Edrich? On a hiding to nothing, son. Never known anything like it. What year was it, after the war, at Lord's, we got rid of Robertson, we got rid of Brown, and then those two buggers came together and they must have made something like a thousand. I'd been bowling all bloody day and the skipper comes up to me and he says, Go on, Arthur, have one more go.

One more go? I said. I haven't got any legs left. One more go, says the skip, go on, Arthur, just one more go. Well, I had one more go and then I dropped dead.

*Wisden* reports: May 1948. Lord's. Middlesex: Robertson c Hazell b Buse 21. Brown c Mitchell-Innes b Buse 31. Edrich not out 168. Compton not out 252. Middlesex declared at 478 for 2 fifty minutes before the close of play on the first day. Wellard's analysis; Overs 39. Maidens 4. Runs 158. Wickets 0.

He moved to Eastbourne with his wife in 1977. Once, finding myself in the area, I rang him and arranged to meet him for a drink. I walked into the pub. It was empty, apart from a lone big man, erect at the bar. He was precisely dressed, as always: tweed jacket, shirt and tie, grey flannels, shoes well polished. He passed a glass to me: the glass, like the ball, tiny in his hands. No, he didn't bother much about club cricket in the Eastbourne area. Anyway, his legs were bad. All the old stagers were dropping like flies. Harold Gimblett had topped himself. He was always a nervous kind of man, highly strung. Remember his first knock for Somerset? Made a hundred in just over the hour. He did it with my bat. I lent it to him, you see. He was only a lad.

Yes, he watched a bit of the game on television. Viv Richards was world class. Mind you, Bradman would take a lot of beating, when you came down to it. But Hobbs was probably the best of the lot.

Arthur played for England against Australia at Lord's in 1938. He took 2 for 96 and 1 for 30, scored 4 and 38 (including a six into the Grandstand). He gave me his England cap and the stump he knocked over when he bowled Badcock.

# Military Matter

SIMON RAVEN

Whenever I review the days which I passed as a soldier, I am always slightly shocked to recall how many of the least edifying or dignified scenes in which I took part were somehow connected with cricket, whether during play itself or the social aftermath. There was the shame-making time when an exigent demand from a bookmaker was served on me actually at the wicket, while I was batting for the Regiment in front of the Colonel-in-Chief and a Field-Marshal; or there was the derisory occasion in Berlin at which a two-innings match against the King's Own Yorkshire Light Infantry had to be converted into a three- and then a four-innings match (so incompetent or 'tired' were the batsmen on either side) in order to provide some sort of spectacle for the visitors invited to meals or drinks on the ground during the two days allotted. For students of human oddity, however, a history which may have a more subtle appeal is the Very Strange Case of Major-General Frothbury . . .

One day in Kenya in the autumn of 1955 my Regiment fielded an Eleven against the Nairobi Club for a whole day's match on the latter's ground, which adjoined the commodious club-house. Our own team consisted almost entirely of officers who had been brought down into Nairobi from their distant and isolated companies in the Aberdare mountains especially for the occasion. The logistic extravagance entailed was entirely justified, it appeared, by the importance of the match, which was in fact a ponderous exercise in public relations between the Regiment and the Colonial Service, the Nairobi Club side being largely made up of district officers or commissioners, with a sprinkling of Kenya policemen. There were, in consequence, many spectators of high rank or sycophantic inclination, among them Major-General Frothbury.

As there were no official umpires for the match, competent volunteers from the audience took shifts of an hour or so, and eventually, late in the afternoon, Frothbury expressed a genial wish to take a turn. It was assumed by all, and asserted by his demeanour, that he had at least an adequate knowledge of the Laws of Cricket, and after five staff officers had struggled for the honour of helping him into a white coat he duly took post at the 'Club end' of the wicket.

The state of the game was delicate. The Nairobi Club had declared at 3.30 for 232 runs, leaving us until 7 p.m. (three hours, if we allow for the break between the innings and a brief tea interval) to beat this total. Although the fast outfield was in our favour, we had none of us had much practice at playing on matting wickets, and the Nairobi Club bowling was reputed to be very tight. By 5.30, when Frothbury strutted on to the ground to umpire, we had made 121 for 5, which put us well up with the clock but otherwise in bad case, as the two men now at the wicket were our last two batsmen of substance, and once they were out the enemy would be right into our tail. One of them was a young National Service subaltern called Kenyon, a correct and neat player without, however, much power behind his strokes; the other was the only non-commissioned chap on our side, a certain Sergeant Jellico, whose brisk natural talent was marred by an unorthodox grip (left hand at the top of the handle and right hand rammed down on to the shoulders of the bat).

General Frothbury proceeded to take against both of them. As Kenyon told me afterwards, when they were at the bowling end together Frothbury would make remarks like, 'Get on with it, will you, and stop finicking about', regardless of Kenyon's clear tactical duty as anchor-man, which was not 'to get on with it' but to stay put, and also regardless of the regulation which forbids the umpire to advise or rebuke the players save only in respect of the Laws. Sergeant Jellico received more conspicuous treatment: the

General took his bat from him and demonstrated the orthodox grip. When the Sergeant, unrepentant, continued to use his own, the General put on an affronted scowl which deepened and darkened when Jellico drove two balls in succession for four and slammed the last of the over past deep mid-wicket for three.

This meant that Jellico must now face the first ball of the next over, which would be bowled from Frothbury's end. The first ball the Sergeant received, a real sod as Kenyon said later, narrowly missed his off-stump.

'I told him about his grip,' said Frothbury to Kenyon. 'If he gets himself out he's no one to blame but himself.'

'I think he's had it too long to change, sir,' said Kenyon.

'Nonsense. Too swollen-headed to take advice. What's his name?'

Kenyon told him.

'Jellico,' said the General, storing it away. 'Nothing I hate more than a conceited NCO.'

The second ball of the over was far less savage and was propelled in a huge arc over the bowler's head for six. The third was swept away off the leg-stump, dangerously but effectively, for four. Frothbury's face worked in discontent. The fourth was slashed hissing towards cover but must, as it seemed, pass wide and to his left.

'Come on, sir,' Jellico called.

Both batsmen started for the run; but before they had taken two strides cover had miraculously gathered the ball with his left hand.

'BACK,' shouted Jellico. He stopped dead and dived back towards his crease.

But for Kenyon it was much harder to stop. He had been backing up properly as the ball was bowled and was therefore going at a much greater momentum than Jellico. However, he juddered to a halt and turned . . . too late, as cover-point had flipped the ball straight back to the bowler, who crisply broke the wicket.

'How's that?' the bowler said.

'Out,' said the General.

Kenyon began to walk.

'Not you,' said Frothbury. 'The other man. Sergeant Jellico.'

'But sir,' said Kenyon, 'the wicket was broken at my end.'

'The end to which he was running.'

'We hadn't crossed, sir,' said Kenyon, and continued on his way.

'You come back here,' yapped the General, while Kenyon, a decent but feeble young man, started to dither.

The captain of the Nairobi Club XI now walked up to Frothbury and said, very pleasantly, 'Slight misunderstanding, General. Often tricky, this kind of thing. But the non-striker's wicket was broken, and since the batsmen hadn't crossed . . .'

'– It's me,' said Kenyon, trying to be firm, 'that's out.'

He turned and marched away.

'YOU COME BACK,' squealed the General like an electric saw. And then, to the Nairobi Club captain: 'Just teaching that sergeant a lesson. He called the run, then he funked it. He should have kept straight on and let young Kenyon get to his end. Anyway, he needs pulling down a peg.'

The Nairobi Club captain smiled a ghastly smile and took a deep breath.

'I'm afraid that has nothing to do with it, sir. The Laws of Cricket state . . .'

'. . . That the umpire's decision is final,' snapped Frothbury, who was not a General for nothing. 'You come back here, Kenyon. Sergeant Jellico is out.'

The Nairobi Club captain beckoned wearily to the other umpire – a GSO II in Frothbury's headquarters, who cravenly deposed that his attention had been distracted by a mosquito and that he had missed the incident altogether.

It was at this stage that somebody at last behaved rather well. Sergeant Jellico, realising that unless the General had his will there would be no more cricket that day, strode from the wicket looking neither to right nor to left but (so the loungers under the fans of the pavilion bar subsequently asserted) blinking very slightly with disappointment, for after all he had been batting with zest and valour and might well have won us the match.

\*

If the Frothbury affair was a powerful instance of human malice in action, then the following piece of pure Maupassant, which occurred a year or so earlier, illustrates very vividly the malice of the gods.

The match against the Hussars at Brunswick lasted exactly two overs, during which nothing much happened except that my friend Andrew Wootton, a non-cricketer who had volunteered, in a lean season, to take the field for the sake of the outing, was observed by all to be wearing black socks and grey gymshoes with his off-white flannels. At the end of the second over it had begun to rain, and after we had hung around for three and a half hours it was agreed that the match should be abandoned. One of our hosts then volunteered to show us round Brunswick. After a quick circuit in our regimental bus, our guide suggested that the bus should be parked centrally and the cricketers released to find what amusement they might until a stated hour of rendezvous.

'If you like,' he said to myself and Andrew, 'I can show you the brothel quarter. It's still there, walls and all. There's a very pretty Gothic gate.'

'Oh yes, please,' squawked a round-faced ensign called Jack Ogle, who was good at overhearing things; and so off we went in the rain, Andrew Wootton loping along indifferent to wet in the front, while our guide, tubby Jack and myself jostled for places under our only umbrella.

'At the bottom end they display themselves in the windows,' said our guide. 'The top end is more tasteful. It's madly out of bounds, of course. If the MPs catch us we're for it.'

'How can they catch us in civilian clothes? We might be any old tourists.'

'They're trained to sniff out Army personnel. Not hard in our case – we're all wearing regimental ties or blazers. They'd recognise them a mile off, then ask to see our identity cards. Luckily it's pretty early – they generally come out at night. But even so,' said our mentor, 'we don't want to hang about.'

Nor did we. Everyone was speedily accommodated in a 'more

tasteful' house at the top end of the street, and very shortly we were reunited outside the front door. All of us, that was, except Jack Ogle.

After ten minutes,

'He must be playing extra time,' said Andrew, who was looking exceedingly glum. 'Failure to score, do you think? Or is he having a second innings?'

'All I know,' I droned dismally, 'is that I'm sick of standing here in this bloody rain shitting myself lest the Red Caps arrive. Let's leave him to find his own way back to the bus.'

'*Not* quite the thing,' said our host, 'to leave one's chums behind in a cat house. Not in our crowd, at any rate.'

'Nor in ours,' I apologised. '*Tristitia post coitum* setting in rather heavily, I'm afraid.'

It set in even heavier during the next fifteen minutes. The rain got harder and our nerves got tauter. Andrew began a long discussion on the chances of our having caught the pox. By the time he had finished they seemed about 66 to 1 in favour. Just as he was concluding this lowering exegesis Jack Ogle appeared at last, looking self-conscious. We hustled him straight out through the pretty Gothic gate and not until we were a quarter of a mile away did anyone speak.

'What on earth were you doing?' I said. 'Having another round?'

'I could only just afford the first.'

'You certainly spun it out,' said Andrew.

Jack giggled.

'Not on purpose.' He giggled again. 'I didn't mean to tell you,' he said, 'but I can't not. Just as I was getting there in fine form, the wireless by her bed started playing God Save the Queen. For some reason, you see, she was tuned into the BAOR network. As soon as she heard it, she started barking orders like a Gauleiter. "Up get," she shouted. She made me get off the bed and stand to attention, then she clamped on her knickers and hung a towel on my john. "Him we may not see while your Royal Anthem die Orchestre do play," she thundered. But of course all this was so putting off that it went straight down and the towel fell off when there were still two bars to go. "To the wall turn," she shouted, and whisked me round and stood me in the corner. God, I did feel a prick.'

'What there was left of it . . .'

'As soon as the bloody thing stopped, she flew out of her knickers and on to the bed, all ready to go again. But I just couldn't get tuned up. All that shouting. I was worried about you chaps too.'

'So what happened?'

'She showed me some special pictures. Goings-on in a girls' orphanage. Still no good.'

'How very depressing!'

'You still haven't heard the worst. I've only just realised it myself.' He opened his coat and examined his shirt, closely and despairingly, as if willing it to change colour or something of the kind. 'After we'd given it up as a bad job,' he said, 'I was in such a hurry to get out to all of you that I forgot to put on that sweater I was wearing.'

'Pity. But not the end of the world.'

'*My mother gave it to me.* Oh God,' wailed Jack, 'it took her three months of loving care and labour to knit it – and I've gone and left it in a Kraut knocking shop where I couldn't even come.'

# The Spoty Dick XI

ANDREW SINCLAIR

There were six of us at Dirty Dick's in the Corfu docks – and six at the Spoty Dog. Five really, because there was Sam. He had never recovered since the night he was counted out. I mean, when it's a bar bill, it must be wrong. What's gone down never adds up. Barmen are the original creative accountants. But Sam was so paralysed that he paid up from the floor he was using as a pillow. He's been horizontal ever after.

'Sam for scorer,' I said.

'And umpire,' Roger said. He's the one with the two hollow legs, where he lays away his scotch to age.

'He can't see straight,' I said.

'Howzat?'

'You mean he could still raise a finger when the other side was in?'

'Out!' Roger shouted. 'Out! Out! Out!' He'd learnt how to appeal on the picket line at Grunwick.

Without Sam, there were eleven of us, the magic number. The only time we ever got out of Dirty Dick's and the Spoty Dog up the hill to the Liston was on Sunday afternoons, when the Byron Club played the Gymnasium or the Gymnasium played the Byron Club. I mean, Corfu isn't big enough to hold more than two cricket clubs – and now there were three. The Spoty Dick XI. English to the gutrot. We invented the game, didn't we? We couldn't leave it to the Greeks.

It must have been the Queen's Birthday that made us decide to throw down the gauntlet. Actually, it was a beer-mat. After drinking a few dozen loyal toasts, Reg took his darts pencil from behind his ear, cleaned it in his ear, and wrote on the back of that Heineken bottle wasted on paper: *The Spoty Dick 11 Chalenge the K.K.K. (Korfu Kriket Klub) to a K.O. Champ Match Two to Five Sat. Winner Buys Drinx.*

Fat Bill, who last knew he had toes when he stubbed them on a landmine at the Battle of the Bulge, waved the flag and said he wasn't going to lose the bloody game, so the Greeks better buy the drinks. Old Lob agreed: 'W. G.,' he said, 'Ranjit, Bradman, Sir Len – I've had 'em all, I've had 'em all. Jus' you bowl me at the sun end and I'll have 'em all.'

I was made captain, see. It was my cap, which looked like a marmalade sandwich made with green and blue bread. When I'd had a few, I'd put it on and tell the boys about the centuries I'd hit for the Freeport Wanderers. The truth was, I'd found the cap in a locker I happened to be passing. It had just stuck to my hand – a sort of levitation and glue effect. And if you get in the way of a bloody miracle, you have to accept it.

The team did not look too good if you thought about it. And if you didn't think about it, you'd have nightmares. For openers, Fat Bill and Hutch. The Greek bowlers wouldn't get Bill out because they wouldn't be able to see the stumps once he got a leg in front of them. And as for Hutch, well, he twitched so much if he didn't have a glass in his hand that he might snick a few over the slips with his propeller wrists. The middle-order batting was solid. Once round Reg's beer belly, twice round the Castello; Roger's bottom had flattened so many bar stools that it was called the bum-roller; and as for Scrubber's thick skull – if a bouncer took it off, he might get smarter. I came in at number six to steady the buffs, while the tail-end looked like a Manx cat – Nobby with the shakes, Steve with the squitters, Podge with double vision, Crackenthorpe with piles, and Old Lob with his wheel-chair.

The day of the match was all sticky shirt and glue, thunder and flash. There had to be a deluge to clear the air. I never felt more wet on my skin since Crackenthorpe sipped at the wrong drink and threw a glass of water over me, yelling that I'd poisoned him.

Our general turn-out wasn't up to Lord's. Podge in our one white shirt was a walking Yellow Peril. Nobby wore gymshoes, but they didn't match and had no toecaps. Reg's army surplus jacket could have doubled for the big top. And they were the Bristol Cream of the Spoty Dick XI.

The KKK looked as if they had stepped off a yacht or a lynching party. White they were, and all over. Silk caps, bleached blouses with those little alligators on the right tit, shorts with vertical creases or long bell-bottoms, and kidskin loafers. With white hoods on, they would have been burning us tramps from the palm trees round the Liston.

Instead, they won the toss. I was using my two-headed shilling with Her Majesty's profile on both sides because I'm so patriotic. But the KKK captain was too quick for me. When I flipped it up, he caught it in mid-air and gave it the twiceover. So I had to call 'Tails' and pretend it was a joke. He might have thought I wasn't sporting. When you're nabbed in the act, that's the only time you have to play fair.

They didn't have openers, they had a pair of executioners. Not that Crackenthorpe is Larwood or Botham by half. His first run-up was all the way from the car-park that's one of the boundaries, but when he reached the crease, he had a coughing fit and chucked up the softest dolly you ever did see. The ball landed halfway up the Castello. Six. The next eleven balls Crackenthorpe delivered were six wides and five slow long-hops. After one over 40 runs for no wicket.

Nobby didn't do much better. His shakes were meant to produce human googlies – the batsman so hypnotised with the St Vitus dance at the bowler's end that he never noticed the slow sphere drifting down on to his bails. Not so the KKK Grand Wizard at the far end. He waited till Nobby's floaters were coasting down like puff balls and put 'em away. Two overs, 70 for nought.

I wasn't flapped. I was as cool as a straight Worcester Sauce with a dash of cayenne. 'Old Lob,' I called. 'From the sun end.' I couldn't see how he could trundle the ball to the far wicket from his wheel-chair, but old bowlers never die, they simply chunter on. He rolled forward to the crease and shot up his right hand in an underarm Nazi salute. The ball flew up like a clay pigeon and seemed to hover just where the sun was leering between the storm clouds. It hung there till we were all dazzled. Then it came down in a bolo punch on the batsman's right peeper, while he was still squinting skywards for it. And down he went, arse over stump.

'Hit wicket!' I yelled. 'Seventy for one.'

Old Lob's second ball was even better. It seemed to climb straight up and never come down. The other opener was halfway down the pitch trying to snatch a quick single before it descended, when it dropped like a brick on the back of his neck. As he pitched forward, the ball bounced back. Old Lob reached down for it from his wheel-chair, but it flicked off his fingers on to the stumps.

'Run out!' I screeched. 'Seventy for two.'

The third ball was the corker. Old Lob's lumbago got him at the bottom of his downswing, locking his shoulder and elbow. The ball sped like a startled stoat along the coconut matting. The new batsman jabbed down his bat too hard on the baked ground and it bounced up again. The ball scuttled underneath and banged into the middle stump.

'Bowled!' I hollered. I couldn't believe it. Seventy for three. A geriatric hat-trick.

Yet fate had snatched our false teeth from the jaws of victory. Old Lob's bowling arm had seized up. And the sun had gone in. The score went to 200 in the next five overs. We had to use our fail-safe procedure. While Scrubber bent behind the umpire pretending to do up his carpet slippers, Roger did his classic bum-roller fall on old whitecoat from the front. The umpire was crushed between numbskull and beer-belly. He let out a last gasp like a zeppelin full of ack-ack and was carried off, while we carried Sam on and held him up at the bowler's end.

'Lift your finger, Sam,' I hissed in his ear, 'when you hear "Howzat?"'

'Howzat?' he asked.

'No, Sam. If I say "Howzat?" then you lift a finger.'

'I never lift a finger unless I can help it.'

'You can't help it, Sam,' I said and lifted his finger for him to show him how.

Of course, I put myself on. With Sam as umpire, I reckoned on a snappy six wickets for no runs. But I'd reckoned without Sam. As I trudged towards the crease, he slipped out of Podge's grip at mid-on and fell in front of my legs. As I tripped, I flung out my arms and slung the ball like a grenade into the lughole of the batsman at my end. He landed on top of me as I landed on top of Sam.

'Howzat?' Roger screamed. 'Out! Out! Out!'

The batsman was out. The projectile in his ear had laid him cold. And Sam, now propped between a close mid-on and a closer mid-off with me bowling round the wicket and the three of them, soon polished off the tail. As the KKKs seersuckered fools struck my limping half-volleys towards the stone arches of the Corfu Bar, we'd all shout 'Howzat?' and mid-on would lift one of Sam's fingers for him – and mid-off would lift another just to make sure. When the scorer protested, Sam was deaf to all pleas. Podge had pulled out his hearing-aid.

At 200 for 8 they declared. It was either that or cancelling the match by objecting to our umpire. Though how anyone could object to Sam, who was so consistent and always treated a batsman as a lost cause, I can't imagine. With Sam, you knew what you were getting. The finger every time. May the sun never set on the good old British Umpire.

Now it was our turn to bat. It was the Luftwaffe against Grandad's Army. They were on a *blitzkrieg* to nothing. They couldn't see the stumps for Fat Bill all right, so they bombed the ball into his spare parts until he retreated to square leg and let his wicket be smashed to rubble. Twitching Hutch whirled his bat everywhere the ball wasn't until a yorker put him out of his misery. Reg scored our first run by getting the ball wedged in his midriff and carrying it in his flab to the other end of the pitch; but Roger, facing a fizzer, sat on the stumps and reduced them to kindling, while Scrubber ducked into a long hop and was given out 'Head Before!'

Four wickets for one run. My turn to rally the rout. I sent Old Lob rolling off to the car-park boundary while I ambled to the middle. There was a black thundercloud behind the Royal Palace at the bowler's end, and I couldn't see a thing. So I didn't do a thing. The first ball hit me fair between wind and water, hope and hernia. Just then, there was a terrible clap of thunder. Everyone looked up, and I kicked the ball down to long leg where Old Lob was waiting.

We had a chance. By the time the lightning flashed and the fielders looked round again, Old Lob had secreted the ball under his wheel-chair while Roger and I were passing each other as regularly and stately as ships in the night. The fielders searched everywhere, looking high and low through the café tables and the tyres of the parked cars. But they weren't going to kick over a cripple, were they now? So we just went on trundling up the runs. Thirty, forty, fifty . . . We might have made a hundred if Roger hadn't hit the matting in a cold sweat at 66, putting an end to the longest run in the history of cricket.

Naturally, when Old Lob moved his wheel-chair and found the ball, the KKK weren't too happy. Those Greeks don't know what a sporting chance is – it's something you take as far as the rules will bend over. They seemed to think we had taken advantage, so they fairly hurled down the fast stuff. Nobby shook so much, he wasn't a good target, but his stumps were. After the first bouncer changed his phrenology, Steve rushed back to the loo where he had been cowering until he was called. As for unlucky Podge with his double vision, he stepped back from the ball he thought was real and was brained by the ball he thought wasn't. And when Crackenthorpe was struck on his piles by a rising leg-cutter, you'd have thought he was auditioning for an Olympic Madame Butterfly, the way he sped off screaming soprano.

That left Old Lob and me with 136 to make. It looked all up with the Spoty Dick XI, but never say die till you meet the Final Score-board. Even the KKKs weren't going to divebomb a Methuselah in a wheel-chair, so they threw up a soft one to Old Lob, who swung his bat with his good hand and sent up a skier.

And then it happened. I don't know who's up there looking down on us and regretting why He made us. I can only tell you what I saw – cross my heart and hope to have another drink. Under the skier the KKK captain set himself. His huge hands were spread open for the gift from heaven like a steam shovel waiting for manna. Then there was a crackle and a whizz and a bang. Something flared through the Greek captain's hands, scorching them black, and burned a hole in the ground at his feet. As he screeched and leapt away, something else fell down the smoking hole deep into the earth.

Well, it was a steal, wasn't it? While Old Lob rolled to and fro in his wheel-chair, I walked it. He was the first cripple who ever made 136 not out. We could see the fielders rolling up their sleevelets and reaching down the scorched hole, but the cricket ball had fallen so far down the path driven by the meteorite that no one could get it out.

Superstitious chaps, those Greeks. When the Greek captain was having his hands bandaged and was buying us our drinks – that's what strangers *always* do here, you know – he said Zeus must have been looking after us, slinging a thunderbolt down like that. It wasn't cricket. Well, I said, that's what you get from being too stuck up, isn't it just? And he had to say yes.

So that was how the Spoty Dick XI fought for the honour of England and won on the field of the Liston. You've got a funny look in your eye. Either you don't believe me or you're dying of dehydration. May my mother have her last breath if a lying word has passed my lips. Well, now you mention it, yes – I did lay the dear soul to rest over twenty years ago. But if you'll stand me a triple, why, I'll tell you how we trounced the West Indies.

# Cricket in Poetry

GODFREY SMITH

It is curious but true that the worst cricket poem is also the most celebrated. Still, to describe it as poetry at all is to give it an accolade it may not have earned. The one piece of verse (handier term) that everyone knows is by Sir Henry Newbolt. The first four lines go:

> There's a breathless hush in the Close tonight –
> Ten to make and the match to win –
> A bumping pitch and a blinding light,
> An hour to play and the last man in

So far, so good. 'Breathless hush' is hackneyed, and 'the match to win' is tautologous. On the other hand, it must be allowed that 'a bumping pitch and a blinding light' does convey a lively impression of the sort of conditions we all remember if we have played any sort of cricket. True, bumping is imprecise – every ball bumps if it pitches at all – but we know what he means. So the scene is vigorously set for the *dénouement* of the game. Then, though, comes the ludicrous bathos that has nevertheless ended up in the *Oxford Dictionary of Quotations*: 'But his Captain's hand on shoulder smote – "Play up! Play up! and play the game!"'

No captain worth his salt would now issue orders as daft and imprecise. 'Drop your bat on everything and leave it all to Blenkinsop' would be a sight more sensible; or even 'For heaven's sake don't get run out or you're for the high jump, mate.' But: 'Play up and play the game' – what sort of a captain would say that?

Well, just conceivably, a captain at Clifton (Newbolt's school) around the year 1880. I wasn't there so I wouldn't know. What renders the poem totally absurd is the second stanza.

The scene now shifts to some distant outpost of the Imperial Raj. The British Army is evidently up against it. The sand of the desert is sodden red, the Gatling machine-gun has jammed and the Colonel is dead. Things look pretty bleak. The regiment is blind with dust and smoke, the river of death has brimmed his banks, England's far and Honour a Name. Nevertheless:

> . . . the voice of a schoolboy rallies the ranks:
> 'Play up! Play up! and play the game!'

This is intolerable. Newbolt never saw a shot fired in anger or he would hardly have perpetrated such patent balderdash. Nevertheless, the absurdity, set in the aspic of the age it was written, was to bring him instant fame. In his book *Play Up and Play the Game*, published in 1973, Patrick Howarth traces the honours that fell thick upon Newbolt: Companion of Honour; honorary degrees from Bristol, Glasgow, St Andrews, Sheffield, Toronto, Oxford and Cambridge; the esteem of such eminent contemporaries as Robert Bridges, A. J. Balfour, H. G. Wells, Sir Edward Grey. 'Of all these distinctions and all this acclaim,' says Howarth, 'it can be said that they stemmed wholly from the publication of a relatively small number of poems, of which the one whose stanzas end "Play up! Play up! and play the game!" was fairly representative.'

And yet, Nemesis was waiting just around the corner. 'Already in the 1930s, when I was a schoolboy,' Howarth continues, 'Newbolt's verses had become a subject of ridicule among the sophisticated young and even the not very young. Early in the 1970s I asked a group of intelligent and fairly well-read young people who had just graduated from Cambridge University . . . what the name of Sir Henry Newbolt meant to them. The answer was in effect nothing.'

The reverse might be said of Francis Thompson, who wrote the only poem to vie with 'Play Up' in popularity. This God-intoxicated, drug-dependent drifter seldom wrote a line that was not deeply poetic, and the haunting thrall of 'At Lord's' does not need the security of a cricket anthology: it would earn its place in any volume of Victorian poetry. The celebrated stone-waller Barlow and his big-hitting partner 'Monkey' Hornby, Lancashire openers in Thompson's young days, are eternally caught in the mind's eye; the sound has been lost but the effect is only to accentuate the dream-like quality of the nostalgic vision:

> For the field is full of shades as I near the shadowy coast,
> And a ghostly batsman plays to the bowling of a ghost,
> And I look through my tears on a soundless-clapping host
>   As the run-stealers flicker to and fro,
>     To and fro:
>   O my Hornby and my Barlow long ago!

Not much cricket poetry can approach that in its lyrical intensity; the obvious danger of much verse recalling long days in the sun is that it may tend to sound like one of those beer commercials we get on ITV in high summer: the players are strolling from the field in the hazy heat into a cosy pub conveniently selling Courage's. It is what Cyril Connolly scathingly called The Worthington Touch – a wodge of sentimental treacle gumming up art. Yet the hazard can be mastered, and then excellent poetry is made.

John Arlott, for instance, brought poetry to his expertise in the commentator's box, just as he brought expertise to his poetry. 'The Old Cricketer'

> Leaps once more, with eager spring,
> To catch the brief-glimpsed, flying ball
> And quickens to its sudden sting:
> The brightness dies; the old eyes fall,
> They see, but do not understand,
> A pursed, rheumatic, useless hand.

He shares the recurring obsession of many cricket poets with the mystery of great strokeplay. In his poem to Hobbs on his 70th birthday:

There was a wisdom so informed your bat
To understanding of the bowler's trade
That each resource of strength or skill he used
Seemed but the context of the stroke you played.

Well said: and there is another fine image in 'On a Great Batsman':

he moves to charm
The ball down-swirling from the bowler's arm

Yet it is not only the batsman's art that moves Arlott: the precise sound of summer is beautifully caught in 'Cricket at Worcester, 1938':

Like rattle of dry seeds in pods
The warm crowd faintly clapped;

Just so: Arlott is, as it were, bowling well within his natural pace. The trouble with very eminent writers is that they seem curiously off form when they essay a snatch of verse on cricket. William Blake, for instance:

That Bill's a foolish fellow;
He has given me a black eye.
He does not know how to handle a bat
Any more than a dog or a cat;
He has knock'd down the wicket,
And broke the stumps,
And runs without shoes to save his pumps.

Nor can Byron truthfully be said to be at his best in 'Cricket at Harrow':

Together we impell'd the flying ball;
Together waited in our tutor's hall;
Together join'd in cricket's manly toil.

However, there is a happy exception: great humorous writers do well on this sort of pitch. P. G. Wodehouse, in 'Missed', offers us not great poetry, but a good laugh:

> I was tenderly dreaming of Clara
> (On her not a girl is a patch)
> When, ah horror! there soared through the air a
> Decidedly possible catch.

which of course he dropped. Another rabbit to offer us rich entertainment is John Betjeman:

> 'The sort of man we want must be prepared
> To take our first eleven. Many boys
> From last year's team are with us. You will find
> Their bowling's pretty good and they are keen.'
> 'And so am I, Sir, very keen indeed.'

We can sense the gathering disaster already:

> 'Let's go and get some practice in the nets.
> You'd better go in first.' With but one pad,
> No gloves, and knees that knocked in utter fright,
> Vainly I tried to fend the hail of balls
> Hurled at my head by brutal Barnstaple
> And at my shins by Winters. Nasty quiet
> Followed my poor performance.

And he is bowled first ball in the trial match, disgraced, and demoted to the seventh game. It is very sad for Betjeman, but very funny for us. A cricket triumph, on the other hand, like Conan Doyle's may have intrinsic interest – he really did dismiss W. G. Grace – but his poetry is nowhere near as good as his bowling:

> With the beard of a Goth or a Vandal,
> His bat hanging ready and free,
> His great hands on the handle,
> And his menacing eyes upon me.

There are not too many anti-cricket poems, but Lewis Carroll wrote one which still quivers with social outrage:

> Amidst thy bowers the tyrant's hand is seen,
> The rude pavilions sadden all thy green;
> One selfish pastime grasps the whole domain,
> And half a faction swallows up the plain;

And yet cricket as social leveller is well explored. Whether the French aristos would have ever gone in their tumbrils to the *tricoteuses* if they had played cricket with their peasants we shall never know. Listen to Francis Brett Young:

Lord Frederick had royal blood in'en, so 'twere said,
For his grammer were Nelly Gwyn, King Charles's fancy,
But when Billy and him walked out to the pitch, side by side,
You couldn't tell which were the farmer and which the gentleman,
The pair on' em looked that majestic and when they got set
You'd a'thought they was brothers born, the way they gloried
In blasting the bowling between 'em.

And the social spread of cricket is neatly noted in G. Rostrevor Hamilton's quatrain:

Where else, you ask, can England's game be seen
Rooted so deep as on the village green?
Here, in the slum, where doubtful sunlight falls
To gild three stumps chalked on decaying walls.

In a world where it is easy to see everything changing for the worse, I think it only fair to say that the poetry of cricket gets better: leaner, sharper, and much less sentimental. True, there will always be a gap between the natural player and the natural writer. Gavin Ewart puts it well:

I can't imagine a century
    being made by Spender.
Was Fuller ever more
    than a good tail-ender?

You can't see Angus Wilson
    driving firmly through the covers;
the literary ladies
    prefer playing games with lovers.

It's sad to see how little
    the literati
have really achieved at cricket –
    though hale and hearty

but modestly omits mention of himself. The truth is that no game has such chroniclers. It lives on in the collective folk-memory:

> A play drops poignantly into its last night.
> A novel needs those lapsing paragraphs
> to tie the knots and bows
> round the gone lives, the feelings we felt.
> But never elsewhere as here the slow
> white glide into a destiny of pastness.
> What more alive than shelves of tomblike Wisdens?

asks Brian Jones, one of the new wave of good young cricket poets.

How fortunate to be Hornby or Barlow or Hobbs, skilfully and eternally encapsulated. Here's Alan Ross, to my mind the finest living cricket poet, on Hammond:

> Never mind the earthbound heaviness
> Of hip, of shoulders, his cover-drive
> Evokes airiness, an effortless take-off.

I'd like to end with a complete short poem by Ross, because in its understated concision it seems to me to sum up what cricket is all about:

Bailey bowling, McLean cuts him late for one.
I walk from the Long Room into slanting sun.
Two ancients halt as Statham starts his run.
Then, elbows linked, but straight as sailors
On a tilting deck, they move. One, square-shouldered as a tailor's
Model, leans over, whispering in the other's ear:
'Go easy. Steps here. This end bowling.'
Turning, I watch Barnes guide Rhodes into fresher air,
As if to continue an innings, though Rhodes may only play by ear.

# Memoirs of a Cricketeer

JULIAN SYMONS

The heading is not a printer's or publisher's error. A cricketeer's memoirs are not those of a cricketer. Before defining the nature of a cricketeer, however, perhaps I should say something about my memories of cricket.

I was taken to see my first county cricket match not many years after the end of the First World War, by my brother Maurice. I was eleven or twelve, Maurice was eight years older, and we took with us sandwiches, fly biscuits and lemonade. We lived at Clapham, so it was natural to go to the Oval. Surrey were playing Yorkshire, and after getting off the bus we passed the sports shop run by the former Surrey and England batsman Bobby Abel. The old man, now blind, sat outside the shop responding to the greetings of those who passed by to the ground.

I have deliberately refrained from checking dates, feeling that such memories as mine should preserve their imprecision, but it was the year in which Surrey had a promising new fast bowler named Sadler, who duly played his part in dismissing Yorkshire for a low score. My local patriotism was strong, and I was elated. I stood with Maurice outside the pavilion when Yorkshire came out to field, and was shocked to hear Macaulay say to Waddington (both of them fast or medium-fast bowlers): 'We're going to get these boogers out.' The shock came from the language, for although I was familiar with 'bugger', I did not expect to hear such godlike figures as cricketers use the word. My recollection is that Yorkshire did get the boogers out, and that within a year or two Sadler's promise had faded.

This was the first of many youthful visits to the Oval. There was a time when I could name the whole Surrey team of the period: Hobbs, Sandham, Mr A. Jeacocke, Mr D. J. Knight, Shepherd, Mr D. R. Jardine, Ducat, Mr P. G. H. Fender, Peach, Fenley, Sadler, Hitch, Strudwick . . . I fear that I am mixing up the early and late twenties, but Surrey's characteristic bowling weakness in the decade is apparent. I became distantly but passionately devoted to one or two of the team, at this time Ducat and Peach, and longed for them to do well. Ducat was one of the few players to have represented England at cricket and football, Alan Peach a standard county cricketer of the time, a hard-hitting middle-order batsman and medium-pace bowler. The fact that I never saw either of them play with distinction did not affect my loyalty.

It was a loyalty, however, that did not extend from county to country. By 1926, when I watched the last day of the final Test match, in which the newly-appointed captain A. P. F. Chapman won back the Ashes, I longed for the Australians to beat England, and was disgusted when they were dismissed for 120-odd, chiefly by Larwood and Rhodes. This anti-patriotic feeling about cricket, and indeed much else, swelled in the thirties. Four years after that Australian defeat, I was delighted when at Lord's Ponsford, and more particularly Bradman, hammered the English all over the ground, happier still when near the end of the day the cry 'Put Woolley on' was answered, and he was battered even more savagely than the other bowlers. That innings of Bradman's, with another when against Middlesex he went in after tea and got a century before stumps, remain in my mind as the finest batting performance I have seen. Bradman, with some justification, replaced Ducat, Peach and Leicestershire's Ewart Astill as a cricketing idol.

By this time, however, I was involved in playing cricket, upon the whole an unwise activity for a cricketeer. I was a poor batsman (my bat of course bore the name of an Australian, C. G. Macartney, rather than Hobbs or Sutcliffe), an adequate field, no bowler. What could be done except make me captain? My position was a little reminiscent perhaps of Major Lupton's, who had to be made Yorkshire's captain in the thirties because he was the only available amateur, but always batted number eleven. Unlike Lupton, however, whose field placings and bowling changes were dictated by such old hands as Emmott Robinson, my handling of the team (generally regarded, not least by me, as masterly) was dictatorial, with only the rarest consultations about placings or changes of bowling. In a cricketing career that lasted some seven years my highest score was 37.

All this seems longer ago, even, than it is. My anti-English feeling survived into the late forties, when I followed admiringly the Australian achievements on Bradman's last tour, but after that it disappeared. I was among the applauding crowd at the Oval in 1953 when Hutton's men at last won back the Ashes, clapping hands as loudly as any. Perhaps Bradman's disappearance from the scene, and Surrey's ascendancy in the fifties, had something to do with this change of heart. Since then, in any case, my patriotism has been unswerving. My enthusiasm for watching cricket, however, has declined. Although I have a member's card for Kent – based on residence rather than a shift of allegiance – I rarely go to matches, and doubt if I could watch a full day of county cricket with pleasure as I did up to a few years ago. I am content to see even Test matches on the box, and enjoy most the sixty-over match that can be completed in a single day.

None of this affects my keenness as a cricketeer, a word that it is time to define. A cricketeer is one devoted to playing simulated cricket, either purely on paper, through a board game, or in some physical form usually involving a dining-table. A true cricketeer will not only play such games, but will introduce contemporary cricketers into them and will keep careful records, for preference in a cricket scorebook. Most cricketeers have a passion for figures, a passion that to those outside the cricketeering circle will seem meaningless. The only cricket annual in the house at present, my collection of *Wisden* having been passed on to my son Mark, is the *Playfair Cricket Annual* for 1967. This excellent little book is kept in a lavatory, where it provides immensely interesting information for the figure- and record-minded. My own interest is chiefly in the obscure and unremembered. What about R. R. Bailey of Northamptonshire, who took five wickets in an innings three times in his first four matches in 1964, yet two years later had not been given his county cap, and in 1966 played in only ten matches, taking twenty-five wickets? I recall his name vaguely, but why didn't he get his county cap in that first season, and what happened to him? What stories are hidden behind the figures in the *Annual* for Lancashire's A. M. Beddow (not re-engaged, played in four matches during the season, making 25 runs) and Worcester's King, who 'made his debut for the county in three matches as a batsman, but will not play again'?

My cricketeering life began at school, with the simplest of paper cricket games. This is played by opening a book and scoring by means of interpretation of the alphabet, 'c' usually meaning caught, 'f' bowled, 'k' stumped and 'v' run out, while other letters signify runs scored, byes, or no run at all. That sentence contains eleven dismissals and so would complete an innings, but the game may be complicated by giving the early batsmen further chances through spinning a coin, and also by having one super-batsman, a Richards, Chappell or Boycott, who is out only if the spun coin comes down heads twice in succession. This version of paper cricket has, so far as I know, no name, and it is for one player. No skill is involved, but I fear that the impulse to cheat by rejecting the page randomly selected because at a glance it is seen to contain too many dismissals for one's favoured team (there is always a favoured team) is strong.

There are other cricket games based on passages from books, but those to be played solo pall after a time, and I was very lucky to find a fellow player in Mark. George Orwell once wrote to me that one of the pleasures of having children is that through them you relive your own childhood. At the time the phrase meant little to me, but I think I understand it now. From an early age Mark shared my enjoyment of games that simulate reality, and for that matter of games that don't. He took immediately to H. G. Wells's game with toy soldiers, 'Little Wars,' and we spent many happy hours setting out armies, placing mock trees, rivers and houses, advancing troops, firing guns, and fighting a battle that rarely took less time than a morning and an afternoon. He became an enthusiastic cricketeer, with my own liking for analyses and percentages, so that one feature of our paper cricket games was the keeping of batting and bowling averages for the whole of a Test series. In the course of time he also became, unlike me, a very good school and club cricketer.

The best passages-from-books cricket game that I know was bought by me at the Oval one day when I was there with Mark. Rain had stopped play, and I bought this ingenious game, which consisted of no more than a piece of cardboard that gave complicated instructions about how each letter in the alphabet affected the batsman, with variations that strongly favoured the better batsmen. We sat in a stand at the Oval and began to play there and then, while the rain fell. Even this game, however, had little element of skill, and concentrated upon the batsmen at the expense of the bowlers.

Before dealing with the best games for cricketeers, I will swerve aside for a couple of paragraphs to deal with table cricket games that call for skill and timing. All of those I know are in some degree unsatisfactory (I have never played cricket Subbuteo, which some recommend), either because they require a perfectly smooth and level surface, or because infringement of the rules is easy and profitable. Take, as a typical example, a game called Balyna, no longer to be seen in the shops. The ball was rolled down a metal gully, either from the top for a fast bowler or half-way down for a slower one. Spin could be imparted by a twist of the fingers as one bowled. The bat was a little round blob of metal suspended on a piece of cord that could be drawn back, and then released to go forward as the ball was bowled. Placing of the little hoops representing fieldsmen involved some skill, and if the ball went through a hoop the batsman was caught. The game was played on a green cloth, with areas marked for one, two or three runs. A protective band round the edge of the pitch was the boundary.

Some of the game's limitations will be obvious. There were

only two means of dismissal, bowled and caught, and for the true cricketeer there is something unsatisfactory about the use of a metal gully and a blob suspended on a piece of string. But still, Balyna had much to recommend it. If you edged the ball it would go towards the slips, you could attack the bowling by lifting your bat high, or defend by barely moving it. A stone-waller could be winkled out by a slow spinner who would induce him to give a catch. Unfortunately, though, the permissible limits for a bowler were hard to define. Spin could be imparted, but speed must not be added by pressure on the ball or a flick of the nail while bowling, and the distinction between rolling the ball down the gully and giving it a flick which gave extra speed and might even make it bounce was a subtle one, liable to cause prolonged and angry disagreement. Mark and I (need I say?) played the game in its proper spirit, but others did not.

Back after this diversion to the best cricket games I know, games which lack any physical element. The first of them is Stumpz, the second Card Cricket, and they have similarities. Stumpz involved a pack of cards for the bowler marked 'Good Length', 'Half Volley', 'Long Hop' and so on, and cards for the batsman containing a variety of strokes from 'Blocked', 'Played Forward' and 'Played Back' to off- or on-drives. The bowler could pitch the ball on the off, the wicket or the leg, and would place his field accordingly. He could switch the card indicator to bowl off-breaks, leg-breaks, googlies or straight balls. Faced by a straight half-volley on the wicket a batsman could if he wished, and if the state of the game demanded it, simply block the ball. A half-volley could not be cut or pulled – the game belonged to the thirties and the existence of the hook stroke was not acknowledged, although of course a half-volley could not have been hooked any more than it could be pulled. The most likely stroke would have been an off- or on-drive. The card then turned up might show a boundary or any other number of runs, although there was no score if a ball was hit to a square on the board which had a fieldsman on it. If the batsman was unlucky the card might say 'L2 catch', which meant that he scored two runs, but was caught if a fieldsman had been placed on square L2.

I first played Stumpz when living in a house with H. B. Mallalieu, a fellow-poet of the thirties. We changed some of the cards and modified a rule or two, so that skill was increased and luck diminished. Our games were mostly Kent v Surrey and Australia v England, but we grew more ambitious and started a county championship. Perhaps this was going too far. We certainly never completed the championship, and with my departure from the house the game was lost. It was, I believe, never very popular, and production soon stopped. A quarter of a century later I bought another set through *Exchange and Mart*, and played it with Mark.

Shortly after the rediscovery of Stumpz, however, it was partly replaced in my affections by Card Cricket, which was produced by the excellent magazine *Games and Puzzles*. This resembled Stumpz in having a bowling and a batting pack, of 110 and 108 cards respectively, plus a chart which showed what kind of strokes could be played to each ball. (The pull had now been replaced by the hook.) There were, however, some clever variations on the original Stumpz idea. The bowler picked up six cards for each over, and could bowl them in what order he wished. A top-grade batsman picked up seven cards, a number reduced for lesser players to six, five, and in the case of the last batsman four. He replaced a card after each one that he played, and ran a chance of being out if he had no card that would play a certain type of ball, like a short-pitched bumper. As the rules suggest: 'If a batsman has shown difficulty in playing off the back foot, the bowler should try to bowl as many short balls as possible to this batsman.' There was a time-limit in overs, and allowance was made for declarations, innings defeats, and stoppages through rain.

Card Cricket, like Stumpz, had its limitations, among them the fact that no differentiation could be made between types of bowling. Scores were too low (between 100 and 150 per innings), and the element of luck too strong, although this could be modified as it could in Stumpz. Such limitations sprang in part from the time factor. A game took around three hours, and no doubt its devisers felt that this was long enough. Originally they had more than 4,000 cards, to cover all kinds of bowlers and left- or right-handed batsmen, but obviously this was felt not to be practical. But both Stumpz and Card Cricket are very good games that will be enjoyed by any cricketeer lucky enough to come across them.

One is always, however, looking for perfection, and I am sure something nearer to it could be achieved. There are twenty or more war games of immense complexity, with names like Waterloo and Stalingrad, and enough buyers exist for them to flourish. A cricket game of similar complexity would find its devotees. It would take account of the state of the pitch and the changes in it over three or four days. It would make possible differentiations between various kinds of bowlers and batsmen, it would embody everything that could possibly happen in the game of cricket, and although its basis must be luck, the element of skill would be much greater than that in any of the cricket games I have played. It would be more likely to take eight hours than three, which means that like almost all of the war games it would probably be played over more than one day.

Do such thoughts seem ridiculous, do the occupations of cricketeers appear much too far from green grass, the sound of bat on ball, the run-stealers flickering to and fro? They are not so far. Remember that all these games, played on board and table, with books or cards, come to life for the cricketeer only when he replaces the numbers one to eleven with the names of real players, past or present, Australians, Englishmen or West Indians, and fights again battles that have been lost and won, hoping to change the result as the wargamer attempts to improve on the tactics used at Waterloo. Cricketeering is a form of day-dreaming, to be sure, but behind the day-dream lies devotion to actuality, a love of the game of cricket.

# *Sibson*

## PETER TINNISWOOD

I believe that the links between cricket and the history of the theatre have been sadly neglected.

My friend, the Brigadier, has some thoughts on this matter.

I am pleased to present them, unexpurgated and unadorned:

It was my father who many many years ago instilled into me feelings for the theatre which I hold still to this very day.

How can I describe those feelings?

How can I do justice to the loathing, the nausea and disgust I hold for the whole panoply of self-conceit and vainglory supported by an unruly horde of parasites, braggarts and pomaded pansies?

I except from these strictures, of course, Mr John Inman, brother of the fine Pakistani Test cricketer, Mr Inman Khan.

And that doyen of the English stage, Sir Alf Richardson, father and grandfather respectively of the two cricketing brothers, Peter and Derek.

And that splendid duo of comedy actors who exercised our chuckle muscles for so many years in the Aldwych farces, Dame Vera Lynn and R. C. Robertson-Glasgow.

But back to my father and his abiding interest in all matters of a Thespian nature.

Apart from being Chief Inspector of bicycles and tandems to the East Bengal Customs and Excise Service my father also achieved considerable distinction as an amateur inventor.

He it was who invented the inflatable toothpick for the use of lifeboatmen.

He it was who invented the luminous arch support for the use

of explorers during the perpetual darkness of the Arctic winter –
a device also used by opening batsmen during the perpetual
darkness of Old Trafford Test matches.

It was in his capacity as an inventor that my father first met
that giant of the English stage, that female colossus, who charmed
us, enchanted us and captured our hearts for more than six
generations.

I refer, of course, to Mrs Chester Dromgoole.

Her beauty was unrivalled.

Her wit was unparagoned.

How well I remember seeing her as a very young boy (it was I
who was the young boy, of course) in the play, *Arsenal and Old
Lace*.

Among the distinguished cast members were Mr Rutland
Barrington, father and grandfather respectively of the late Surrey
and England batsman, Mr Ken Barrington, and the bewitching
Miss Winifred Emery, sister of that most sensitive and subtle of
English actors, Mr Dick Emery, who coined a catchphrase,
which originated in remarks made by Sir Donald Bradman to
Mr Harold Larwood during the celebrated and infamous 'body-
line' series in Australasia:

'Oooh, you are awful, but I like you.'

My father had been summoned to a weekend house party at
the country residence of Mrs Chester Dromgoole to demonstrate
to her his latest invention, the portable wig.

Mrs Dromgoole, always a fitness fanatic, had recently been
playing the arduous part of Othello in Shakespeare's play of a
very similar name.

In order to achieve maximum physical soundness she had
taken to training with members of the Chelsea Association
Football Club.

The constant heading of a sodden football had caused an un-
sightly bald patch to appear on the crown of her pate, thus
necessitating the intervention of my father and his latest cranial
creation.

Mrs Dromgoole expressed herself delighted with the wig,

which served the dual purpose of concealing her trichopathic deficiencies and providing a warm and comforting night bed for her beloved Boston terrier, named after Julius Caesar, who coined another of cricket's immortal catchphrases:

'Come two, Brute.'

My father never ceased to talk with affection and enthusiasm of the blissful four days he spent at that gracious stately home set in the heart of the rolling green hills of rural England.

Dear old 'Weskers' – the company that weekend was dazzling.

Statesmen, diplomats, politicians, great soldiers strolled the gravelled paths, lingered in the exotic conservatories and gossiped on the fine-cropped lawns.

Among the distinguished guests, my father noticed a young Boer statesman and one of the most promising young soldiers in the French army, later to become a field-marshal.

It was this duo who were to prove the inspiration for that immortal comic paper cartoon strip, Smuts and Joffre.

Over breakfast that first morning my father shared a table with those two eminent men of letters, Sir Sacha Distel, and his brother, Edith.

Later on the same day my father played a game of shuttlecock and battledore with a certain Irishman by the name of Wilde, who was partnered by a Frenchman by the name of Proust.

My father was partnered by Lord Kitchener.

The sodomites won.

The perfect weekend was marred for my father by only one thing; the presence of a Norwegian playwright, who had achieved a certain success in his own country as the author of the play, *Piers Gynt*.

His name was, I believe, Sibson.

Sibson's gloomy mien, his dark brooding silences and the shapeless, shabby raincoat he wore constantly despite the noble, blazing English sun cast a sullen blight on the company which was not to be assuaged despite Mrs Dromgoole's heroic efforts to entertain with her impersonations of Mr Charles Marowitz reciting the early works of Strindberg.

My father well remembered his first encounter with Sibson, who was seated at an exquisite rosewood and tupelo escritoire in the writing room.

'What-ho, Sibson,' said my father. 'Scribblin' again, eh?'

Sibson fixed my father with a pair of cold watery blue eyes and said:

'Sir, I am writing a play in which the heroine refuses to discover herself, and her conflicts and her tragedy are the results of this refusal.

'Longing for life and yet afraid of it, she refuses to admit this fear and convert the energy of her conflict into action.

'And so at the centre of the play will be a mind turning upon itself in a kind of vacuum.'

'I see,' said my father. 'And are you using washable ink in your fountain pen?'

Many years later my father saw this play, *Edna Gobbler*, in the company of two of the most august members of the cricketing establishment, Mr H. D. G. Leveson Gower and Sir Pelham 'Plum' Warner, creator, among many other things, of the immortal catchphrase:

'Mind my bike.'

During the second act Sir Pelham, who had found increasing difficulty accommodating his nether regions, clad as they were in cricket pads and abdominal protector, in the narrow confines of the orchestra stalls, said in a very loud voice:

'Who are all these bloody Norwegians, anyway?'

'Sir,' said my father. 'One is a puisne judge. The other is a scholar engaged in the history of civilisation. And the chap with the big nose is his wife.'

'Splendid pair of shoulders on her,' said Leveson Gower. 'Wonder if she'd like to open the bowling for me at the next Scarborough Festival.'

And with that the gentle snores of two of the most distinguished administrators in the history of the summer game echoed gently around the theatre.

They were disturbed only when some damn fool let off a pistol shot at the end of the play, causing Sir Pelham to spill half a box of mint-flavoured chocolate dragees down the front of his MCC blazer.

I mention this incident only to emphasise a point that has often been overlooked by the so-called experts and self-appointed arbiters of public taste – the overriding influence exercised by cricket on the most momentous and significant movements in the history of the drama.

For example, it was during the weekend at the residence of Mrs Chester Dromgoole that Sibson conceived the central theme of his most famous play.

A lot of rot has been spoken about this, and I intend to put the record straight here and now.

The facts are these:

On the Sunday afternoon as was customary at these house parties Mrs Dromgoole split her guests into two teams to take part in a game of cricket.

Sibson was nowhere to be found.

It was the butler, Billington, who finally discovered him skulking in the attic dressed in shabby great coat, woollen gloves and a dirty, reddish-brown wig.

On being summoned to Mrs Dromgoole's presence and informed of her desire that he take part in the cricket match, Sibson threw up his hands and cried:

'But, merciful God, one doesn't do that kind of thing.'

It took all the tact of my father's hostess to persuade him to don Free Foresters' cap and I Zingari sweater, although he jibbed at wearing cricket flannels, protesting:

'One should never put on one's best trousers to go out to battle for freedom and truth.'

On seeing him take a net with Dame Flora Robson and her brother, the eminent drama critic, Sir Harold Robson, my father well understood Sibson's reluctance.

For his aptitude for the game could be summed up in three well-chosen words:

'No bally good.'

The two teams were captained respectively by Lord Harris and Lady Campbell-Bannerman, a noted purveyor in her own right of top-spinner and chinaman.

Sibson opened the batting for Lady Campbell-Bannerman's side and with typical Scandinavian two-eyed stance faced the first ball sent down by Lord Harris himself.

The noble Lord, bowling over the wicket, sent down a short-pitched ball which rose sharply from the pitch and struck Sibson flush in the groin.

Much was the merriment of the spectators as the melancholic father of all subsequent plays concerned with the inner experience of the individual and the assessment and revaluation of his past at some ultimate turning-point of his soul's pilgrimage hopped on one leg clutching his private parts.

When he had regained his breath, Sibson pointed feebly at Lord Harris and cried:

'Go round, Peer.'

This Lord Harris did and, bowling round the wicket, struck Sibson a formidable blow on the right temple.

It was obvious now to one and all that his Lordship was determined to humiliate and humble the Norwegian for the gloom and despondency he had caused to settle on the company in the previous days.

The third ball struck Sibson on the chest.

The fourth, a beamer, caused him to fling himself full-length on the pitch.

The fifth knocked out his two front teeth, and the sixth, the most perfect of yorkers, wrecked his castle.

Sibson had not troubled the scorer.

And as he stormed back to the pavilion swinging his bat angrily, muttering dark Scandinavian curses and grinding his remaining Nordic teeth, we realise now only too well the origin of his most celebrated of plays.

I refer, of course, to *The Wild Duck.*

# My First Dates With Cricket

ALEC WAUGH

My love, I think I should say, my passion for the game of cricket began at the start of my sixth year. I was born in July 1898 and I can pinpoint the date. On the morning of 28 October my father came into my bedroom and announced that during the night a baby brother had been born. 'Fine,' I said. 'He'll be the wicket-keep.'

My parents lived in West Hampstead, at No. 11 Hillfield Road. It had a long and very narrow garden. First there was a lawn, then beyond a willow tree, a vegetable garden. When my father or the cook bowled to me and I missed the ball, I had to search for it among the cabbages. Time was wasted. I needed a wicketkeeper badly. Alas, Evelyn never realised the high ambitions I had cherished for him. He was soon to develop a deep-rooted detestation of all organised athletics, particularly of cricket. I am afraid I must hold myself to blame for this. In the meantime my own devotion to the game intensified.

In 1903 Middlesex was the champion county. I cannot remember this. But in the autumn the county's chief bat, P. F. Warner, was appointed captain of the MCC side in Australia. From this point 'Plum' Warner became my hero. Every evening my father brought home the green *Westminister Gazette* that contained the scores of the day's cricket. Soon I knew the names of all the players, English and Australian; they became the protagonists of the nursery matches in which I recreated the battles that were being waged in Adelaide and Sydney. I marked out the wicket under the window that faced the wall, and tossed the ball above the door, playing it on the rebound.

Each chair bore a fieldsman's name, English or Australian, as the case might be. If the ball landed without bouncing in a chair, the batsman was declared caught. Evelyn's cot was in the far corner of the room; if a ball landed there the batsman scored six but was given out. Gradually over the years – we did not leave the house until 1907 – the bouncing of the ball above the door wore a hole in the fabric, and my father was subjected to an extra charge for 'wilful damage'. I kept the analysis of the various bowlers and in the process acquired an efficiency in elementary mathematics that astonished my first headmaster.

In May I was taken to Lord's for the first time. Warner's XI from Australia was matched against the MCC. I cried when Warner's wicket fell. In August I saw Middlesex take the field for the first time, against Surrey. It was the match that Middlesex would always soonest win. My father took me on the Saturday. We watched from the Mound. Middlesex needed some 250 runs. Wickets fell steadily. But Macgregor, the captain, was still in with 43 runs against his number. A. E. Trott came in at number nine with 50 runs still needed and hit his first ball for three. Macgregor came down the pitch and spoke to him. 'He's warning him to go steadily,' my father said. He did. Forty minutes later he was 27 not out with Middlesex the winners by three wickets.

Next summer I saw my first Test match – the Lord's match, the second in the series with F. S. Jackson captaining England, J. Darling the Australians. I went with my parents on the second day, after lunch. The ground was packed. Not a seat nor any standing room. We stood behind the screen. My father walked behind the crowd. 'Would you let my little boy in?' he asked. 'He's only six and he's never seen a Test match.' I was lifted over the crowd and given a seat on the ground. I have seen photographs of the match. There is a white smudge just to the right of the screen. It must be me. I watched there for two hours, while my parents behind the screen saw nothing.

'Plum' Warner was still my hero. He was to remain it until that famous late August evening of 1920 when Middlesex won the championship and 'Plum' was carried shoulder high to the pavilion. Has Lord's known a more emotional moment? I question it.

Every schoolboy has his own special hero or heroes. It is a very special feeling. It is proprietary, in a peculiar way that has been expressed by, of all unlikely poets, Francis Thompson. What a long journey from 'The Hound of Heaven'! It is very short. It is called 'At Lord's'. He rarely, he says, goes to the matches of the 'southran folk though the red roses crest the caps I know'. He would be listening to the clapping of a shadowy host as the run-getters flicker to and fro. 'O my Hornby and my Barlow long ago.' It is the use of the word 'my' that gives it its special magic. It reveals the personal belonging of the schoolboy to his hero. It is a great poem, I think, only comprehensible to an Englishman, to a special kind of Englishman.

I had, as a schoolboy, a second series of loyalties, to Somerset and to S. M. J. 'Sammy' Woods. My father was a Somerset man, his father the doctor at Midsomer Norton. My mother, the daughter of an Indian civil servant, was born at Chittagong. Her mother, as a widow, married a parson who was for many years the vicar of Bishop's Hull, a village less than two miles from Taunton. Evelyn and I divided our summer holidays between our grandparents' two houses. My father had inspired his in-laws with a love of cricket and I was to see many fine matches at the Taunton ground. Somerset were never within eight places of winning the championship, but it was said that no county could be sure of winning the championship till they had tackled or failed to tackle Somerset. In the early 1900s Yorkshire lost only three matches in three seasons. Two of them were against Somerset. In one of them Somerset were bowled out for 87, Yorkshire scored over 300, but Somerset won by 279 runs, and the card was printed in gold lettering. I saw Somerset beat Surrey there by three wickets in 1909. The next match was against Kent; Somerset suffered from the inevitable reaction and fielded out the whole of the first day and half of the second and on the third day had to follow on. But Somerset as so often had a surprise up its sleeve. A. E. Lewis made over two hundred runs and that great fieldsman K. L. Hutchings dropped three catches in the deep.

Most of Somerset's wickets in those years fell to slow left-arm bowlers. My father published a book of verses, 'Legends of the Wheels', commemorating the joys of bicycling. One line ran: 'Will scour the market-place to know what wickets Tyler took today'. But during most of this time the dominant figure in Somerset cricket was the captain, Sammy Woods. He was a tremendous lion of a man. Born in Australia in 1868 he came to England to finish his education: if education is the right word with which to define his intermittent conflicts with examiners. He combined in his accent a highpitched Australian swing with a West Country burr. In 1888, when the Australians were over, he was called upon as a fast bowler in all three Tests. In his four years at Cambridge he took 36 Oxford wickets and in one of these years there was very little play. He was also to play cricket for England against South Africa, and he played rugby football for England. He was a great trencherman with a thirst that it was hard to quench. When Cambridge were entertaining a visiting team of almost international capability, he invited half of the team to a breakfast of hot lobsters and draught beer. The visitors quailed, so Woods ordered them coffee and eggs and bacon, and Woods and Macgregor settled for the beer and lobsters. Woods then proceeded to bowl them out.

He was a legend. I remember my father returning from a day at Lord's and saying to my mother: 'Would you like to kiss this hand before I wash it? It has shaken hands with Sammy Woods.'

We had an earthenware water jug that had on the outside medallions of Gregor Macgregor, Sammy Woods, and I think William Gunn. It was made by Doulton and there is an example of it in the pavilion at the Oval.

'Plum' Warner was never to be replaced in my devotion, but in 1910 I was to acquire another hero, a Middlesex player I need hardly add. I had gone to see the Middlesex and Essex match at Lord's. I got there after lunch on the first day. Essex had made 93 for 2. In the first over Tarrant got a wicket, a catch in the slips. 'Plum' tossed the ball to a very young player. It was the first time that I had seen him. I looked at my score-card. J. W. Hearne. He was thin and small. He took a short run and his arm went over quickly. It was not an easy or very attractive action. His second ball was driven for two. Then the fireworks began. Within forty minutes he had taken seven wickets without having a run scored off him. 'Plum' was to write of him a year or two later: 'On his day and in his hour he is unplayable.' A year later he went to Australia with the MCC and scored a century in his second Test match. In 1913, 1914 and 1920 he scored over two thousand runs and took over a hundred wickets. His obituary notices in 1965 referred to his mammoth partnerships with Hendren, comparing them to Compton and Edrich's partnerships after the Second War, but his partnerships with Tarrant before the First War were even more remarkable. Tarrant, too, was making his 2,000 runs and taking 100 wickets in a season. In those three war years Tarrant and J. W. Hearne were Middlesex.

'Young' Jack was never a strong man. He missed what should have been his best years, 1915–18. He never did as much in Test matches as he should have done. His health kept breaking down. He was picked for England for the last time at Trent Bridge in 1926. Only forty-five minutes' play was possible, and Hobbs and Sutcliffe made some 35 deliberate runs. Young Jack was reported as being rather more than 'rather ill' – in the pavilion. Over the years he gave me more pleasure than any cricketer I have watched.

I had other opportunities too of watching Middlesex cricketers. The Hampstead cricket club was known as the nursery of Middlesex cricket; its ground in the Lymington Road had only been a few yards away from my parents' first home above a dairy in the Finchley Road and was only a short walk from our second home in Hillfield Road. I spent a lot of time there, particularly in the summer of 1907 when I had an attack of whooping cough and could not go to school. My father's link with it was S. S. Pawling,

William Heinemann's partner. He was never quite good enough for county cricket, though he played three times for Middlesex. But he was a formidable performer under the 'umbrageous elms' of the club ground. Nicknamed 'the skipper', he was a great blond giant of a man, and was the hero of Frank Danby's novel *Joseph in Jeopardy*. Frank Danby, the mother of Gilbert Frankau, provided one of the scandals that were accepted in Victorian London. She and Pawling are mentioned in Arnold Bennett's Journals. The highly decorated family tomb that was awaiting her in the West End Lane cemetery exercised a great fascination on my boyhood. I noticed it when I was being taken for a walk there by Evelyn's nurse. I took my father to see it. 'I have,' I said, 'a very terrible thing to show you.' A few years ago I took my wife, Virginia Sorensen, to see it. She was appropriately impressed. Gilbert is there now, though Pamela, a Roman Catholic, of course is not.

In the 1880s and early 90s Hampstead numbered not only A. E. Stoddart and Gregor Macgregor among its members but also the Australian 'demon' bowler F. R. Spofforth, who would regularly get his 200 wickets a year at less than half a dozen runs apiece. F. R. O'D. Monro, a cousin of the poet Harold, wrote a book about the club that contained the full score of a match that I remember against MCC in the summer of 1907. A. E. Trott was playing for MCC. Eighteen wickets fell in the day. Hampstead led on the first innings and there was an exciting finish as Trott endeavoured to get them out a second time. He just failed. I was sorry when my father built his own house at North End, Hampstead, and I no longer went to Lymington Road.

During my summer holidays with my grandparents I never went to see the county play at Bath, perhaps because there were no matches there in August, but mainly I think because Midsomer Norton had a flourishing village side of which my grandfather was the president. All the members of the eleven were familiar figures to my father. He refers to them in his autobiography by name, and the Waugh family watched the matches every

Saturday. The captain of the village was a mining engineer from the north. He had three sons, one of my own age, the other two slightly older. He arranged boys' matches during the summer and it was under his captaincy that I played my first games in adult company. I made a 25 for him when I was fourteen and the following year I made a 65. During the 1914 summer term I looked forward to an August of cricket at Midsomer Norton. I felt that I should now be promoted to a regular place in the village side, not just in the schoolboy matches. I had during June earned a place in the Sherborne school eleven. I had played against Dulwich College, which had A. E. R. Gilligan as its captain and A. H. H. Gilligan as its best bat. It was an exciting summer for me. I was second in the Sherborne batting averages and Middlesex were challenging Kent and Surrey at the head of the county championship.

My father met me at Waterloo when I came back for the summer holidays. 'Let's go to the Oval,' I said. 'Surrey are playing Sussex.' I had hopes that they might be beaten. They very nearly were, thanks to a fierce spell of bowling by K. H. C. Woodroffe – a brilliant young amateur who was not to survive the war. I was hopeful, though. Surrey would be rattled by that narrow win. Surrey's next match was against Kent at Blackheath. 'Let's go down,' I said.

We went on the Saturday by train. We travelled in the same carriage as Philip Trevor, the *Daily Telegraph* correspondent. We took a fourwheeler at the station, at the usual rate of 'a bob a nob'. 'I don't know why I'm bothering to come down,' Trevor said. 'They probably won't print my report. It's the last match I'll be watching.' The certainty of war was by now accepted. During the morning two telegrams were brought out to players. 'Calling-up orders, I bet,' said Trevor. 'I've already got mine. I know where I'll be on Monday. Oh, well hit!' he added. 'Fourpence to pay' as cover-point failed to cut off a drive.

The drama of this present match was ebbing. On the second day Hobbs and Hayward had put on over 200 runs in one of their finest partnerships. At the start of the season Hayward had been out of form, and his place in the side had become unsure. But he was finishing in his best style. By mid-afternoon a draw was certain, with Surrey taking points for a lead on the first innings. The precise result that a Middlesex supporter would most have welcomed. It did not seem to matter now.

It had been a sunny morning, but the sky clouded over in the afternoon. At five o'clock it began to rain. It seemed appropriate that the last Saturday of peace should end like this, with grey skies, a light rain falling and stumps drawn early.

The return match late in August was played at Lord's. The Oval had been commandeered by the military. Hayward was again in form: over 90 runs. *Wisden* said: 'Hayward was lucky, but few men could have played such an innings on such a wicket against the Kent slow bowlers.' It was the last time I saw him bat. P. G. H. Fender was to hit a hurricane 48. A. P. Freeman played for the first time for Kent. Just as that last Saturday at Blackheath had seemed an appropriate finale to a world about to end, so did Surrey's appearance on this older field seem an appropriate symbol of a world of change. Would it ever be the same again, I wondered. I don't think it has, not quite.

# A Deaf Man Looks At Cricket

DAVID WRIGHT

First recollections, and I realise that I see the game as ceremony. White figures on a red background, the fielders dispose themselves, in memory, like a corps de ballet. I am aged five or so, at the old Wanderers' ground, long since absorbed by the Johannesburg railway station. My grandfather, magnificent in a club blazer (he'd played for Kimberley against Lord Hawke's XI in the nineties), sits remotely enthroned in the curlicued Edwardian wrought-iron balcony of the cricket pavilion, tin-roofed and painted red. The playing-field beaten earth, the same red shade; the pitch green matting. Umpires change stations; the fielders cross over; stately as a minuet.

My next recollection of cricket – again at the Wanderers – is more precise. Plump, agile, fiery of hair and face, A. P. F. Chapman leaps to take an impossible slip catch. It is a Test match; had I a *Wisden* by me I'd be able to give the exact date. Probably the early thirties. My grandfather, though still 'the best-dressed man in South Africa', was by then impoverished, bankrupted by the stock-market crash of 1929. My own circumstances had altered too, I having turned stone deaf after a bout of scarlet fever. This was to send me to England, and for good, a year or two later: to Northampton, which possessed the only school in the then Empire that catered for the secondary education of the deaf in those days.

Emigrating to England from Africa at the age of fourteen was fairly traumatic. Cricket played on grass for one thing. It didn't seem proper – amateurish somehow. No way of telling how the ball would bounce. Then the light – variable, undependable; long summer evenings when one couldn't believe the clock, the sun horizon-high well after supper and bedtime; and as for the weather – 'no two days alike, unless it's raining'.

Yet it was at Northampton, a squalid conglomerate of tanneries and brick terrace-houses, county town of England's middle shire, that I became hooked on cricket as a spectator. Odd, because Northants then competed fiercely, and had for years, with Leicestershire for the honour of second-bottom place in the county cricket championship table: an elevation which it seldom attained. Its county ground was besieged by regiments of low brick houses, from whose exiguous back yards flight after flight and squadron after squadron of pigeons would take to the air as soon as the shoe factories had disgorged their slaves, the birds' owners. Parked cars, whose windows winked the sun, often to the distraction if not destruction of visiting batsmen, flanked the pitch. This un-distinguished but pleasant playing-field we were allowed to attend most Wednesday afternoons throughout the summer term, if there were a match. It was there I beheld, in flesh and blood, those gods who had been names only in my Johannesburg prep school; names with which we conjured in games of paper cricket played with dice: Verity, Hendren, Sutcliffe, Larwood, Ham-mond, Bowes, and Voce. It was there I first saw – the whole town turning out for them – the conquering Australians: Pons-ford, Woodfull, Bradman – what a let-down, the latter! He was bowled for two runs – which unprecedented event, reported with awe next morning in *The Times*, induced our headmaster to assemble the entire school and announce that never again, perhaps, would any one of us be likely to witness a happening newsworthy enough to win a headline on the principal page of so eminent a newspaper. Innocent days.

In the thirties Northants had one noted player – I think it was he who took Bradman's wicket. This was Clark, a red-haired fast bowler, said to be even faster, on his day, than the legendary Larwood; and blessed or cursed with a fast bowler's irascible disposition (one reason, it was said, why Test selectors would look beyond him when picking an England eleven). That temper I witnessed – once, memorably, when Notts were playing, and

Larwood himself, not then so fast, perhaps, as he had been in that still-reverberating leg-theory series in Australia, with his first ball sent Clark's middle stump cartwheeling foolishly into the wicket-keeper's gloves; which so inspired, or inflamed, the Northants redhead that he went through the opposition, when their innings came, like a whirlwind; reserving for the unhappy Larwood a ball that, searing the grass where it touched, left that batsman staring, his wicket a smoking ruin.

Undependable in the field, no use with a bat, ludicrous with a ball, I never became a player; but for all that attained a place in the school's first, and I have to say only, XI. The school roll-call never exceeded twenty-four pupils; and nearly half of those were under ten years old. Nonetheless we had an XI, which played weekly matches against the local hearing schools, or scratch sides raised by a former county player that could include, besides absolute rabbits, real first-class cricketers who happened to be temporarily unemployed; for despite our small numbers, we had a formidable reputation. The match of the year was against the 600-strong Northampton Grammar School. Officially we were supposed to be taking on its second XI; but usually – so ashamed were they of losing to us – their team was well laced with players from their First XI. If they generally beat us, that was no dishonour; but sometimes, not often, we won. The venue for these matches was discreet – perhaps because the Grammar School did not wish their occasional defeats by us to be too public. It was fenced on one side by high brick walls facing the Little Billing Road, and on the other by a magnificent vista: the placid valley of the river Nen, that lay below the high ground on which stood the Northampton Lunatic Asylum, in whose precincts the game was played. The most famous inmate of this asylum had been the poet John Clare. In my time, though I did not know it then, it housed James Joyce's daughter Lucia. For all I know she may have been one of the spectators when we were playing, for the patients had the freedom of the asylum grounds and often came to watch.

Deafness is no handicap at cricket – probably the reverse, since no noise can disturb the batsman's concentration. The disadvantages are few – you can't hear the umpire shout 'No-ball', and so miss the chance of hitting a six without risk; and because you can't hear the other batsman call, runnings-out tend to be more frequent. But the most exceptional, though not the best, batsman that I ever saw was a deaf man. He was also one of the school's most remarkable pupils, having arrived there almost totally uneducated at the age of sixteen, unable even to do simple arithmetic; yet within a few years he was to matriculate, enter London University, and there collect first a BSc. and later a doctorate; this at a time when the number of deaf-born university graduates – not just in England but the entire world – could be counted on the fingers of one hand. All this he achieved through dogged, meticulous concentration; and this is what made him, in turn, the mainstay of the school XI. In spite of his poor vision (he wore pebble lenses) it was almost impossible to get him out. His batting was of a piece with his character – tenacious, orderly, diligent, unbelievably persevering. For every kind of ball – long hop, full toss, short length, good length, off-break, leg-break, he had one and the same stroke: a perfectly executed forward play in classic Victorian style. He never missed the ball and he broke the bowlers' hearts.

I left school for Oxford just before the Second World War broke out and suspended county cricket for five mortal years. At Oxford I took up rowing. I watched no cricket, though even in wartime there must have been some to watch. At any rate it was at Oxford that I made the first of the two appearances on a cricket field that I have so far vouchsafed the public since leaving school. In desperate need the captain of the college cricket team pressganged three or four unattended oarsmen, myself among them, to make up a complement to meet the Oxford University Women's XI. I will not reveal whether it is shame or gallantry that disinclines me to disclose who won. It was fifteen years before I made my next appearance on a cricket field. That was at Chester, on the Roodee. My wife was then in the mobile theatre, the Century, that toured the northern towns every summer. At Chester its visit coincided with that of Bertram Mills' Circus.

Naturally, a match was arranged between the two companies; not unnaturally, it was a dramatic occasion. It was also the one and only time that I ever covered myself with glory on a cricket field, for I bowled no less a batsman than Coco the clown, himself and in person. He, however, returned the compliment when it was our turn to bat. Each of us was out first ball.

In 1942 I went down from Oxford, to settle in London where I was to live for the next quarter of a century. I was lucky enough to find a flat over a bombed-out electric-appliance shop in Great Ormond Street ('That's in Bloomsbury?' the dean of my college remarked when I told him my new address. 'A very *wild* place!'). My evenings, however, were spent in Soho; but my days – in summer, that is, when I had the money and the time – at Lord's or the Oval; nearly always at the former, for like most Londoners I would not if I could help it go south of the river. Towards the end of the war, despite the GI invasion, cricket began to revive. I can claim to have been present when a flying bomb, passing over-head at Lord's, failed to distract the attention of either the players or the spectators from the game in hand; though I have to con-fess that as I was unable to hear either planes or sirens I knew nothing about the incident till I read of it in the papers the next morning.

To recall the great summer of 1947, the summer of Compton and Edrich, recreates for me the gold and shadows of an eternal afternoon. The ground is Lord's and I am lying on the grass somewhere, or standing hour after hour outside the Tavern; the weather ever warm and the evenings ever clear; they cannot always have been so, but that is how it seems. I see the familiars of those endless afternoons, sentinel figures by the fence opposite the Tavern doors, the hard men from the George and the Third Programme: Bob Pocock, Reggie Smith, René Cutforth and Louis MacNeice; the latter half-hiding behind a pint jar of bitter his curiously broken teeth, intent eyes watching over its brim the bowler running up to the wicket from the Nursery End.

But to return to cricket itself. I have often been asked how deafness affects one's enjoyment as a watcher, and found it difficult to answer. One reads much about the click of bat on ball, and the rest of it; sounds I've never heard and don't miss, though all aver they are part of the pleasure. On the other hand I do enjoy the West Indian steel bands, which I *can* hear! but they are not part of the mythology. And, talking of West Indian steel bands, the only time I ever did hear the human voice was at a Test match against the West Indies. One day in 1963 I was at Lord's cricket ground; Ted Dexter had just come in to bat. He put a couple of runs on the board with the air of a man who means to get another 98 before lunch. Suddenly he was bowled. While the bails were still flying, coats, hats, cushions, umbrellas, sandwiches, for all I know babies even, were hurled into the air by some nine or ten thousand West Indians in the free seats where I was watching. Up went a simultaneous roar of delight. Hearing that sound, for me not very loud but like a croaking bark, was a queer and spooky experience. I have never forgotten it.

I do notice, because of deafness, things that may elude the ordinary spectator: for the deaf do not notice more, they notice differently. I can generally read, for instance, the batsman's frame of mind – apprehensive or confident – transmitted by the involuntary tapping of his bat on the crease as he awaits the delivery of a ball. One can sometimes tell if he has made up his mind, even before the ball has left the bowler's hand, to smite or try to smite it to kingdom come. It was always a joy to watch Hutton, perhaps the most elegant of tappers, increase the tempo of his beat as the bowler neared the point of delivery, till it almost became part of his stroke. The dour Sutcliffe was another whose frame of mind was easy to 'read' in this way, though that was between balls, when it was his habit to stroll up the pitch and do a bit of 'gardening'; thoughtfully, or on occasion annoyedly, patting down imaginary divots and excrescences; or sweeping away invisible loose blades of grass.

Sight is not all, I know; I remember going to a Test match at Headingley with a blind friend – a cricket fan, though on that occasion he was only accompanying me because it was past three in the afternoon, and he wanted to go on drinking. There was little he missed of the game, I found; even though he was aided by the commentary coming from his transistor radio. Well do I recall our journey from the pub to the ground at Headingley. As I steered my friend there a car drew up beside us, out of whose window popped a lady's head enquiring the way to somewhere or other. What a card she drew, poor woman. One of us was blind and could not tell, the other was deaf and could not hear . . .

Yet what my blind friend got out of the game eludes me. The appeal of cricket has always seemed to me to be spectacle: not excitement, though I suppose that no other game, bar tennis, can work up to such long-drawn-out and intense orgasms of suspense. I find I watch cricket for its aesthetic element, high-falutin' though this sounds. For instance it is the pleasure I find in watching the action of certain bowlers, not necessarily the most famous or effective, that draws me. For example Goddard of Gloucestershire, who used to bowl, as George Barker once remarked, 'like a snake'. Even after more than quarter of a century I can recreate in my mind's eye the dozen or so most perfect overs I have ever seen in my life, maiden overs in which not a wicket fell nor a run was scored. Few now will have heard of or remember the bowler, for he died of cancer at the age of thirty-one. He was N. B. F. Mann, 'Tufty' Mann; and when I saw him he was playing for South Africa in a Test at Lord's. A slow, mortally accurate bowler, he pitched the ball, an all but unplayable ball, again and again on the identical spot; for the batsman it must have been like the Chinese water-torture. The action, the slow engine-smooth run-up, delivery, and millimetre-shaving precision of the pitch and movement of the ball were pure delight, acting on the eye as I imagine a passage of music does on the ear.

As a substitute for music, I watch ballet; the dance, for me, is music made visible. Cricket I watch for almost the same reason, except that its music, so to speak, is abstract. As I remarked at the beginning, I see the game as ceremony.

## A Poet at the Tavern

### L.M. 1907–1963

Your verse half rubbish, I thought. But at Lord's
We used to meet, for once on common ground,
Watch Graveney and Cowdrey make a stand,
A sweetly hammered ball disturb the feeding birds.
It was a game as marginal as ours,
Bounded by laws it takes genius to transcend;
Whose transfigured masters, blade in hand,
In a green circle became as gods.

You would not deny its players their honours
Deserved for a perfection of its kind;
And who am I, now, to deny you yours,
Now gone so long, gone now so long beyond
Reach of any word or of change of heart or mind
Or of those long afternoons and shades?

# Contributors

DRUMMOND ALLISON, born 1921 in Caterham, Surrey, killed in action 1943. Poet. Posthumously published volumes: *The Yellow Night* (1944), *The Poems of Drummond Allison* (1980).

KINGSLEY AMIS, born 1922 in London. Poet and novelist. Lecturer in English at Swansea University, 1949–61; Fellow of Peterhouse, Cambridge, 1961–63; Hon. Fellow of St John's College, Oxford, 1976. Publications include: (verse) *A Frame of Mind* (1953), *A Case of Samples* (1956), *A Look Round the Estate* (1967), *Collected Poems, 1944–1979* (1979); (novels) *Lucky Jim* (1954), *That Uncertain Feeling* (1955), *I Like It Here* (1958), *Take a Girl Like You* (1960), *One Fat Englishman* (1963), *The Anti-Death League* (1966), *Girl 20* (1971), *Ending Up* (1974), *The Alteration* (1976), *Jake's Thing* (1978), *Russian Hide-and-Seek* (1980). Edited *The New Oxford Book of Light Verse* (1978). Recreations: music, thrillers, television.

SIR ALFRED AYER, FBA, born 1910 in London. Philosopher. Grote Professor of the Philosophy of Mind and Logic at London University, 1946–59; Wykeham Professor of Logic at Oxford University and Fellow of New College, 1959–78; Fellow of Wolfson College, Oxford, since 1978. Publications include: *Language, Truth and Logic* (1936), *The Foundations of Empirical Knowledge* (1940), *Philosophical Essays* (1954), *The Problem of Knowledge* (1956), edited *Logical Positivism* (1959), *The Concept of a Person and Other Essays* (1963), *The Origins of Pragmatism* (1968), *Metaphysics and Common Sense* (1969), *The Central Questions of Philosophy* (1974), *Part of My Life* (1977), *Perception and Identity* (1979), *Hume* (1980).

BERYL BAINBRIDGE, born 1934 in Liverpool. Novelist and playwright. Novels: *A Week-End with Claude* (1967), *Another Part of the Wood* (1968), *Harriet said . . .* (1972), *The Dressmaker* (1973), *The Bottle Factory Outing* (1974), *Sweet William* (1975), *A Quiet Life* (1976), *Injury Time* (1977), *Young Adolf* (1978), *Winter Garden* (1980). Plays: *Tiptoe through the Tulips* (1976), *The Warrior's Return* (1977), *It's a Lovely Day Tomorrow* (1977). Recreations: painting, sleeping.

MELVYN BRAGG, born 1939 in Wigton, Cumberland. Novelist and Broadcaster. His novels include: *For Want of a Nail* (1965), *The Second Inheritance* (1966), *Without a City Wall* (1968), *The Hired Man* (1969), *A Place in England* (1970), *The Nerve* (1971), *Josh Lawton* (1972), *The Silken Net* (1974), *A Christmas Child* (1976), *Autumn Manoeuvres* (1978), *Kingdom Come* (1980). Editor and presenter on television of *Read All About It*, *The Lively Arts*, and *The London Weekend Television South Bank Show*. Screenplays include *Isadora*, *The Music Lovers* and *Jesus Christ Superstar*. Recreations: walking, books.

GAVIN EWART, born 1916 in London. Poet. His books include: *Poems and Songs* (1938), *Londoners* (1964), *Pleasures of the Flesh* (1966), *The Deceptive Grin of the Gravel Porters* (1968), *The Gavin Ewart Show* (1971), *Be My Guest!* (1975), *No Fool Like an Old Fool* (1976), *Or Where a Young Penguin Lies Screaming* (1978), *The Collected Ewart, 1933–1980* (1980). Recreations: listening to music, playing cricket once a year.

ROY FULLER, born 1912 in Failsworth, Lancashire. Poet. Solicitor to the Woolwich Equitable Building Society, 1938–69, since then a director. Oxford Professor of Poetry, 1968–73; Governor of the BBC, 1972–9. Queen's Gold Medal for Poetry, 1970. Publications include: *Poems* (1939), *The Middle of a War* (1942), *A Lost Season* (1944), *Savage Gold* (1946), *Epitaphs and Occasions* (1949), *Collected Poems* (1962), *New Poems* (1968), *The Reign of Sparrows* (1980), *Souvenirs* (memoirs) (1980). Recreations: 'none worth mentioning'.

JACKY GILLOTT, born 1939 in Lytham St Annes, Lancashire, died 1980. Novelist, journalist and broadcaster; her novels include *Salvage* (1968), *War Baby* (1971), *A True Romance* (1975), *Crying Out Loud* (1976), *The Head Case* (1980).

ROBERT GITTINGS, born 1911 in Portsmouth. Poet and biographer. Fellow of Jesus College, Cambridge, 1935–40; Honorary Fellow, 1978. Producer and scriptwriter at the BBC, 1940–63. Chief publications: *John Keats* (1968), *Young Thomas Hardy* (1975), *Collected Poems* (1976), *The Older Hardy* (1978). Recreations: most outdoor pursuits except blood-sports.

SIMON GRAY, born 1936 on Hayling Island, Hants. Playwright and novelist. Lecturer in English at Queen Mary College, London University, since 1965. His plays include: *Wise Child* (1968), *Sleeping Dog* (1968), *Dutch Uncle* (1969), *The Idiot* (from the novel by Dostoievsky, 1971), *Spoiled* (1971), *Butley* (1971), *Otherwise Engaged* (1975), *Two Sundays* (1975), *Dog Days* (1976), *Molly* (1977), *The Rear Column* (1978), *Close of Play* (1979), *Stage Struck* (1980), *Quartermaine's Terms* (1981). Novels: *Colmain* (1963), *Simple People* (1965), *Little Portia* (1967); (as Hamish Reade) *A Comeback for Stark* (1968). Recreations: watching cricket and soccer, swimming.

RONALD HARWOOD, born 1934 in Cape Town. Novelist and play-wright. Was a professional actor for seven years. His publications include: (novels) *All the Same Shadows* (1961), *The Guilt Merchants* (1963), *The Girl in Melanie Klein* (1969), *Articles of Faith* (1973), *The Genoa Ferry* (1976), *César and Augusta* (1978); (stories) *One. Interior. Day* (1978); (biography) *Sir Donald Wolfit* (1971); (plays) *Country Matters* (1969), *The Ordeal of Gilbert Pinfold* (from the novel by Evelyn Waugh, 1977), *A Family* (1978), *The Dresser* (1980). Presenter of *Read All About It* on BBC Television, 1978–9. Recreations: tennis, cricket.

MICHAEL HOLROYD, born 1935 in London. Biographer and essay-ist. Publications include: *Hugh Kingsmill* (1964), *Lytton Strachey*

(1967–8), *Unreceived Opinions* (1973), *Augustus John* (1974–5). Chairman of the Society of Authors, 1973–4; Chairman of the National Book League, 1976–8. Is currently engaged on a biography of Bernard Shaw. Recreations: listening to stories, avoiding tame animals, being polite, music, sleep.

TED HUGHES, born 1930 in Mytholmroyd, Yorkshire. Poet. Publications include: *The Hawk in the Rain* (1957), *Lupercal* (1960), *Wodwo* (1967), *Crow* (1970), *Gaudete* (1977), *Remains of Elmet* (1978), *Moortown* (1979); also several children's books, notably *The Iron Man* and *How the Whale Became*. Queen's Medal for Poetry, 1974. Recreations: fishing.

HAMMOND INNES, born 1913 in Horsham. Novelist and traveller. Publications include: *Wreckers Must Breathe* (1940), *The Lonely Skier* (1947), *The Blue Ice* (1948), *The White South* (1949), *Campbell's Kingdom* (1952), *The Mary Deare* (1956), *The Land God Gave to Cain* (1958), *Harvest of Journeys* (travel, 1959), *The Doomed Oasis* (1960), *Atlantic Fury* (1962), *Sea and Islands* (travel, 1967), *The Conquistadors* (history, 1969), *North Star* (1974), *The Big Footprints* (1977), *The Last Voyage* (Cook) (1978), *Solomon's Seal* (1980). Recreations: cruising, ocean racing, forestry.

P. J. KAVANAGH, born 1931 in Sussex. Poet and novelist. Publications include: (verse) *One and One* (1960), *On the Way to the Depot* (1967), *About Time* (1970), *Edward Thomas in Heaven* (1974), *Life Before Death* (1979); (novels) *A Song and Dance* (1968), *A Happy Man* (1972), *People and Weather* (1979); (autobiography) *The Perfect Stranger* (1966); (for children) *Scarf Jack* (1978), *Rebel for Good* (1980).

HARRY KEMP, born 1911 in Singapore. Poet; retired lecturer in mathematics. Took part in a record opening stand of 244 for Stowe School v Cryptics. Publications include: *The Left Heresy* (1939), *Poems as of Now* (1969), *Poems as of Then* (1972), *Poems in*

*Variety* (1977), *Ten Messengers* (1977), *Verses for Heidi* (1978). Recreations: fishing, music, collecting paintings, making country wines.

THOMAS KENEALLY, novelist, b. 1935 in Sydney. Publications: *The Place at Whitton* (1964), *The Fear* (1965), *Bring Larks and Heroes* (1967), *Three Cheers for the Paraclete* (1968), *The Survivor* (1969), *A Dutiful Daughter* (1971), *The Chant of Jimmie Blacksmith* (1972), *Blood Red, Sister Rose* (1974), *Gossip from the Forest* (1975), *The Lawgiver* (1975), *Season in Purgatory* (1976), *A Victim of the Aurora* (1977), *Ned Kelly and the City of the Bees* (1978), *Passenger* (1979), *Confederates* (1979). Recreations: swimming, sailing, hiking.

LAURIE LEE, born in Stroud, Gloucestershire. Poet and autobiographer. Publications include: (verse) *The Sun My Monument* (1944), *The Bloom of Candles* (1947), *My Many-Coated Man* (1955); (travel) *A Rose for Winter* (1955); (autobiography) *Cider with Rosie* (1959), *As I Walked Out One Midsummer Morning* (1969), *I Can't Stay Long* (1975). Recreations: music, travel.

SIR BERNARD LOVELL, FRS, born 1913 at Oldland Common, Gloucestershire. Scientist. Professor of Radio Astronomy in the University of Manchester, and Director of Jodrell Bank Experimental Station (now Nuffield Radio Astronomy Laboratories) since 1951. Hon. Foreign Member American Academy of Arts and Sciences, Hon. Member Royal Swedish Academy; Guggenheim Astronautics Award, 1951, Churchill Gold Medal, 1964. Vice-President Lancashire CC. Publications include: *Science and Civilization* (1939), *Radio Astronomy* (1951), *Meteor Astronomy* (1954), *The Individual and the Universe* (Reith Lectures, 1958), *Discovering the Universe* (1963), *The Story of Jodrell Bank* (1968), *Out of the Zenith* (1973), *The Origin and International Economics of Space Exploration* (1973), *P. M. S. Blackett – A Biographical Memoir* (1976), *In the Centre of Immensities* (1978), *Emerging Cosmology* (1981). Recreations: cricket, gardening, music.

LEO MCKERN, born 1920 in Sydney, New South Wales. Was at first a painter, 1937–40; after Army service took up acting professionally in 1944; arrived in England 1946. His many stage roles include Touchstone, Ulysses, Quince, Toad in *Toad of Toad Hall*, the Common Man (and Cromwell on Broadway) in *A Man for All Seasons*, Peer Gynt, Iago, Volpone, Shylock and Vanya. His TV appearances include J. M. W. Turner, Socrates, Mr Boffin in *Our Mutual Friend* and Rumpole in *Rumpole of the Bailey*. Recreations: sailing, photography, swimming, painting.

ARTHUR MARSHALL, born 1910 in Barnes. Schoolmaster at Oundle, 1931–54, Private Secretary to Lord Rothschild, 1954–8. Has written for the *New Statesman* since 1935; contributes a fortnightly column to the *Sunday Telegraph*; regular broadcaster and appearer on television, notably in *Call My Bluff*. Publications include: *Nineteen to the Dozen* (1953), *Salome, dear, NOT in the Fridge!* (1968), *Girls Will Be Girls* (1974), *I SAY!* (1977). Recreations: reading, sitting in the sun.

MICHAEL MEYER, born 1921 in London. Translator and biographer. Has translated sixteen plays by Ibsen and sixteen by Strindberg. Other publications include: (edited) *Eight Oxford Poets* (with Sidney Keyes, 1941), *Collected Poems of Sidney Keyes* (1945); (novel) *The End of the Corridor* (1951); (plays) *The Ortolan* (1967) *Lunatic and Lover* (1978); (biography) *Henrik Ibsen* (1967–71). Gold Medal of the Swedish Academy, 1964. Is currently engaged on a biography of Strindberg. Recreations: real tennis, eating, sleeping.

SIR FRANCIS MEYNELL, born 1891 in London, died 1975. Book designer, publisher and poet. Founder of the Nonesuch Press, 1923; typographic adviser (unpaid) to HM Stationery Office, 1945–66; director-general of the Cement and Concrete Association, 1946–58. Publications include: *The Typography of Newspaper Advertisements* (1929), *The Week-End Book* (1933), *English Printed*

*Books* (1946), *Poems and Pieces* (1961), *My Lives* (autobiography, 1971).

GERALD MOORE, born 1899 in Watford. Studied piano in Toronto and toured Canada as a boy pianist; on his return to England devoted himself to accompanying and chamber music, and has been associated with most of the world's leading singers and instrumentalists. Neville Cardus wrote of him that he 'has shaped an entirely new chapter in the history and evolution of the concert performer'. Hon.D.Litt., Sussex University, 1968; Hon. Mus.D., Cambridge University, 1973. Publications include: *The Unashamed Accompanist* (1943), *Careers in Music* (1950), *Am I Too Loud?* (1962), *The Schubert Song Cycles* (1975), *Farewell Recital* (1978), *Poet's Love* (1981). Recreations: reading, bridge, gardening.

V. S. NAIPAUL, born 1932 in Trinidad, lives in Wiltshire. Novelist. After leaving Oxford he worked for two years as a freelance broadcaster and for nearly two years edited a weekly literary programme for the BBC World Service. His publications include: (novels) *The Mystic Masseur* (1957), *A House for Mr Biswas* (1961), *The Mimic Men* (1967), *In a Free State* (1971, Booker Prize), *Guerillas* (1975), *A Bend in the River* (1979); (nonfiction) *The Middle Passage* (1962), *An Area of Darkness* (1964), *The Loss of El Dorado* (1969), *The Overcrowded Barracoon* (1972), *India: A Wounded Civilization* (1977), *The Return of Eva Peron* (1980).

HAROLD PINTER was born in London in 1930. He wrote his first plays, *The Room*, *The Birthday Party* and *The Dumb Waiter*, in 1957 and achieved his first great success with *The Caretaker* in 1960. Since then he has written four more full-length plays, *The Homecoming* (1964), *Old Times* (1970), *No Man's Land* (1974) and *Betrayal* (1978), as well as a number of shorter plays for the stage, radio and television. For the cinema, his screenplays include *The*

*Servant, Accident, The Go-Between, A la Recherche du Temps Perdu,
The Last Tycoon* and *The French Lieutenant's Woman*.

SIMON RAVEN, born 1927 in London. Novelist and playwright.
After leaving Cambridge, he was a regular army officer for four
years, serving in Germany and Kenya. His novels include: *An
Inch of Fortune* (1950), *Feathers of Death* (1959), *Brother Cain* (1959),
*Doctors Wear Scarlet* (1960), *Close of Play* (1962), *The Rich Pay
Late* (1964), *Friends in Low Places* (1965), *The Sabre Squadron*
(1966), *Fielding Gray* (1967), *The Judas Boy* (1968), *Places Where
They Sing* (1970), *Sound the Retreat* (1971), *Come Like Shadows*
(1972), *Bring Forth the Body* (1974), *The Survivors* (1976), *Roses of
Picardie* (1979). Stories: *The Fortunes of Fingel* (1976). Non-fiction:
*The English Gentleman* (1961), *Boys Will Be Boys* (1963). His TV
dramatisations include *Point Counterpoint* (1968), *The Pallisers*
(1974), *Edward and Mrs Simpson* (1978) and *Love in a Cold Climate*
(1980). Recreations: cricket, travel, reading.

ANDREW SINCLAIR, born 1935 in Oxford. Novelist and historian.
Fellow of Churchill College, Cambridge, 1961–3. Publications
include: *The Breaking of Bumbo* (1958), *My Friend Judas* (1959),
*Prohibition* (1962), *Gog* (1967), *Magog* (1972), *Jack: a Biography of
Jack London* (1977), *The Facts in the Case of E. A. Poe* (1979).
Directed the film of *Under Milk Wood* (1971). Recreations: old
cities, old movies.

GODFREY SMITH, born 1926 in London. Novelist and columnist.
Has worked for the *Sunday Times* for thirty years; edited its
Magazine for seven years, its Review for three. Novels: *The Flaw
in the Crystal* (1954), *The Friends* (1957), *The Business of Loving*
(1961), *The Network* (1965), *Caviare* (1971), *The Cries of London*
(1981).

JULIAN SYMONS, born 1912 in London. Crime writer, historian,
biographer. Publications include: (crime stories) *The Thirty-First
of February* (1950), *The Colour of Murder* (1957), *The Progress of a*

*Crime* (1960), *The End of Solomon Grundy* (1964), *The Man Who Killed Himself* (1967), *The Blackheath Poisonings* (1978); (history and biography) *A. J. A. Symons, his Life and Speculations* (1950), *Thomas Carlyle* (1952), *The General Strike* (1957), *The Thirties* (1960), *Bloody Murder: A History of the Crime Story* (1972), *The Tell-Tale Heart* (biography of Edgar Allan Poe, 1978). Recreations: walking in cities, cricketeering.

PETER TINNISWOOD, born 1936 in Liverpool. Novelist and playwright. Novels: *A Touch of Daniel* (1968), *Mog* (1970), *I Didn't Know You Cared* (1973), *Except You're a Bird* (1974), *The Stirk of Stirk* (1974). Plays: *The Investiture* (1971), *Wilfred* (1980), *The Day War Broke Out* (1980). Numerous plays for TV and radio, including *Tales from a Long Room* (1980). Is currently working on a musical version of his Brandon novels for the National Theatre.

ALEC WAUGH, born 1898 in London. Novelist. He has written over fifty books, including *The Loom of Youth* (1917), *Kept* (1925), *The Balliols* (1934), *No Truce with Time* (1941), *Island in the Sun* (1956), *A Family of Islands* (1964), *My Brother Evelyn and Other Profiles* (1967), *Married to a Spy* (1976). Recreation: watching life go by. Died 1981.

DAVID WRIGHT, born 1920 in Johannesburg. Poet. Publications include *To the Gods the Shades* (collected poems, 1976) and *Metrical Observations* (1980). Translations include *Beowulf* and *The Canterbury Tales*. Edited several anthologies, including *The Penguin Book of Romantic Verse*, *The Penguin Book of Everyday Verse*, and *Edward Thomas: Selected Poems and Prose*. Gregory Fellowship in Poetry at Leeds University, 1965–7. Recreation: walking.